BEST of the BEST
from
Virginia
COOKBOOK II

Selected Recipes from Virginia's
FAVORITE COOKBOOKS

Susan Constant *was the largest of three ships led by Captain Christopher Newport on the 1607 voyage that resulted in the founding of the first permanent English settlement in North America, Jamestown, in the new colony of Virginia. Replicas of the ship and her sisters,* Godspeed *and* Discovery, *are docked in the James River at Jamestown.*

BEST of the BEST
from
Virginia
COOKBOOK II

Selected Recipes from Virginia's
FAVORITE COOKBOOKS

Edited by
Gwen McKee
and
Barbara Moseley

Illustrated by Tupper England

QUAIL RIDGE PRESS
Preserving America's Food Heritage

Recipe Collection ©2007 Quail Ridge Press, Inc.

Reprinted with permission and all rights reserved under the name
of the cookbooks, organizations, or individuals listed below.

Library of Congress Cataloging-in-Publication Data

Best of the best from virginia cookbook ii : selected recipes from virginia's favorite cookbooks / edited by
GWEN MCKEE and BARBARA MOSELEY ; illustrated by Tupper England.
p. cm. – (Best of the best state cookbook series)
Includes index.
ISBN-13: 978-1-893062-89-4
ISBN-10: 1-893062-89-9
1. Cookery 2. Cookery, American--Southern style I. McKee, Gwen. II. Moseley, Barbara.
TX715.B48565155 2007
641.5--dc22

2007009614

First edition
Printed in Canada

Design by Cynthia Clark
Cover photo: Monticello © Virginia Tourism Corporation
Back cover photo by Greg Campbell

This book is available at a special discount on bulk purchases for promotional, business,
and educational use. For information, contact:

QUAIL RIDGE PRESS • 1-800-343-1583
email: info@quailridge.com • www.quailridge.com

Contents

PHOTO © BUDDY MAYS / VIRGINIA TOURISM CORPORATION

Monticello, located near Charlottesville, was the estate of Thomas Jefferson, principal author of the United States Declaration of Independence, third President of the United States, and founder of the University of Virginia. The house is of Jefferson's own design and the only home in the United States that has been designated a World Heritage Site.

The Quest for the Best
by Gwen McKee

I am frequently asked how the idea for the BEST OF THE BEST STATE COOKBOOK SERIES came about, and how it got started.

It all began with my love for cooking and entertaining, which I have been doing all of my married life. Having collected a variety of cookbooks, most of which have splatters or turned-down pages or notations on the recipes, one day it occurred to me that if I could compile all these earmarked favorite recipes, it would be an incredible cookbook! And wouldn't it be even more special if I could get favorite recipes from the best cookbooks from all over each state—the Best of the Best! Wow! The idea consumed me and became a passion. I knew I had to pursue this quest.

In the days before Internet, faxes, cell phones, or even inexpensive long-distance calling, the only way to gather everything I needed was to strike out and do my research in person. I started in my home state, and that is how *Best of the Best from Mississippi* became the first BEST OF THE BEST cookbook in 1982.

Completing the first cookbook was a lot of work, and I knew if I wanted to tackle Louisiana next, with all its cookbooks, I would need help.

My golfing buddy Barbara Moseley and I were always talking about food and recipes on the golf course, and I knew she was an excellent cook. Besides being my sounding board for all the decisions I faced with *Best of the Best from Mississippi,* she had a lot of office savvy and experience, and was not working at the time. So I asked her if she would be interested in helping me with the *Best of the Best from Louisiana.* Without a moment's hesitation, she replied, "When do we leave?" We left the next day, and we have been hitting the road ever since.

Until the distance to states far from our Mississippi home base necessitated flying and renting a vehicle, we traveled in our big van (we have worn out four) all over each state, our mission being to find out what people in that state liked to cook and eat. We tasted as we went, and talked to people everywhere about what they liked to cook and eat. Invariably, local cookbooks captured the area's cuisine beautifully, and their creators were excited to share specific favorites.

From the very beginning, we established goals. We would search for cookbooks that captured local flavor with kitchen-friendly recipes that anybody anywhere could cook and enjoy. We would make the books user friendly, and edit for utmost clarity. Our criterion for including a recipe was threefold; it had to have great taste, great taste, and great taste!

We went from Louisiana to Texas, then to other southern states that were in close proximity. After four years and four books, we began to say to each

Gwen McKee and Barbara Moseley

other, "Do you think we'll ever finish the whole United States?" Over the next 22 years of travel and research, we had poured through hundreds of thousands of recipes from more than 10,000 cookbooks, and had visited every state in the country.

In 2005, we were finally able to say, "We did it!" The BEST OF THE BEST STATE COOKBOOK SERIES now covers all fifty states. The result is more than 19,000 recipes gathered from every corner of our country. With more than two million copies sold, we are very proud that the series is known as the definitive source for state and regional cooking. (A free booklet entitled *We Did It!* that tells the story of how the series was developed is available upon request.)

Because it has become so much a part of our lives, and to further continue our motto of "Preserving America's Food Heritage," we have begun to revisit states, finding outstanding new cookbooks with more wonderful recipes to showcase and share. Journey with us to Virginia through the pages of this book, and catch the flavor and excitement of the Birthplace of Our Nation as Barbara and I did.

Gwen McKee

Contributing Cookbooks

All American Recipes
Berea's Home Cooking Favorites
The Best of Virginia Farms Cookbook
Celebrate Virginia!
Celebrating Our Children Cookbook
Children's Party Book
Church Family Favorites
The Colonial Williamsburg Tavern Cookbook
Come Cook with Us
Cookin' for the Cure
Cooking with ARK Angels
Cooking with Grace
Country Cookbook
Country Home Favorites
Country Treasures
Culinary Secrets of Great Virginia Chefs
Delightfully Seasoned Recipes
Discovery Tour 2006 Cookbook
Favorite Recipes: Barbara's Best Volume II
Favorite Recipes: Bayside Baptist Church
The Fine Art of Dining
First Family Favorites
Food, Family, and Friendships
Food to Die For
For Men Who Like to Cook, Want to Cook (or Have To!)
From Chaney Creek to the Chesapeake
G.W. Carver Family Recipes
Garden Gate Recipes
Gather 'Round Our Table
Grandma's Cookbook
Granny's Kitchen
The Hall Family Cookbook
The Ham Book
Holiday Fare
In Good Company
It's Delicious!
Joy in Serving
Just Like Mama's
Kids in the Kitchen
Kitty Caters

Contributing Cookbooks

A Laugh & A Glass of Wine
Long Hill Bed & Breakfast
Loving, Caring and Sharing
Mrs. Rowe's Favorite Recipes
My Table at Brightwood
Not By Bread Alone Cookbook
Oh My Stars! Recipes that Shine
Our Best To You!
Philippine Cooking in America
Pungo Strawberry Festival Cookbook
Recipes from Home
The Riggs Family Cookbook
Sharing Our Best
The Smithfield Cookbook
Tangier Island Girl
Taste & See
A Taste of Heaven
A Taste of Prince William County Cookbook
Taste of the Town II
A Taste of Tradition
A Taste of Virginia History
Taste Trek!
Tasty Treasures from Johnson's Church
Thought for Food
Tidewater on the Half Shell
Toast to Tidewater
Tried and True Recipes
Very Virginia
Vesuvius, Virginia: Then and Now
Vintage Virginia
Virginia Cook Book
Virginia Fare
Virginia Hospitality
Virginia Seasons
Virginia Traditions
The Westwood Clubhouse Cookbook
What Can I Bring?

Beverages and Appetizers

The George Washington Memorial Parkway stands as a memorial to George Washington. It connects historic sites from Washington's home at Mt. Vernon, past the nation's capital, to the Great Falls of the Potomac, where Washington demonstrated his skill as an engineer for the Patowmack Canal Project.

Cranberry Ice and Pineapple Shrubs

In colonial Virginia, shrubs were popular fruit juice concoctions spiked with alcohol and vinegar. Shrubs have evolved into nonalcoholic fruit juice beverages served over crushed ice, frozen fruit ice, or sorbet. Make the cranberry ice a day ahead and serve this recipe in a punch bowl or individual glasses.

FOR THE CRANBERRY ICE:

1 (16-ounce) can whole-berry
  cranberries

2 cups sweetened cranberry juice,
  or cranberry juice cocktail

Place the cranberries and cranberry juice in a blender and purée. Pour into ice cube trays for individual shrubs, or into a 1-quart container for a punch bowl presentation, and freeze.

FOR THE SHRUBS:

24 ounces soda water
1 quart pineapple juice,
  preferably fresh, chilled

2 limes, thinly sliced, for garnish

For a punch bowl presentation, pour soda water and pineapple juice over cranberry ice and garnish with lime slices.

For individual shrubs, pour 2 ounces soda water into each glass and top off with pineapple juice, leaving enough room for 1–2 cubes cranberry ice. Add cranberry ice to each glass and garnish with lime slices. Allow cranberry ice to melt and soften a few minutes prior to serving. Serves 10–12.

Holiday Fare

My Favorite Punch

3 (12-ounce) cans frozen orange juice concentrate, undiluted
3 (12-ounce) cans frozen lemonade concentrate, undiluted
2½ pounds sugar
Water to cover sugar
6 (46-ounce) cans pineapple juice
1 small bottle lime juice concentrate (this is the secret ingredient!)
Ginger ale (3 quarts per gallon of juice)

Thaw frozen concentrates. Make a simple syrup by pouring sugar into a saucepan and covering with water; bring to a boil. Remove from heat and cool. Blend all juices and simple syrup in a large container. When blended, store in gallon jugs in refrigerator. Keep refrigerated for at least 3 days. At serving time, add 3 quarts cold ginger ale to each gallon of juice mixture.

Kitty Caters

Jeanne's Punch

1 or 2 liters peach juice
1 or 2 quarts peach ice cream
2 liters ginger ale

Pour juice into punch bowl. Spoon in ice cream. Add ginger ale. Stir. Serve. May add fruit slices for garnish.

Taste Trek!

Citrus Slush Punch

2½ cups sugar
6 cups water, divided
1 (12-ounce) can frozen orange juice
1 (12-ounce) can frozen lemonade
1 (46-ounce) can pineapple juice
2 (2-liter) bottles ginger ale, chilled

Over high heat bring sugar and 3 cups water to a boil, stirring until sugar dissolves. Remove from heat. Stir in frozen orange juice and lemonade; add pineapple juice and remaining 3 cups cold water until blended. Pour into 2 (9x13-inch) pans. Cover and freeze overnight, until mixture is firm.

Cut into small squares and place in 2-gallon punch bowl. Pour chilled ginger ale slowly over squares; stir until punch is slushy. Makes 65 (½-cup) servings.

Taste of the Town II

Banana or Chocolate Milk Shakes

1 banana, peeled and sliced, or 6 chocolate sandwich cookies
1 tablespoon vanilla ice cream
1 tablespoon honey
⅔ cup cold milk
⅓ cup plain yogurt

For banana shake, put all ingredients, except chocolate cookies, in blender, put lid on, and whiz it for about 1 minute. The milk shake should be evenly mixed and creamy. Pour and serve immediately.

For chocolate shake, eliminate bananas and substitute chocolate cookies; proceed as above.

Taste & See

Wassail

½ cup sugar
½ cup water
12 whole cloves
2 cinnamon sticks

1½ quarts orange juice
2 cups grapefruit juice
1 quart apple or cider juice
1 orange

Combine sugar, water, and spices in deep saucepan; simmer 10 minutes. Strain this mixture, then add orange juice, grapefruit juice, and cider. Reheat and serve hot from punch bowl. For garnish, slice orange and float on top. Serves 16.

Hint: Use a star-shaped cookie cutter to cut each orange slice and float in punch bowl.

Discovery Tour 2006 Cookbook

Spanish Coffee

1 jigger Tia Maria liqueur
½ jigger brandy
1 cup hot brewed coffee

2 tablespoons sweetened whipped cream

Stir Tia Maria and brandy into coffee. Top with whipped cream. Serves 1.

In Good Company

Early in the 16th century, Spanish explorers discovered the Chesapeake Bay while in search of the fabled (and nonexistent) Northwest Passage to India. They gave the land now known as Virginia the name "Ajacan." Several failed attempts at establishing a mission in Virginia spelled the end of Spanish ventures to colonize the area, but the English were successful in establishing a permanent settlement at Jamestown in 1607.

Toasted Almond Party Spread

1 (8-ounce) package cream
cheese, softened
1½ cups shredded Swiss
cheese
⅓ cup Miracle Whip

2 tablespoons chopped green
onion
⅛ teaspoon ground nutmeg
⅛ teaspoon pepper
⅓ cup sliced almonds, toasted

Preheat oven to 350°. Combine all ingredients; mix well. Spread mixture in 9-inch pie plate or quiche dish. Bake 15 minutes, stirring after 8 minutes. Garnish with additional toasted almonds, if desired. Serve with assorted crackers or toasted bread cut-outs.

Country Cookbook

Delicious Olive Nut Spread

2 (3-ounce) packages cream
cheese, softened
½ cup mayonnaise
1 cup chopped salad olives

2 tablespoons olive juice
Dash of pepper
½ cup chopped pecans

Mash cream cheese with a fork; add mayonnaise and blend well. Stir in olives, juice, and pepper. Fold in pecans. Refrigerate several hours before serving. Keeps well in refrigerator. Serve with crackers or bread rounds.

Long Hill Bed & Breakfast

Virginia was named to honor Queen Elizabeth of England, who was often referred to as the "Virgin Queen."

Shrimp Salad Spread

1 (7-ounce) can medium shrimp, drained
1 (8-ounce) package cream cheese, softened
½ cup mayonnaise
2 dashes garlic salt
2 slices onion, finely chopped
2 shakes Worcestershire

Break shrimp into small pieces. Add remaining ingredients and mix. Chill and serve with crackers or small cocktail bread.

Delightfully Seasoned Recipes

Shrimp Spread

1 (8-ounce) package cream cheese, softened
½ cup sour cream
¼ cup good mayonnaise
1 cup seafood cocktail sauce
1 (8-ounce) package shredded mozzarella cheese
¾–1 pound salad shrimp (ready to eat)
3–4 spring onions, tops included, finely chopped
1 small tomato, seeds removed, finely chopped

In small mixing bowl, beat cream cheese, sour cream, and mayonnaise until smooth. Spread cream cheese mixture on a round serving platter. Cover cream cheese with cocktail sauce and sprinkle with mozzarella cheese, shrimp, onions, and tomato, in that order. Cover and chill. Serve with crackers or small pieces of assorted toasted bread.

Country Home Favorites

Cream Cheese with Jezebel Sauce

Great replacement for pepper jelly. Also a wonderful gift idea. May also be served with roast beef or pork.

1 (18-ounce) jar pineapple
  preserves
1 (18-ounce) jar apple jelly
1 (5-ounce) jar prepared
  horseradish

1 (1-ounce) can dry mustard
1 tablespoon cracked
  peppercorns
1 package cream cheese (any
  size)

In a bowl, combine preserves, jelly, horseradish, mustard, and peppercorns, mixing well. Pour into airtight containers. Cover and store in refrigerator. Serve over cream cheese as a spread accompanied with crackers. Yields approximately 4 cups of sauce.

Virginia Seasons

Cheese Ball

2 cups shredded sharp Cheddar
  cheese, room temperature
2 (8-ounce) packages cream
  cheese, softened
2 tablespoons chopped onion

¼ cup chopped green pepper
1 (8-ounce) can crushed pineapple,
  drained dry
1 teaspoon seasoned salt
2 cups chopped pecans, divided

Mix cheeses, onion, pepper, pineapple, salt, and ⅓ the pecans, and shape into cheese ball. Roll ball in remaining pecans.

Berea's Home Cooking Favorites

Brie with Brown Sugar

Very attractive.

1 small round of Brie
3 tablespoons butter
3 tablespoons brown sugar

3 tablespoons chopped nuts
  (pecans or walnuts)
1 tablespoon honey

Microwave Brie on HIGH for 15 seconds. Place on serving dish. Combine butter, brown sugar, nuts, and honey in a small microwave container. Microwave on HIGH for 15 seconds. Spread on top of Brie. Serve with sliced apples and plain crackers. Yields 8 servings.

Virginia Fare

Roasted Red Pepper and Artichoke Torte

2 red bell peppers
3 bagels, chopped
2 tablespoons olive oil
2 (8-ounce) packages cream
  cheese, softened
1 (15-ounce) carton ricotta
  cheese
1 (10¾-ounce) can condensed
  cream of celery soup

2 eggs
2 tablespoons chopped green
  onion
1 tablespoon dried Italian
  seasoning
1 clove garlic, minced
1 (15-ounce) can artichoke hearts,
  drained, chopped
Fresh spinach

Wash red bell peppers, deseed, and devein. Place skin side up on a broiler pan and broil until you can handle them. Remove peppers and peel off blackened skins. Skins should come off easily. Chop peppers and set aside for use in recipe.

Preheat oven to 375°. While peppers are roasting, chop bagels and combine with olive oil. Spray a 9x2½-inch springform pan with cooking spray. Press bagel mixture into springform pan and bake 15 minutes. Cool.

In mixer bowl, combine cheeses, soup, eggs, green onion, Italian seasoning, and garlic. Mix well. Spread ½ cheese mixture over bagel crust. Top with artichokes and ½ the roasted peppers. Spread remaining cheese over peppers. Top with remaining red peppers. Bake at 375° for 1 hour or until set in the middle. Cool. Refrigerate 6–8 hours or overnight.

Run knife around edge of torte and remove side of springform pan. Top with chopped fresh spinach in a ring around the edge of the torte. Slice thinly and serve with crackers.

Cooking with ARK Angels

Layered Bruschetta Dip

1 (8-ounce) package cream
  cheese, softened
2 cloves garlic, minced
2 small tomatoes, chopped

⅓ cup sliced green onions
⅓ cup shredded Cheddar
  cheese

Mix cream cheese and garlic; spread onto bottom of 8- or 9-inch pie plate. Top with tomatoes, green onions, and cheese. Cover and refrigerate until ready to serve. Serve with favorite crackers.

Delightfully Seasoned Recipes

Halftime Hot and Spicy Corn Dip

1 (8-ounce) package cream
  cheese
2 tablespoons butter or
  margarine
1 tablespoon garlic salt
2 tablespoons milk

2 tablespoons finely chopped
  jalapeño pepper
1 (8-ounce) can shoepeg corn,
  drained
1 large bag blue corn tortilla
  chips

Cook first 3 ingredients in a saucepan over medium heat until creamy and bubbly. Add milk, jalapeño, and corn; cook, stirring often, until thoroughly heated. Spoon into a serving dish. Serve with blue corn tortilla chips. Serves 8–10.

What Can I Bring?

Chipped Beef Dip

24 ounces sour cream
24 ounces mayonnaise
2 tablespoons dill
2 tablespoons parsley flakes

Small onion, finely chopped
3 (3-ounce) packages chipped beef,
    finely chopped

Combine all ingredients in a large bowl. Chill for 2 hours before serving. Pour into round bread bowl and serve with cubed bread or crackers.

Country Home Favorites

Hot Virginia Dip

Everybody's favorite!

1 cup pecans, chopped
2 teaspoons butter
2 (8-ounce) packages cream
    cheese, softened
4 tablespoons milk

5 ounces dried beef, minced
1 teaspoon garlic salt
1 cup sour cream
4 teaspoons minced onion

Sauté pecans in butter. Reserve. Mix all ingredients thoroughly. Place in 1½-quart baking dish, top with pecans. Chill until serving time. Bake at 350° for 20 minutes. Serve hot with crackers or small bread sticks.

Virginia Hospitality

 The history of American stoneware begins in eastern Virginia in the early 18th century, at the Yorktown factory of entrepreneur William Rogers. Although not a potter himself, Rogers' factory was the first successful American attempt to produce salt-glazed stoneware in the hope of lessening American dependence on Great Britain for utilitarian ceramics. His stoneware rivaled British-made examples in appearance and quality.

Reuben Dip

½ pound corned beef, chopped
½ cup sauerkraut, drained
   thoroughly, chopped
¼ pound Velveeta cheese,
   cubed

¼ pound Swiss cheese, grated
1½ tablespoons Dijon mustard
¾ cup mayonnaise

Mix all ingredients and bake uncovered in a 350° oven for 35 minutes.

The Fine Art of Dining

Ham Dip

1 (16-ounce) carton sour cream
3 tablespoons mayonnaise
1½ teaspoons brown sugar
¼ cup chili sauce

1 tablespoon mustard
1½ teaspoons chili powder
1 cup ground ham

Blend all ingredients well. Refrigerate. Serve with potato chips, crackers, or fresh raw vegetables. For an attractive serving arrangement, cut out interior of a red cabbage, leaving about 1 inch thick sides, to form a bowl. Fill cavity with dip. Arrange on a platter, surrounded with vegetables for dipping. Makes 2½ cups.

The Ham Book

Ham Log

This has a unique flavor that will inspire your guests to ask for the recipe. It can be made several days before using and kept in the refrigerator. It freezes well.

1 (8-ounce) package cream
   cheese, softened
1 tablespoon mayonnaise
½ cup chopped chutney

1 cup ground cooked ham
1 cup chopped pecans or
   pecan-flavored peanuts
Cherries for garnish

Blend cream cheese and mayonnaise with a fork. Add chutney and ground ham. Shape into log form. Sprinkle chopped nuts on wax paper. Roll log in nut mixture until well covered. Wrap in foil and chill until firm. Garnish with cherries and serve with crackers.

The Ham Book

Party Crab Dip

3 (8-ounce) packages cream
   cheese, softened
1 (8-ounce) carton sour cream
½ cup mayonnaise
2 teaspoons dry mustard
1 teaspoon lemon juice

⅓ cup dry white wine
⅓ cup dry sherry
2 pounds crabmeat
Salt and pepper to taste
Paprika

Blend cream cheese, sour cream, mayonnaise, dry mustard, lemon juice, wine, and sherry until smooth; fold in crabmeat. Sprinkle with salt, pepper and paprika. Pour into ovenproof dish and heat in 325° oven about 45 minutes. Serve warm with crackers or toast rounds.

Pungo Strawberry Festival Cookbook

Apple Dip

1 (8-ounce) package cream
   cheese, softened
½ cup packed brown sugar
¼ cup white sugar

1 (7½-ounce) bag bits-of-brickle
   (Heath)
Apple slices
Sprite or ginger ale

Mix cheese and sugars. Fold in brickle; mix well and refrigerate. Set out one hour before serving. Soak apple slices in Sprite or ginger ale to keep them from darkening. Drain before serving.

Just Like Mama's

Taffy Apple Dip

1 (8-ounce) package cream
   cheese, softened
¾ cup brown sugar
¼ cup sugar
1 tablespoon vanilla extract

Chopped honey-glazed nuts for
   garnish
Assorted unpeeled apple slices,
   sprinkled with lemon juice

Mix cream cheese, sugars, and vanilla, blending well. Chill. Before serving, sprinkle nuts on top. Serve with apple wedges.

From Chaney Creek to the Chesapeake

King Charles II regarded the Virginians "the best of his distant children" and elevated Virginia to the position "of dominion" along with England, Scotland, Ireland, and France. Thus one of the state's nicknames is the "Old Dominion."

Simply Sensational Strawberry Salsa

½ Vidalia onion
½ red bell pepper
½ green bell pepper
½ yellow bell pepper
½–1 jalapeño pepper to taste
1 large ripe tomato

½ cup apple cider vinegar
1½ teaspoons garlic powder
1½ teaspoons parsley flakes
12 large ripe strawberries, cut small
1 package Equal sweetener

Dice onion, peppers, and tomato. Marinate ½–1 hour in vinegar. Toss in garlic powder and parsley flakes. Sweeten strawberries with Equal and add to vegetable mixture. Serve very cold with tortilla chips or warm over chicken. Also good as a marinade.

Pungo Strawberry Festival Cookbook

Virginia Ham Fantastics

2–3 (12-count) packages Parkerhouse rolls (or 20 count party rolls)
¾ pound Virginia ham, sliced paper thin
½ pound Swiss cheese slices

1 stick butter or margarine, softened
1–2 tablespoons mustard
2 tablespoons Worcestershire
1 tablespoon dried minced onion
1 tablespoon poppy seeds

Line 11x13-inch baking sheet with foil that has been lightly greased. Place rolls that have been filled with ample slices (cut quarter size) of ham and cheese on the foil-lined pan. Place rolls very close together. Spoon a mixture of butter, mustard, Worcestershire, onion, and poppy seeds over top of rolls. Cover with foil and refrigerate for several hours, or they may be baked right away. When ready to bake, preheat oven to 350°. Leave foil on to prevent scorching, and bake approximately 30 minutes. Serves 8.

Virginia Traditions

Swiss Ham Croissants

The airy, flaky layers of puff pastry almost melt in your mouth while the ham provides salty flavors. These can be baked ahead, frozen, and refreshed just before serving for seemingly effortless entertaining.

1 cup lean, cooked, finely
   minced ham
1 teaspoon country-style
   mustard
1 teaspoon unsalted butter,
   softened

1 pound puff pastry dough
1 egg, mixed with 1 teaspoon
   water

Combine ham, mustard, and butter. On a large floured board, roll out puff pastry into a 7x18-inch rectangle. With a sharp knife, divide into 2 rows of 10 triangles, each about 3½ inches. Place a tablespoon of filling on each triangle. Spread. Roll, pulling top sides out slightly and stretching point into a croissant. Curve slightly and place with final point tucked under on ungreased baking sheet. Brush with egg and water mixture. Bake at 420° for 10–12 minutes or until golden brown. Serve either hot or cold. Yields 10 servings.

Recipe from Otto J. Bernet, Ukrop's Supermarket, Richmond
Culinary Secrets of Great Virginia Chefs

Tortillas with Spinach, Artichokes, and Peppers

1½ tablespoons olive oil
2½ pounds fresh spinach, or 2
  cups frozen chopped spinach
1 sweet red or green bell pepper,
  cut into small pieces
1 (8-ounce) package cream
  cheese, softened

1 cup shredded or cut-up Monterey
  Jack cheese with jalapeños
1 cup artichoke hearts, cut into
  small pieces
6 large or 12 small tortillas (corn
  or flour)
Salsa

In heavy skillet, heat olive oil. Add spinach and pepper; cook until pepper is soft. Add cream cheese; cook and stir until melted and mixture is smooth. Add Monterey Jack cheese and stir until melted. Taste to see if it needs a little salt (hard to tell). Add artichokes. Cook and stir 2–3 minutes. Remove from heat. Steam or heat (briefly in microwave—cover with plastic or wax paper) tortillas to soften. Fill tortillas, roll, and place seam side down in greased baking dish. Bake in 325° oven about 30 minutes. Do not let them get too dry. Let cool several minutes. Cut into serving-size pieces. Spoon salsa over top.

Note: You can make the mixture and keep it in a covered container overnight. If you put it together with the tortillas too early, the tortillas dry out.

Variation: Spread a layer of spinach mixture in greased pie plate. Bake at 325° for 15 minutes. Remove from oven and place on a mat or wire rack for 10 minutes or so. Break eggs and place on spinach mixture. Sprinkle with a little salt and pepper. Sprinkle top with ¼ cup Parmesan cheese. Bake until eggs are set. Sprinkle with paprika.

Long Hill Bed & Breakfast

Artichoke Pie

2 (6-ounce) jars marinated
  artichoke hearts
1 small onion, chopped
1 teaspoon garlic powder
½ cup bread crumbs
Dash of each: salt, pepper, and
  oregano

4 eggs, well beaten
½ pound sharp Cheddar cheese,
  grated
1 tablespoon chopped parsley

Drain juice from 1 jar artichoke hearts; save juice from other jar. Chop artichokes. Sauté onion in reserved artichoke juice; add garlic powder. Add bread crumbs and seasonings to beaten eggs. Stir in cheese, parsley, artichoke hearts, and onion. Pour into greased 9-inch pie plate. Bake at 350° for 20–30 minutes. Serve while hot. Cut into pie slice wedge, and serve on small plates with salad forks.

My Table at Brightwood

Fred's Cocktail Wieners

1 (16-ounce) jar chili sauce
1 (8-ounce) jar grape jelly

2–3 packages Little Smokies
  sausages

Heat chili sauce and grape jelly in a saucepan over medium heat. Add Smokies and let simmer until Smokies are heated thoroughly. Flavor is better if entire mixture is allowed to simmer 30–40 minutes. Dish can also be prepared in a crockpot.

Kids in the Kitchen

Oysters Virginia Beach

½ pound mushrooms, thinly
  sliced
6 tablespoons butter, divided
3 tablespoons flour
1–2 dozen fresh oysters
⅓ cup dry sherry
3 tablespoons sliced green
  onions

3 tablespoons chopped parsley
¼ teaspoon salt
⅛ teaspoon cayenne pepper
⅛ teaspoon garlic powder
½ cup bread crumbs
Bacon, cooked, crumbled
  (optional)
Parmesan cheese (optional)

Preheat oven to 350°. Sauté mushrooms in 2 tablespoons butter; set aside. Melt remaining butter. Stir in flour; cook slightly. Add remaining ingredients except bread crumbs. Place in buttered 1½-quart casserole. Top with crumbs. Bake at 350° for 15 minutes. Ladle into individual shells for serving, and add optional toppings, if desired. Serves 6.

Tidewater on the Half Shell

Marinated Ham Biscuits

2 packages small dinner rolls
1½ pounds thin-sliced ham
½ pound Swiss cheese
1 stick margarine, melted

1½ teaspoons dry mustard
1½ teaspoons poppy seeds
2 teaspoons onion flakes
1½ teaspoons Worcestershire

Slice horizontally complete package of dinner rolls and insert sliced ham and Swiss cheese. Place rolls on a large cookie sheet. In saucepan, melt margarine then remove from heat. Add dry mustard, poppy seeds, onion flakes, and Worcestershire. Brush tops of rolls until entire mixture is used. Bake in preheated 350° oven 15 minutes.

Cookin' for the Cure

Mexican Wontons

**1 pound chicken or ground beef,
  cooked, chopped**
1 package taco seasoning
1 (15-ounce) can black beans
1 (10-ounce) can Ro-Tel tomatoes
**2 cups shredded Mexican cheese,
  divided**
**1 (16-ounce) package wonton
  wrappers (usually found in
  produce section)**
**Garnishes: salsa, sour cream,
  guacamole, etc.**

Mix together all ingredients, using only ½ the cheese. Put wonton wrappers into mini-muffin pan and fill with mixture (omit meat to make vegetarian wontons). Top wontons with remaining cheese. Bake at 350° for 10 minutes. Serve with salsa, sour cream, guacamole, etc.

A Taste of Prince William County Cookbook

Chesapeake Bay Virginia Crab Puffs

**1 pound fresh or 1 (14.5-ounce)
  can crabmeat**
1 cup mayonnaise
½ cup grated onion
1 cup shredded Cheddar cheese
1 tablespoon lemon juice
Pinch of salt
1 package hot dog buns

In a large bowl, combine all ingredients except hot dog buns. Cut rounds from buns using a small cookie cutter or rim of a juice glass, cutting 3 from each half of buns. Spread crab mixture evenly on top of rounds. Broil or bake at 400° about 5 minutes. Makes 48 puffs.

Note: Puffs may be baked and frozen for later use. Before serving, reheat at 400° about 10 minutes.

Virginia Cook Book

Smithfield Crab Fritters

Merging two wildly popular Virginia products—blue crab and Smithfield ham—yields an irresistible starter.

2¼ cups all-purpose flour
1½ cups warm water
¼ cup vegetable oil
1 teaspoon garlic powder
½ teaspoon salt
½ teaspoon black pepper
2 tablespoons Old Bay
  Seasoning

½ pound backfin crabmeat,
  picked over
½ cup chopped scallions
½ cup diced Smithfield ham
3 egg whites, whipped to stiff
  peaks
Peanut oil for frying
Cocktail sauce

In a small bowl, combine flour, water, and oil with a wire whip. Combine with garlic powder, salt, pepper, and Old Bay Seasoning. Gently add crab, scallions, and ham, and mix with a spoon. Fold in egg whites. Drop by large spoonfuls into peanut oil. Fry until firm, or when a toothpick inserted in center comes out dry. Drain. Serve immediately with cocktail sauce. Yields 6 servings.

Recipe from Richard H. Goodwin, Delaney's Café and Grill, Richmond
Culinary Secrets of Great Virginia Chefs

Cheese Straws

1 (10-ounce) brick Cracker Barrel Extra-Sharp Cheddar, grated, room temperature
1 cup butter, room temperature

2½ cups sifted all-purpose flour
1 teaspoon salt
1 teaspoon cayenne pepper

Cream cheese thoroughly, using a strong mixer. Scrape down sides of mixer bowl several times. Add butter, and cream well for about 10 minutes or until light and fluffy. (If possible, at this point, for shorter, tenderer straws, let cheese-butter mixture sit uncovered, outside refrigerator for a day.)

Add flour, salt, and red pepper. Blend well again. Form in strips on cookie sheets with a cookie press, using the disk with the serrated opening. Bake at 350° about 10 minutes or until straws are blushed with brown.

Tips:

(1) Best not to make cheese straws in high humidity.

(2) A strong standing mixer is needed; whisk attachment is suggested.

(3) Cheese, cut in chunks and brought to room temperature, need not be grated before creaming.

(4) Straws will not brown evenly and must be watched carefully; remove end and side pieces, and continue cooking rest of straws.

(5) Straws freeze beautifully for long periods of time.

(6) A double batch does not take twice as long, and takes half the cleanup!

Food to Die For

Spinach Cheese Squares

3 eggs
1 cup milk
1 cup all-purpose flour
1 teaspoon baking powder
1 teaspoon seasoned salt
1 tablespoon chopped onion
2 (10-ounce) packages chopped
spinach, thawed, drained

½ pound Monterey Jack cheese,
grated
¼ pound Monterey Jack cheese
with jalapeños, grated
2 tablespoons butter

Beat eggs with fork in large bowl. Add milk, flour, baking powder, salt, and onion, and mix well. Add spinach and all cheese, and mix. Place butter in a 9x13-inch baking dish and heat to melt. Spread in bottom of dish. Add spinach mixture. Bake at 350° for 35–40 minutes. Allow to cool and cut into squares. Squares freeze well, and can be heated in microwave. Makes about 90 (1-inch) squares.

Note: For a stronger jalapeño flavor, use all Monterey Jack cheese with jalapeños instead of above proportions.

It's Delicious!

Broccoli Balls

1 (10-ounce) package frozen
chopped broccoli, thawed
½ cup butter or margarine,
melted
1 medium onion, finely chopped

½ teaspoon garlic salt
½ cup grated Parmesan cheese
1½ cups chicken-flavored stuffing
mix
3 eggs, beaten

Mix all ingredients in large bowl. Chill one hour. Roll into small balls. Place on a greased baking sheet. Bake at 325° until lightly browned, 10–15 minutes.

Note: These balls freeze beautifully unbaked.

Loving, Caring and Sharing

Egg Rolls

1 pound hot sausage
3 tablespoons sugar
¼ cup vinegar
Pepper to taste
1½ teaspoons salt
Dash of red pepper
1 pound popcorn shrimp
Cornstarch to thicken

1 head cabbage
2 carrots
1½ green bell peppers, chopped
1 large onion, chopped
2 or more packages egg roll
  wrappers (found in produce
  section)

Fry sausage until done; drain. Add sugar, vinegar, pepper, salt, red pepper, shrimp, and enough cornstarch to thicken the mixture. Grind (or shred) cabbage and carrots; add chopped green pepper and onion in large bowl. Pour hot sausage mixture over vegetables to break them down. Let set one hour or more.

Place corner of egg roll wrapper toward you. Place 2 large tablespoons of mixture about halfway on the wrapper. Roll one time to cover mixture and fold left side over mixture, then right side. Roll up and seal. It will end like an envelope. Mix a little cornstarch and water to seal sides and ends. This keeps them from coming unfolded.

Freeze each one individually either by putting in small zip-lock bag or wrapping in plastic wrap. Keep frozen until ready to deep-fry. Deep-fry at 350° until golden brown, about 5 minutes. Serve with Sweet and Sour Sauce.

SWEET AND SOUR SAUCE:
1½ cups white corn syrup
¼ cup ketchup
1 tablespoon mustard

1 teaspoon sugar
1 tablespoon white vinegar

Mix all ingredients with wire whisk and serve with Egg Rolls.

Just Like Mama's

Sugar Coated Peanuts

1 cup granulated sugar
½ cup water

2 cups raw shelled peanuts,
skins on

Dissolve sugar in water in saucepan over medium heat. Add peanuts and continue to cook over medium heat, stirring frequently. Cook until peanuts are completely sugared (coated and no syrup). Pour and spread on an ungreased cookie sheet. Bake at 300° for approximately 30 minutes, stirring at 5-minute intervals.

Our Best to You!

Hugs and Kisses

¼ cup butter or margarine,
**   melted**
1 tablespoon Worcestershire
1 teaspoon seasoned salt
1 cup pretzel sticks (bite-size
**   lengths)**
8 cups rice, corn, or wheat
**   square cereal**

Candy-coated chocolate candies,
raisins, butterscotch morsels,
miniature marshmallows,
chocolate chips, or peanut butter
morsels (optional)

Combine butter or margarine, Worcestershire, and seasoned salt, mixing well. Combine pretzels and cereal in large bowl. Drizzle seasoned butter over cereal mixture and mix gently until evenly coated. Spread mixture in 10x14x3-inch baking pan. Bake at 300° for 1 hour, stirring at 15-minute intervals. Spread mixture on paper towels and cool. Add 1 cup of one or several optional ingredients. Makes 10–12 cups.

Children's Party Book

Bread and Breakfast

PHOTO © VIRGINIA TOURISM CORPORATION

In the central Piedmont region of Virginia, fall colors begin to appear by mid-October. With 15.8 million acres of Virginia being forested, you are sure to see the splendor of her multi-hued backdrop of fall color, while at the same time, enjoying the state's varied array of outdoor recreational activities.

Southern Raised Biscuits

Delicious—a cross between a biscuit and a yeast roll.

1 envelope dry yeast
¼ cup warm water
5 cups all-purpose flour*
3 tablespoons sugar
5 teaspoons baking powder

½ teaspoon baking soda
1½ teaspoons salt
¾–1 cup shortening
2 cups buttermilk

Dissolve yeast in warm water. Sift dry ingredients into a large bowl. Cut in shortening. Add buttermilk, then yeast mixture. Stir until thoroughly moistened. Turn out onto floured board and knead a minute or two. Roll out into ¼-inch thickness and cut with biscuit cutter. Place on greased baking sheet. Let rise 30 minutes. Bake at 425° for 15 minutes or until brown. Brush tops with melted butter. Makes 60 (2-inch) biscuits.

*May substitute self-rising flour for all-purpose flour; omit baking powder and salt.

Note: Dough may be refrigerated in a covered bowl (Tupperware container) and taken out as needed. Will keep in refrigerator 5–6 days. These biscuits are really better after they have been refrigerated. Makes good ham biscuits.

Granny's Kitchen

Sweet Potato Biscuits

¾ cup canned or mashed
  cooked sweet potatoes
¼ cup shortening, melted
3 tablespoons sugar

⅔ cup milk
4 teaspoons baking powder
½ teaspoon salt
1½ cups all-purpose flour

Preheat oven to 400°. Heat sweet potatoes in a medium saucepan; remove from heat. Stir in shortening and sugar. Add milk, baking powder, salt, and flour, stirring to make a soft dough. Pat dough into a ½- to 1-inch thickness with hands, and cut into 2- to 3-inch rounds. Place on lightly greased baking sheet, and bake until brown. Makes approximately 24 biscuits.

Celebrate Virginia!

Creasy's Hot Rolls

1 cup warm water
½ cup sugar
1 package dry yeast
1 egg, beaten

3 cups self-rising flour
3 cups all-purpose flour
½ teaspoon salt
2 tablespoons shortening

Mix warm water with sugar, dry yeast, and egg. Add to mixture the flours, salt, and shortening. Mix well, adding warm water as needed. Let rise to double in bulk. Punch down and make out into rolls. Let double in size, then bake 20 minutes at 375°.

If you wish not to use all at once, let the mixture rise to double in bulk; punch down and cover with heavy towel and place in refrigerator. Use all dough within 4 days.

Country Cookbook

Sour Cream Dinner Rolls

1 (8-ounce) carton sour cream
½ cup butter or margarine
½ cup plus 1 teaspoon sugar,
 divided
1¼ teaspoons salt
2 packages yeast

½ cup warm water
1 teaspoon sugar
2 large eggs
4 cups all-purpose flour
2 tablespoons melted butter

Heat sour cream, butter, ½ cup sugar, and salt till butter melts, then cool to 105°–115°. Proof yeast in warm water with a teaspoon of sugar, then add to cooled sour cream mixture. Stir in eggs and gradually add flour. Cover and chill 8 hours.

Roll out dough to ¼-inch thickness and cut with a 2- to 3-inch biscuit cutter. Brush tops with melted butter, crease center of each roll with a knife, and fold over; press edges to seal. Place in greased pan and let rise 45 minutes or till doubled in size. Bake at 375° for 10–15 minutes or till golden brown. Makes about 4 dozen.

A Taste of Heaven

Yeast Rolls

3 eggs
1½ cups sugar
1 cup Crisco oil
1 cup milk

2 cups hot (boiling) water
3 teaspoons salt
3 packages dry yeast
7–8 cups all-purpose flour

Beat eggs; gradually add next 5 ingredients; mix thoroughly, then add yeast and beat slowly until dissolved. Fold in flour and knead on floured surface. Put in greased bowl and let rise until double in size. Knead and make into rolls; let rise. Bake at 350° for 15 minutes, then at 325° for 15 minutes. Makes 7–8 dozen rolls.

Garden Gate Recipes

Sweet Potato Yeast Rolls

⅔ cup shortening
⅔ cup white sugar
1 cup cooked mashed
   sweet potatoes
1 cup scalded milk
1 teaspoon salt

2 packages dry yeast, dissolved in
   ½ cup lukewarm water
2 eggs, well beaten
Enough all-purpose flour to make
   a soft dough (about 6 cups)

Mix shortening, sugar, sweet potatoes, milk, and salt together. Add yeast; mix well. Add eggs. Add flour and knead well. (It may not take all of the flour to make a nice soft dough.)

Put in large greased bowl; cover with damp cloth. Let rise in warm place. Punch down. After it has been punched down, dough may be refrigerated for later use. Knead again and make out rolls; let rise. Bake at 400° for 12-14 minutes, or until golden brown.

Tasty Treasures from Johnson's Church

Poppy Seed Bread

3 cups all-purpose flour
1½ teaspoons baking powder
1½ teaspoons salt
2¼ cups sugar
3 eggs

1½ cups milk
1½ cups oil
1½ tablespoons poppy seeds
2 teaspoons vanilla
2 teaspoons butter flavoring

Mix together all ingredients. Beat 2 minutes. Pour into greased and floured 5x9-inch loaf pan. Bake for approximately 1 hour at 350°.

GLAZE:
¾ cup sugar
¼ cup orange juice

1½ teaspoons vanilla
½ teaspoon butter flavoring

Mix together and pour over hot bread. Let stand 30 minutes. Remove bread from pan.

Recipes from Home

Foundation Sweet Dough

2 packages yeast
½ cup plus 1 tablespoon sugar
1 cup lukewarm water
1 cup milk
6 tablespoons Crisco

1 teaspoon salt
7 cups sifted all-purpose flour,
  divided
3 eggs, beaten

Dissolve yeast and 1 tablespoon sugar in lukewarm water. Scald milk. Add Crisco, remaining sugar, and salt. Cool to lukewarm; add 2 cups flour to make a batter. Add yeast mixture and beaten eggs; beat well. Add remaining flour or enough to make soft dough. Knead lightly and place in greased bowl. Cover and let sit in warm place free from draft. Let rise until double in bulk, about 2 hours. (Dough may be used for sweet rolls, loaves of bread, or Cinnamon Buns.)

CINNAMON BUNS:

1 recipe Foundation Sweet
  Dough
6 tablespoons butter or
  margarine, melted
1½ cups brown sugar

2 tablespoons cinnamon
1 cup raisins
4 tablespoons milk
1 cup sifted powdered sugar
¼ teaspoon vanilla

When sweet dough is light, punch down and divide into 2 equal portions. Roll out into oblong pieces ¼ inch thick. Brush with melted butter and sprinkle with brown sugar, cinnamon, and raisins. Roll up as for jellyroll. Cut in 1-inch slices. Place cut side up about 1 inch apart in large, shallow greased baking pan. Cover and let rise in warm place, about 1 hour. Bake 20 minutes at 400°. While cinnamon buns bake, add milk slowly to sifted powdered sugar to make a smooth, fairly thick paste. Add vanilla. While cinnamon buns are warm, pour icing over them.

Berea's Home Cooking Favorites

Coffee Ring

1 package dry yeast
½ cup warm water
¼ cup plus 1 teaspoon sugar, divided
3 tablespoons butter
1 egg, slightly beaten
1 cup warm milk
1 teaspoon salt

3½ cups all-purpose flour
1–2 tablespoons butter, melted
1–2 tablespoons brown sugar
1–1½ cups mixture of raisins, nuts, and dried fruits (apricots, apples, pears, etc.)
½ cup confectioners' sugar
2 tablespoons evaporated milk

Mix yeast in warm water with 1 teaspoon sugar added. Add butter to warmed milk. Stir to melt butter. Add egg and yeast mixture to milk. Add dry ingredients (remaining sugar, salt, and flour). Mix until dough holds together in soft ball. Knead a few turns on lightly floured surface. Turn into greased bowl and let rise until double in size. Roll out on floured surface to about ¼ inch in thickness.

Spread rectangle of dough with melted butter and brown sugar. Add a mixture of raisins, nuts, and/or dried fruits. Roll up like a jelly-roll and form into a circle on baking sheet. Snip slits in top of ring at intervals around the ring. Let rise again. Bake 30 minutes at 350°. Let cool. Top with glaze of confectioners' sugar and evaporated milk.

Kitty Caters

Born May 29, 1736, in Hanover County, Patrick Henry is perhaps best known for the speech he made in the House of Burgesses on March 23, 1775: "Is life so dear, or peace so sweet, as to be purchased at the price of chains and slavery? Forbid it, Almighty God! I know not what course others may take; but as for me, give me liberty or give me death!" This speech is credited by some with single-handedly instigating the Revolutionary War.

Sweet Potato Puffs

1 (16-ounce) can sweet potatoes,
   drained, mashed
2 packages crescent rolls
1 stick margarine

1 cup sugar
1 cup Sprite
Cinnamon to taste

Put 1 tablespoon sweet potatoes in each crescent triangle. Wrap and seal edges of crescents together. Place in 9x13-inch baking dish. Melt margarine in small saucepan. Add sugar and Sprite. Bring to a boil and pour over sweet potato puffs. Sprinkle with cinnamon. Bake at 350° for 30 minutes.

Recipes from Home

Cherry Lemon Muffins

1 cup dried cherries
2 cups all-purpose flour, divided
2 teaspoons baking powder
1 teaspoon baking soda
½ teaspoon salt
5 tablespoons sugar

1 egg
1 cup buttermilk
5 tablespoons butter, melted
Juice from 1 lemon
Lemon zest from 1 lemon

Preheat oven to 375°. In a food processor, place dried cherries sprinkled with 2 tablespoons flour to separate them. Pulse to chop. In a large bowl, sift together flour, baking powder, baking soda, salt, and sugar. In another bowl, lightly beat the egg. Add buttermilk, butter, lemon juice, and zest. Combine well. Add chopped cherries. Stir buttermilk mixture into flour mixture just until dry ingredients are moistened. Pour into greased muffin tins. Bake 20 minutes or until muffins are golden brown. Makes 12.

Tried and True Recipes

Strawberries and Cream Bread

1¾ cups all-purpose flour
½ teaspoon baking powder
¼ teaspoon baking soda
½ teaspoon salt
¼ teaspoon cinnamon
½ cup butter
¾ cup sugar

2 eggs
½ cup sour cream
1 teaspoon vanilla
1 teaspoon almond extract
1 cup coarsely chopped
  strawberries
¾ cup chopped walnuts

Combine flour, baking powder, baking soda, salt, and cinnamon. In small bowl, cream butter. Gradually add sugar and beat until light. Beat in eggs, one at a time. Beat in sour cream, vanilla, and almond extract. Stir into flour mixture only until dry ingredients are moistened. Fold in strawberries and nuts. Grease 4x8-inch loaf pan. Turn mixture into pan. Bake at 350° for 60–65 minutes, or until wooden pick inserted in center comes out clean. Let stand in pan 10 minutes. Turn out onto a rack to cool. Makes 1 loaf.

Pungo Strawberry Festival Cookbook

Banana Nut Bread

½ cup granulated sugar
2 tablespoons brown sugar
5 tablespoons margarine,
  softened
1⅓ cups mashed ripe bananas
  (3 or 4 bananas)

1 egg
2 egg whites
2½ cups all-purpose flour
1 teaspoon baking soda
½ teaspoon salt
⅓ cup chopped walnuts

Preheat oven to 375°. Spray large loaf pan with nonstick cooking spray; set aside. Beat sugars and margarine in large bowl with electric mixer until light and fluffy. Add bananas, egg, and egg whites. Sift together flour, baking soda, and salt in medium bowl; add to banana mixture. Stir in walnuts. Pour into prepared loaf pan. Bake 1 hour or until wooden pick inserted in center comes out clean. Remove from pan. Cool on wire rack 10 minutes. Serve warm or cool completely. Makes 1 loaf (16 servings).

Sharing Our Best

PHOTO © VIRGINIA TOURISM CORPORATION

Mount Vernon was named for Admiral Edward Vernon, Lawrence Washington's commander in the British Navy. Lawrence was George Washington's older half-brother who owned the family estate at the time. George inherited the property in 1761.

Apple Bread

2 sticks sweet butter, softened
2 cups sugar
2 teaspoons cinnamon
4 eggs
4 tablespoons milk
2 teaspoons vanilla

4 apples, peeled, chopped
4 cups all-purpose flour
½ teaspoon salt
½ teaspoon baking soda
4 teaspoons baking powder

Beat softened butter well. Add sugar to cinnamon and beat with butter until fluffy. Add eggs, milk, and vanilla, and beat. Add apples and mix. Mix together flour, salt, baking soda, and baking powder. Combine mixtures and mix until blended. Pour batter in 2 well-greased loaf pans. Bake at 350° for 50–55 minutes. Cool 15 minutes, then remove from pans. Pour Glaze over warm loaves.

GLAZE:

1 cup powdered sugar
1 teaspoon cinnamon

4 tablespoons sweet butter
2 tablespoons water

Mix sugar and cinnamon. Melt butter and add water. Add butter mixture to sugar mixture and mix until smooth. Pour over warm loaves. Makes 2 loaves.

Note: Apple bread freezes well.

It's Delicious!

 Built of wood in a neoclassical Georgian architectural style, the plantation home of George Washington—Mount Vernon—is is set on 40 wooded acres located in Fairfax County, overlooking the Potomac River. The house was built by the Washington family about 1735, and was Washington's home from 1747 until his death in 1799. Washington transformed the house's modest frame from one-and-a-half to two-and-a-half stories and extensively redecorated the interior. The north and south wings of the house were begun just before the start of the Revolutionary War. The very last room, the Large Dining Room, was completed after the war's end. The mansion has been restored, with much of the original furniture, family relics, and duplicate pieces of the period based upon Washington's detailed notes.

Parmesan Garlic Bread

1 package yeast
¼ cup warm water
2 cups milk
2 tablespoons sugar
2 tablespoons shortening
2 teaspoons salt

⅛ teaspoon cayenne pepper
5½ cups plain flour, divided
1 cup grated Parmesan cheese
¼ cup margarine, melted
2 teaspoons garlic salt

Soften yeast in water. Scald milk. Combine sugar, shortening, salt, and pepper in large bowl. Add hot milk. Stir until sugar dissolves and shortening melts. Stir in about 2 cups flour. Beat well. Add yeast. Stir in cheese and enough flour to make a soft dough. Stir well. Add flour until you have a stiff dough. Knead well until shiny. Shape into a ball. Place in lightly greased bowl. Cover and let rise in warm place 1½ hours or until double.

Punch down. Divide dough in half. Cover and let rest 10 minutes. Roll out each section of dough into a 10x16-inch rectangle. Brush with butter. Sprinkle with garlic salt. Cut dough into 2x4-inch pieces. Stack side by side in greased loaf pans. Let rise 1 hour. Bake in 400° oven 30 minutes, or until brown.

Recipe submitted by Mrs. Josephine Stamper, Smyth
Country Treasures

Savory Party Bread

1 unsliced loaf French or Italian
   bread (can use presliced if
   slices are thick)
1 pound Monterey Jack cheese,
   sliced
½ cup butter, melted
½ cup chopped scallions
2 tablespoons sesame seeds

If cutting unsliced bread, do not make cuts all the way to the bottom of loaf. Insert cheese slices between cuts. Combine butter and scallions. Place bread on a long enough sheet of aluminum foil to cover. Pull foil up around ends and sides of loaf. Pour butter and scallions evenly over loaf. Pull foil up to cover top of loaf. Bake at 350° for 15 minutes. Uncover top. Bake 10 minutes longer. Perfect with Italian food.

My Table at Brightwood

Jalapeño Hush Puppies

1½ cups cornmeal
½ cup all-purpose flour
1½ teaspoons baking powder
1½ teaspoons salt
½ teaspoon black pepper
¾ cup milk
1 egg, beaten
3 tablespoons vegetable oil
¼ cup chopped jalapeños

Combine dry ingredients. Add remaining ingredients and stir until well blended. Drop by teaspoonfuls into hot oil until golden brown. Drain on paper towels.

From Chaney Creek to the Chesapeake

Upscale Cornbread

By heating the pan and melting the butter in it, you sort of fry the outside of the cornbread and make it crunchy and delicious.

8 tablespoons margarine	1 (14-ounce) cream-style corn
3 eggs	1 cup sour cream
2 boxes Jiffy Corn Muffin Mix	

Put margarine into a 9x13-inch baking dish and put into a 350° oven to melt margarine and heat dish. While dish is heating, beat eggs in a separate bowl and add corn muffin mix, corn, and sour cream. Mix. Pour batter into heated baking dish onto the melted butter. Bake 30–40 minutes, until cornbread is nicely browned and crispy around the edges of the pan. It will pull away from the pan slightly when it is done.

Kitty Caters

Ham and Cheese Bread

2 cups all-purpose flour	1 cup buttermilk
½ teaspoon baking powder	⅓ cup margarine, melted
½ teaspoon baking soda	2 eggs
1 cup shredded medium or sharp Cheddar cheese	1 cup ground ham

In a large bowl, combine first 4 ingredients, blending well. In a medium bowl, mix buttermilk, margarine, and eggs. Add to flour mixture. Stir in ham. Grease bottom of a loaf pan. Pour batter into pan and bake at 350° for 45 minutes or until toothpick inserted in center comes out clean.

Virginia Cook Book

Spoon Bread

5 eggs
4 teaspoons baking powder
¼ cup cornmeal
1 tablespoon sugar

½ teaspoon salt
2 cups milk
2 tablespoons melted butter

Beat eggs and baking powder in bowl until foamy. Stir in cornmeal, sugar, salt, milk, and butter. Bake in greased pan at 350° for 40 minutes, until lightly brown.

For Men Who Like to Cook, Want to Cook (or HAVE to!)

Old Virginia Spoonbread

4 cups milk
1 cup yellow cornmeal
1½ teaspoons salt
½ cup water

4 egg yolks, beaten
⅛ teaspoon cream of tartar
4 egg whites

Scald milk. Mix cornmeal and salt with water and stir into milk. Cook until thickened. Remove from heat. Add a small amount of hot cornmeal mixture to egg yolks, then stir yolks into hot cornmeal.

Add cream of tartar to egg whites. Whip until stiff but moist. Fold whites into cornmeal and pour into a 2-quart greased pan. Bake at 350° for 30 minutes or until light brown and a knife inserted in center comes out clean.

Virginia Seasons

Virginia is one of four states technically designated as commonwealths (sharing the title with Massachusetts, Pennsylvania, and Kentucky).

Quick Eggs Benedict

2 English muffins
4 slices Virginia ham
4 eggs

1 (10¾-ounce) can Cheddar
cheese soup, undiluted
Paprika for garnish

Split, butter, and toast muffins. On each muffin half, place a slice of ham. Fry eggs and place one on top of each ham muffin. Heat soup, and spoon desired amount over each muffin. Garnish with paprika. For lunch or supper, serve with broccoli spears.

The Ham Book

Smithfield Ham Quiche

A new twist on basic quiche. Great served with fresh fruit for weekend guests.

1 cup grated Swiss cheese
1 cup chopped Smithfield ham
½ cup chopped onion
1 (9-inch) pie shell, unbaked
1 (12-ounce) can evaporated
  milk

3 eggs
1 cup hot cooked quick grits
1 tablespoon chopped parsley
½ teaspoon salt
¼ teaspoon dry mustard
⅛ teaspoon cayenne pepper

Preheat oven to 375°. Sprinkle cheese, ham, and onion over bottom of pie shell. Beat remaining ingredients together and pour into pie shell. Bake 45–50 minutes, or until knife inserted into center comes out clean. Cool 10 minutes before serving. Yields 6 servings.

Virginia Fare

Famous since the mid-1700s for its salt-cured hams, Smithfield recently (2002) celebrated the 100th birthday of its oldest ham, which was cured in 1902. This ham, which is on display still today at the Isle of Wight County Museum, may very well be the world's oldest edible dried meat.

Egg Bake

16–20 slices English muffins or
    white bread (crusts removed)
½ pound thinly sliced Cheddar
    cheese
½ pound thinly sliced Swiss
    cheese
½ pound thinly sliced deli ham

8 eggs
3 cups milk
½ teaspoon dry mustard
½ teaspoon salt
1½ cups cornflake crumbs
¼ cup butter, melted

Grease a 9x13-inch baking pan. Butter one side of bread and place in a layer in bottom of baking pan. Place a layer of Cheddar, then a layer of Swiss, then a layer of ham; repeat all layers. Mix eggs, milk, mustard, and salt; pour over top of layers. Push down to make sure it soaks through the bread. Refrigerate 8–12 hours (or overnight). Before baking, sprinkle with cornflake crumbs and drizzle with butter. Bake at 350° for 1 hour.

All American Recipes

Egg and Cheese Bake

½ cup butter or margarine
1 cup Bisquick
1½ cups cottage cheese
2 cups grated Cheddar cheese or
    combination of cheeses
1 teaspoon dried onion or
    2 teaspoons fresh

1 teaspoon dried parsley flakes or
    1 tablespoon fresh
¼ teaspoon salt
6 eggs, lightly beaten
1 cup milk

Melt butter in a 9x13-inch baking dish. Combine remaining ingredients and carefully pour onto melted butter, spreading evenly. Bake at 350° about 40 minutes.

Long Hill Bed & Breakfast

Apple-Sausage Pie

1 cup Bisquick
¼ cup ice cold water
2 tablespoons flour
1 teaspoon cinnamon
½ cup apple juice

1 pound bulk pork sausage (half regular, half hot), cooked, well drained
2 apples, peeled, cored, chopped

Mix baking mix and water until soft dough forms. Roll or pat dough into lightly greased 10-inch pie pan. Mix flour, cinnamon, and apple juice in saucepan. Heat to boiling, stirring constantly. Boil and stir 1 minute. Stir in sausage and apples. Spoon onto dough. Bake at 425° for 25–30 minutes until crust is golden brown.

Long Hill Bed & Breakfast

Apple Sausage Balls

2 pounds pork sausage
1 onion, diced fine
2 tablespoons sage

1 apple, diced fine
2 cups Italian bread crumbs
4 eggs

Blend ingredients together, make into small bite-size balls, and bake at 325° for 40 minutes. Can be frozen and reheated with a small amount of apple juice.

A Laugh & A Glass of Wine

Blue Knoll Cheesy Apple Egg Bake

2 cups sliced peeled Granny
  Smith apples
2 tablespoons cinnamon-sugar
6 slices crisp-cooked bacon,
  crumbled

2 cups shredded Cheddar cheese
2 cups milk
6 eggs
2 cups baking mix

Layer apples, cinnamon-sugar, bacon, and cheese in order listed in a 9x13-inch baking dish sprayed with nonstick cooking spray. Whisk milk and eggs in a bowl until blended. Add baking mix and stir until smooth. Pour egg mixture over prepared layers. Bake at 375° for 40 minutes or until set. Serve with warm maple syrup. Yields 8 servings.

Recipe from Blue Knoll Farm Bed & Breakfast, Castleton
Vintage Virginia

Virginia Ham and Broccoli O'Brien

10–12 slices white bread,
  buttered
2 cups diced baked Virginia ham
1 (10-ounce) package frozen
  chopped broccoli, cooked
1 (24-ounce) package frozen hash
  brown potatoes O'Brien,
  thawed

½ cup chopped onion
3 cups shredded sharp Cheddar
  cheese
6 eggs, slightly beaten
2–2½ cups half-and-half
¼ teaspoon Dijon mustard
Salt and pepper to taste

In an 8x12-inch baking dish, layer in order: bread, ham, broccoli, potatoes, and onion. Top with cheese. In a medium mixing bowl, combine eggs, half-and-half, mustard, salt and pepper; mix well. Pour over top of cheese. Cover and refrigerate 8 hours or overnight. Remove from refrigerator, let stand 30 minutes, then bake, uncovered, at 325° for 1 hour.

Virginia Cook Book

Glorified Grits

2 cups cooked grits
¾ cup shredded Cheddar
  cheese, or 1 roll garlic cheese,
  sliced

1 stick butter
¾ cup milk
2 eggs, beaten
Cornflake crumbs

Spray small casserole dish with Pam. Put in cooked grits. Melt cheese and butter in milk, then slowly stir in beaten eggs. Pour mixture over grits, stir, and bake 25 minutes at 350°. Sprinkle with cornflake crumbs and bake 20 minutes more. Serve hot.

Country Cookbook

Pan-Fried Grits
with Virginia Country Ham

The South is known for its love of grits. This corn is a naturally wonderful starchy side dish for other meals. Chef Kimmel added the intricate flavors of country ham and Cheddar cheese with just a hint of garlic and chives. Shaped in muffin tins, they are finished by pan frying.

1 quart water
1¼ cups grits
2 teaspoons white pepper
1 teaspoon garlic powder
2 teaspoons salt

1 tablespoon dried chives
¼ cup finely chopped Virginia
  country ham
1 cup grated Cheddar cheese
2 tablespoons vegetable oil

In a large saucepan, bring water to a boil. Stir in all ingredients except cheese and oil. Stir until smooth. Cook over medium heat, whipping occasionally, for 15 minutes or until thick. Remove from heat. Mix in cheese. Grease muffin tins with nonstick spray. Fill each to the top with mixture. Let cool. Remove from pans. Split lengthwise. Pan-fry in skillet in hot oil until golden on each side. Yields 9 servings.

Recipe by Mark Kimmel, The Tobacco Company Restaurant, Richmond
Culinary Secrets of Great Virginia Chefs

Baked Cheesy Grits

3 cups water
1 cup grits
½ stick butter
2 eggs, separated
¼ cup milk
½ teaspoon seasoned salt
⅛ teaspoon white pepper
⅛ teaspoon red pepper
¼ teaspoon minced garlic
1 cup shredded cheese, can be Cheddar or mixture of Cheddar and Monterey Jack

Heat water to boiling. Add grits; reduce heat; cook 5 minutes or until thick, stirring often. Remove from heat. Add butter. Beat egg whites and set aside. Add milk to egg yolks and beat; add salt and peppers. Stir garlic and cheese into grits. Add egg mixture to grits. Fold in egg whites.

Bake in greased casserole at 325° for 45 minutes or longer, till firm on top and almost set in middle. Will firm up and settle as it sits. Garnish with sprinkle of cheese or paprika on top.

Long Hill Bed & Breakfast

Sausage Cheese Muffins

1 pound bulk hot pork sausage
1 (10¾-ounce) can condensed Cheddar cheese soup (undiluted)
½ cup milk
2–3 teaspoons rubbed sage
3 cups biscuit/baking mix

In a skillet over medium heat, cook sausage until no longer pink; drain. In a bowl, combine soup, milk, sage, and sausage. Stir in biscuit mix just until moistened. Fill regular greased muffin cups two-thirds full. Bake at 400° for 15–20 minutes or until muffins test done. Yields 2 dozen muffins.

Loving, Caring and Sharing

 About half of all the people in the United States live within a 500-mile radius of Richmond.

Pumpkin Pecan Pancakes

2 cups all-purpose flour	1½ cups solid-pack pumpkin
4 teaspoons baking powder	3 eggs
1 teaspoon ground cinnamon	1 cup milk
½ teaspoon ground nutmeg	¾ cup vegetable oil
¼ teaspoon ground allspice	1 teaspoon vanilla extract
¾ cup sugar	½ cup chopped pecans

Sift dry ingredients together and set aside. Using a large bowl, combine pumpkin, eggs, milk, oil, and vanilla. Add dry ingredients and stir until blended; stir in pecans just before ready to cook.

A hot greased griddle is best for cooking pancakes. Pour ¼ cup batter onto griddle and cook until bubbles form and bottom is brown. Turn and brown other side. Serve with warm pure maple syrup.

Variation: May omit pecans from batter and add to syrup. Heat and pour over pancakes.

Mrs. Rowe's Favorite Recipes

Harvest Apple Pancakes

1 cup all-purpose flour	2 tablespoons sugar
2 teaspoons baking powder	1 egg
¼ teaspoon nutmeg	1 large cooking apple, peeled,
½ teaspoon cinnamon	thinly sliced
2 tablespoons oil	½–¾ cup milk

Combine all ingredients and cook on heated griddle until puffed, then flip and cook until done. Serve with fruit and Apple Sausage Balls (page 54).

A Laugh & A Glass of Wine

Grand Fruit Topping–Granola

1 cup all-purpose flour
½ cup packed brown sugar
½ cup flaked coconut
½ cup coarsely chopped pecans
  or walnuts

1 cup firm margarine or butter
1½ cups Fiber One Cereal

Mix flour, sugar, coconut, and nuts. Pour into ungreased 9x13x2-inch baking pan. Dice margarine or butter into tiny pieces and sprinkle over mixture in pan. Stir in cereal. Bake at 325° for 10 minutes. Remove from oven and stir to continue combining. Return to oven. Bake 10 more minutes. Remove from oven. Stir well. Cool completely. Store in covered container in refrigerator. Makes approximately 5 cups.

Long Hill Bed & Breakfast

Gran's Apples

1 tablespoon citrus juice
1 cup water
3–4 flavorful, medium-size
  apples

2 tablespoons light corn syrup
Lemon wedge
Cinnamon

Using a 4-quart microwavable utensil, combine citrus juice and water. Core apples, but do not peel. Cut into bite-size pieces and place in citrus-water as you chop. This keeps fruit from turning brown. Drain off water and drizzle with corn syrup. Cover and microwave 4–5 minutes (until apples are translucent). Squeeze lemon wedge over apples and stir. Can add additional sweetener, if desired. Sprinkle with cinnamon. Serve warm. Serves 4.

The Fine Art of Dining

Tom's Own Sausage Gravy

1 pound sausage, hot or regular	1½ pints half-and-half
1 teaspoon minced garlic	1 teaspoon beef bouillon
3–4 tablespoons flour	Frozen or homemade biscuits

Crumble sausage in large skillet and brown thoroughly; add garlic. Drain grease from sausage and stir in 3 or 4 tablespoons flour. Pour in half-and-half and beef bouillon. Heat and stir until it thickens. Cover and let simmer for 1–2 hours, stirring occasionally. Let cool; place in refrigerator overnight. Reheat gravy and serve over hot, baked biscuits.

Cookin' for the Cure

Chocolate Gravy

This is delicious with hot biscuits.

2 tablespoons cocoa (heaping)	Milk (approximately 1½ cups)
3 tablespoons flour (heaping)	2 tablespoons butter
1 cup sugar	2 teaspoons vanilla
Pinch of salt	

Mix cocoa, flour, sugar, and salt in saucepan. Over medium heat start whisking, while adding enough milk to make desired consistency; takes a few seconds to get thick. Add butter and vanilla.

The Riggs Family Cookbook

Soups, Stews, and Chilis

After Jamestown burned in 1699, the capital of Virginia was moved to Williamsburg. The Governor's Palace, completed in 1722, was home to seven governors, including Patrick Henry and Thomas Jefferson. At the urging of Jefferson, its last resident, the capital was relocated to Richmond in 1780 for security reasons during the American Revolution.

Rappahannock Crab Bisque

1 stick butter or margarine
3 leeks (white part only), washed,
   halved, thinly sliced
1 garlic clove, minced
½ cup all-purpose flour
4 cups chicken broth
½ cup dry white wine

2 cups half-and-half
½ pound fresh crabmeat
¼ teaspoon salt
¼ teaspoon black pepper
Sliced leeks for garnish (white
   part only)

In a large saucepan, melt butter and sauté leeks and garlic over medium-high heat 3 minutes or until tender, stirring constantly. Blend in flour and cook 1 minute, stirring constantly. Gradually add broth and wine; cook over medium heat, stirring constantly until mixture thickens. Stir in half-and-half, crabmeat, salt, and pepper. Heat thoroughly. Serve garnished with sliced leeks. Yields 6–8 servings.

Very Virginia

Lynn's Crab Soup

1 chicken bouillon cube
1 cup boiling water
¼ cup chopped onion
¼ cup diced celery
¼ cup butter
3 tablespoons flour
1 teaspoon salt
⅛ teaspoon pepper

¼ teaspoon hot sauce
1 teaspoon Worcestershire sauce
1 quart milk
1 pound crabmeat
1 potato, cooked, diced, or 1 can
   diced potatoes (optional)
Chopped parsley

Dissolve bouillon cube in boiling water. Sauté onion and celery in butter. Blend in flour and seasonings. Add milk and bouillon. Cover and simmer over medium heat; do not boil. Add crabmeat. Add potatoes, if desired; top with parsley flakes.

Note: Recipe may be halved, but use all of bouillon cube.

Favorite Recipes: Barbara's Best Volume II

Williamsburg Bisque of Hampton Crab

1 cup crabmeat
1 (10¾-ounce) can cream of
  mushroom soup
1 (10¾-ounce) can cream of
  asparagus soup

1 cup light cream
1¼ cups milk
1 teaspoon Worcestershire
½ cup dry sherry
Dash of Tabasco

Blend all ingredients in blender. Heat but do not boil. Serves 8.

Virginia Seasons

Roasted Butternut Squash Bisque

2 pounds peeled butternut
  squash
2 tablespoons honey
2 tablespoons olive oil
1 cup chopped onion

½ cup chopped candied ginger
2 tablespoons chopped garlic
4 cups chicken stock
1½ cups buttermilk
1 teaspoon salt

Peel squash and dice into 1-inch cubes. In a bowl, toss squash with honey. Spread mixture into a roasting pan and roast in a 450° oven for 20 minutes, stirring occasionally. Heat olive oil in a pot on medium heat. Add onion and sauté until soft. Stir in ginger and garlic, cooking until aromatic. Add roasted squash and chicken stock to cover. Cook until very soft, about 15 minutes. Remove from heat and purée until very smooth (using a food processor or blender). Return bisque to pot and add buttermilk. Bring bisque to a low simmer; do not allow it to boil—this will curdle the buttermilk. Season to taste with salt, and serve. Serves 6–8.

The Fine Art of Dining

Cold Squash Soup

In hot weather, this soup can not be beat!

1 large onion, chopped
2 pounds crookneck squash,
   washed, sliced
6–8 cups chicken broth
2 (8-ounce) packages cream
   cheese, broken into pieces

Salt and pepper to taste
¼ teaspoon sugar
1 teaspoon lemon juice

Cook vegetables in chicken broth. Stir in cream cheese. Add salt, pepper, sugar, and lemon juice. Purée in batches in processor. Chill. If soup is too thick, thin with a little milk. Serves 8–10.

Note: Use Neufchâtel cheese and save calories without forfeiting flavor.

Food to Die For

Summer Soup

1 medium onion
1 medium green bell pepper
2 medium zucchini
2 cups chicken broth

1 cup sour cream
Salt and pepper to taste
Chopped parsley or dill
   (optional)

In 3-quart saucepan, cut up vegetables coarsely. Add broth and simmer 15–20 minutes. Let cool. Reserve broth. Place vegetables in food processor or blender. Purée to desired consistency. Return to broth, and add sour cream; blend well. Season to taste with salt and pepper. Add fresh herbs, if desired. Chill.

Thought for Food

In Virginia, more people work for the U.S. Government than any other industry—about one-quarter of the state's workforce.

Old-Fashioned Cream of Tomato Soup

½ cup butter
½ cup flour
4 cups milk
2½ pounds canned tomatoes,
   diced
1½ cups tomato juice
1½ cups Bloody Mary mix

2½ teaspoons salt
2 teaspoons pepper
½ cup sugar
2 cups heavy cream
Sour cream for garnish
Chopped green onions for
   garnish

Melt butter in a large pot. Add flour and stir to make a roux. Allow to cook about 1 minute, stirring constantly. Do not brown. Add milk and stir until thickened. Add next 7 ingredients and bring to a boil. Reduce heat to medium and simmer 15 minutes. Garnish each serving with a dollop of sour cream and green onions. Serves 12.

Recipe from Heart in Hand Restaurant Caterers, Clifton
A Taste of Virginia History

Cream of Broccoli Soup

1 pound broccoli, fresh or frozen
2 sticks butter
1 cup all-purpose flour, sifted
1 quart chicken stock

1 quart half-and-half
1 teaspoon salt
¼ teaspoon white pepper

Clean broccoli and remove stems. Cut into ½-inch pieces. Steam in ½ cup water until tender. Do not drain. Set aside. Melt butter in saucepan over medium heat. Add flour to make a roux. Cook 2–4 minutes, stirring constantly. Add chicken stock, stirring with wire whisk, and bring to a boil. Turn heat to low. Add broccoli, half-and-half, salt, and pepper. Heat, but do not boil. Serves 8–10.

Tasty Treasures from Johnson's Church

Spinach and Feta Soup

2 tablespoons oil
2 tablespoons butter
2 cups chopped onion
2 teaspoons chopped garlic
2 cups finely chopped fresh
  spinach
4 tablespoons flour
4 cups milk
2 cups chicken or vegetable
  broth

¼ teaspoon white pepper
¼ teaspoon turmeric (or ground
  ginger)
8 ounces crumbled feta cheese
2 cups chopped cooked chicken
  (optional)
Crumbled feta cheese for
  garnish

Pour oil into saucepan. Melt butter in oil over medium heat until bubbly. Stir in onion and garlic; cook 3 minutes or until soft. Mix in spinach; cook an additional 3 minutes. Reduce heat to low. Stir in flour; cook one minute. Stir milk into spinach-flour mixture, very slowly, incorporating approximately ⅛ cup milk into spinach-flour mixture at a time before adding more milk. When all the milk has been added, stir in broth, white pepper, and turmeric. Simmer 20 minutes, stirring occasionally.

Purée mixture in blender; return puréed mixture to pot. Stir in feta; simmer 5 minutes. Stir in chicken, if desired, and simmer an additional 5 minutes. Serve hot. Garnish with crumbled feta cheese. Serves 6.

Toast to Tidewater

Vegetable Beef Soup

1 pound soup meat
1 large meaty soup bone
3 quarts water
1 quart canned tomatoes
1½ cups ketchup, or 1 (6-ounce)
  can tomato paste
4 medium onions, chopped
2 large carrots, chopped or
  sliced
4 large potatoes, chopped
2 stalks celery, chopped
2 cups chopped cabbage
½ cup chopped green bell
  pepper

1 cup green beans
½ cup sliced okra
2 cups corn
2 cups green peas
1 teaspoon sugar
1 teaspoon Lawry's Seasoned
  Salt
1 teaspoon onion powder
1 teaspoon garlic powder
1 teaspoon Ac'cent
Salt to taste (begin with 1
  teaspoon)

Braise soup meat and large soup bone in large heavy stockpot. Add water, tomatoes, and ketchup or tomato paste to pot. Stir to mix well and bring to a boil. Cook until meat is tender. Remove bone and soup meat. Chop meat and discard bone. Add all vegetables except corn and peas. Simmer 1 hour.

Add corn, peas, spices, and chopped meat. Simmer 10 minutes longer. Taste; add additional salt if necessary. If soup is too thick, add additional water. Freezes well. Makes 1½ gallons.

Mrs. Rowe's Favorite Recipes

The wild ponies of Assateague and Chincoteague islands are actually small horses just larger than a Shetland pony. There are two theories of how the ponies came to live on the islands. One legend is that a Spanish galleon wrecked off of Assateague Island and the surviving ponies swam ashore. However, the more likely theory is that early 17th-century colonists let their animals loose on the island to avoid the tax on fenced livestock. Whichever theory is true, Virginia's wild ponies have been living on the islands for hundreds of years.

Hearty Potato Soup

6 medium potatoes, peeled,
sliced
2 carrots, diced
6 celery stalks, diced
1 cup chicken broth
1 cup water
1 onion, chopped

6 tablespoons butter or
margarine
6 tablespoons all-purpose flour
1 teaspoon salt
½ teaspoon pepper
1½ cups milk

In a large kettle, cook potatoes, carrots, and celery in chicken broth
and water until tender, about 20 minutes. Drain, reserving liquid and
setting vegetables aside. In same kettle, sauté onion in butter until
soft. Stir in flour, salt, and pepper; gradually add milk, stirring constantly until thickened. Gently stir in cooked vegetables. Add 1 cup
(or more) of reserved cooking liquid, until soup is desired consistency.
Yields 8–10 servings (about 2 quarts).

Not By Bread Alone Cookbook

Hotel Roanoke's Peanut Soup

The hotel's signature soup has been a favorite of locals and travelers for many generations.

1 small onion, chopped
2 ribs celery, chopped
1 stick butter
3 tablespoons flour
8 cups chicken broth

2 cups peanut butter
1 tablespoon lemon juice
⅓ teaspoon celery salt
1 teaspoon salt
½ cup ground peanuts

Sauté onion and celery in butter in a large saucepan for 5 minutes or
until tender but not brown. Stir in flour and cook until bubbly. Add
chicken broth. Cook until slightly thickened, stirring constantly. Cook
30 minutes, stirring occasionally.

   Strain mixture into a second large saucepan. Add peanut butter,
lemon juice, celery salt, and salt, and mix well. Cook just until heated
through, stirring to blend well. Ladle into soup bowls and sprinkle
with ground peanuts. Serves 10.

Oh My Stars! Recipes that Shine

Virginia Peanut Soup

¼ cup olive oil
½ pound carrots, chopped
    rough
½ pound yellow onions,
    chopped rough
½ pound celery stalks, cut
    rough
¼ cup concentrated chicken
    base
12 cups water

1 pound fresh chicken carcass
¼ cup fresh tarragon leaves
1½ cups clarified butter
½–¾ cup flour
¾ pound creamy peanut butter
¾ tablespoon Kitchen Bouquet
2 cups heavy cream
Salt and pepper to taste
Crushed peanuts for garnish

Preheat oven to 350°. Glaze a medium baking sheet with olive oil. Spread vegetables evenly over pan. Bake 1 hour, turning vegetables occasionally. Combine chicken base with water. Add vegetables, chicken carcass, and tarragon. Simmer 2 hours. Strain mixture thoroughly and refrigerate. After simmering, you should have about 8 cups usable stock. When stock has completely cooled, skim off fat. Melt butter in a medium saucepan. Whisk in ½ cup flour to make a roux, using a little more if necessary. Simmer on very low heat 30 minutes until roux becomes a dusty brown.

Transfer stock to a heavy-bottomed stockpot and begin heating. When stock is just below a boil, add peanut butter, stirring to blend. Add roux, stirring constantly so it doesn't settle on bottom of pan and burn. Stir in Kitchen Bouquet, then cream. Season with salt and pepper. Simmer on low heat another 10 minutes. Remove from stove and run through strainer again. May be stored in refrigerator for later use or served immediately. Garnish with crushed peanuts. Serves 8.

Recipe from Occoquan Inn Restaurant and Tavern, Occoquan
A Taste of Virginia History

Peanuts were first grown commercially in the United States in Virginia. Because of their size and flavor, Virginia peanuts are known as the "Cadillac of peanuts."

Tavern Tortilla Soup

1 tablespoon butter or
  margarine
1 medium-size purple onion,
  chopped
1 garlic clove, minced
2 (14½-ounce) cans chicken or
  vegetable broth
1 (8-ounce) can tomato sauce
1 (28-ounce) can diced tomatoes
1 (4.5-ounce) can chopped green
  chiles, drained
1 (15-ounce) can black beans,
  drained

1 (4-ounce) can yellow corn
  kernels, drained
¼ cup chopped cilantro
¼ teaspoon crushed sweet red
  pepper flakes
1 teaspoon dried oregano
6 corn tortillas, cut into
  ½-inch-wide strips
Vegetable oil
1 cup shredded Monterey Jack
  cheese
Sour cream for garnish

Melt butter in a large saucepan over medium heat; add onion and garlic. Sauté until tender. Add broth and next 8 ingredients. Bring to a
boil; cover, reduce heat, and simmer 20–30 minutes.

Fry tortilla strips in hot oil in a skillet until crisp (may be baked).
Sprinkle tortilla strips and cheese evenly in individual soup bowls;
ladle soup into each bowl. Garnish with sour cream, if desired. Serve
immediately. Serves 6–8.

What Can I Bring?

Tomi's Bean Soup

3 cups chopped fresh kale
1 teaspoon garlic powder
1 (15-ounce) can pinto beans
2 (15-ounce) cans navy beans
1 (14½-ounce) can diced
  tomatoes

2½ cups water
3 beef bouillon cubes
1 teaspoon minced onion

Combine all ingredients in large stockpot; bring to a boil. Reduce heat
and simmer 1 hour.

G.W. Carver Family Recipes

The History of Jamestown

"The Birthplace of a Nation"

Jamestown, settled in 1607, was the first permanent English settlement in the Americas. It is, in essence, the birthplace of our nation. The traditions established at Jamestown—representative government, the rule of law, free enterprise, and cultural diversity—form the basis of American culture as we know it. The year 2007 marks the 400th anniversary of Jamestown.

Listed Below Are Significant Events in Jamestown's History:

1606: In June of 1606, King James I granted a charter to the Virginia Company to establish an English settlement in the Chesapeake region of North America. By December, three ships (the *Susan Constant, Godspeed,* and *Discovery*) had set sail from England with 108 settlers.

1607: On May 14, nearly five months after departing from England, the expedition began building a settlement at a site on the James River. The group was instructed to settle Virginia, and to find gold and a water route to the Orient. The group named their settlement for King James I.

1608: Captain Christopher Newport, commander of the 1607 Jamestown expedition who had sailed back to England, returned to Virginia in January with settlers and goods, marking the first of a series of regular arrivals in the colony. John Smith was elected president of the governing council in the fall. Smith returned to England the next fall (1609) to recover from a gunpowder wound and never returned to Virginia.

1611: Elizabeth City and Henrico were established, marking the beginning of expansion beyond Jamestown.

1613: The first sample of tobacco cultivated by John Rolfe was shipped to England about this time. Tobacco was the "golden weed" that ensured the economic survival of the colony. Pocahontas, the favorite daughter of Powhatan, powerful leader of some thirty Indian tribes in coastal Virginia, was kidnapped by the English.

1614: Pocahontas married John Rolfe after being baptized in the Anglican Church, and an eight-year period of peace ensued between the English colonists and Powhatan Indians. (Pocahontas died in England in 1617.)

1619: The first representative legislative assembly in British America met at Jamestown on July 30th to establish one equal and uniform government over all Virginia that would provide "just laws for the happy guiding and governing of the people there inhabiting."

1624: King James revoked the charter of the Virginia Company, and Virginia became a royal colony.

1699: A fire destroyed Jamestown, and the town declined and eventually ceased to exist. The capital of Virginia was moved from Jamestown to Williamsburg.

Chicken Soup with Egg-Lemon Sauce

**1 (4- to 5-pound) stewing
  chicken
1 onion (optional)**

**1 stalk celery (optional)
Salt to taste
1 cup rice**

Place chicken in heavy kettle. Cover with water and add onion and celery stalk, if desired. Cover and simmer over low heat until tender. Add salt the last hour of cooking. Remove chicken and strain broth. Return broth to heat, and when boiling, add rice; simmer until rice is done, about 20 minutes. Prepare Egg-Lemon Sauce according to method preferred.

EGG-LEMON SAUCE (1):

4 eggs   **Juice of 2 lemons**

Beat eggs until fluffy and gradually beat in lemon juice. Add 2 cups of the hot broth slowly to the egg-lemon mixture, beating constantly. Return soup to heat and slowly stir into mixture.

EGG-LEMON SAUCE (2):

4 eggs, separated   **Juice of 2 lemons**

Beat egg whites until stiff. Add yolks, one at a time, and continue beating. Gradually beat in lemon juice. Add 2 cups of hot broth to egg-lemon mixture, stirring constantly. Return soup to heat and slowly stir into mixture.

EGG-LEMON SAUCE (3):

**4 eggs
1 tablespoon cornstarch**

**Juice of 2 lemons
1 or 2 cups boiling broth**

Beat eggs until fluffy. Beat in cornstarch and lemon juice. Slowly add broth and cook sauce until thickened. Gradually stir mixture into soup. Makes 6–8 servings.

Come Cook with Us

Mexican Chicken Soup

1 onion, chopped
2 cloves garlic, minced
1 tablespoon olive oil
3–4 chicken breasts
1 (14-ounce) can chicken broth
1 (14-ounce) can beef broth
1 (10¾-ounce) cream of chicken
  soup
1 (14½-ounce) can diced
  tomatoes

1 (14½-ounce) can diced tomatoes
  with chiles
2 teaspoons Worcestershire
1 tablespoon steak sauce
1 (10-ounce) package frozen
  corn
1 teaspoon cumin
1 teaspoon chili powder
3 cups shredded cheese

Sauté onion and garlic in olive oil in large Dutch oven or stockpot.
Brown chicken breasts in oil. Remove and shred or chop chicken.
Return to pot. Add rest of ingredients, except cheese, to pot. Simmer
one hour. Stir in cheese and serve. May garnish with more cheese,
sour cream, and tortilla chips.

A Taste of Heaven

Summer Goulash

¼ cup cooking oil
6 large potatoes, peeled, cubed
1 large onion, diced
1 large green bell pepper, cubed
3 carrots, sliced
2 celery stalks, sliced
4 green tomatoes, diced

4 ears corn, cut from cob, or 1
    (10-ounce) package frozen corn
1 cup water or more
½ stick margarine
½ teaspoon sugar
Salt and pepper to taste

Heat oil in Dutch oven and prepare vegetables. Stir vegetables to coat well with oil. Add water, margarine, and sugar. Cover and cook on medium heat until vegetables are tender, adding more water as needed. Stir frequently to prevent sticking. Add salt and pepper to taste.

From Chaney Creek to the Chesapeake

Seafood Gumbo

4 tablespoons canola oil
2 medium onions, sliced
3 stalks celery, sliced
2 pounds okra, sliced
2 quarts stewed tomatoes
Salt, pepper, and garlic salt to
    taste

2 pounds raw shrimp, peeled,
    deveined
1 pound crabmeat
6 cups steamed rice

Heat oil in heavy saucepan. Add onions, celery, and okra, and sauté until brown. Cook over low heat, stirring occasionally until okra does not stick to pan or spoon. Gradually add stewed tomatoes and seasoning. Cover and cook slowly about 20 minutes. Add shrimp and crabmeat, and simmer 45 minutes or more. Serve over rice.

Celebrating Our Children Cookbook

Fiesta Chowder

3 tablespoons flour
1 package fajita seasoning, divided
4 skinless, boneless chicken breast halves, cubed
3 tablespoons oil
1 medium onion, chopped
1 teaspoon minced garlic
1 (15-ounce) can whole-kernel corn with red and green peppers
1 (14½-ounce) can Mexican-style stewed tomatoes
1 (15-ounce) can black beans, rinsed, drained

1 (4.5-ounce) can chopped green chiles
3 cups water
1 cup uncooked instant rice
1 (2¼-ounce) can sliced ripe olives
1 (10¾-ounce) can condensed nacho cheese soup
3 tablespoons chopped fresh cilantro
1 tablespoon lime juice
Sour cream for garnish
Cilantro for garnish
Crushed tortilla chips for garnish

Combine flour and 2 tablespoons fajita seasoning in a heavy-duty zip-top plastic bag; add chicken. Seal and shake to coat. Cook chicken in oil in a large Dutch oven over high heat, stirring often, 4 minutes or until browned. Reduce heat to medium high; add onion and garlic, and sauté 5 minutes. Stir in remaining fajita seasoning, corn, tomatoes, black beans, chiles, water, rice, and olives. Bring mixture to a boil, reduce heat to medium low, cover, and simmer 5 minutes. Remove lid and stir in nacho cheese soup, chopped cilantro, and lime juice. Garnish with sour cream, cilantro, and/or tortilla chips. Serves 8–10.

Tried and True Recipes

The Mariners' Museum in Newport News houses one of the largest maritime collections in the world, with more than 35,000 artifacts. You'll find the museum filled to the crow's nest with prized artifacts that celebrate the spirit of seafaring adventure.

Virginia Bacon and Corn Chowder

6 ears fresh sweet corn
1 quart half-and-half
¼ pound smoked bacon,
chopped into small pieces
1 small yellow onion, finely
chopped

2 ribs celery, finely chopped
2 cups (more or less) chicken
broth
Salt and pepper to taste
¼ cup cornstarch for thickening
(optional)

Cut corn kernels from cobs into a bowl, and reserve. Break corn cobs into halves, and simmer in the half-and-half in a saucepan over low heat for approximately 1 hour.

Sauté bacon in a skillet over medium heat. Add onion and celery, stirring constantly. Cook until onion turns golden, being careful to not burn the bacon. Reduce heat to low. Stir in chicken stock, and simmer 15 minutes. Remove and discard corn cobs, reserving the half-and-half mixture. Stir bacon mixture into half-and-half mixture. Add corn kernels, and simmer 1 hour or longer.

Adjust seasonings with salt and pepper, if necessary. If soup needs to be thickened, combine cornstarch, 1 teaspoon at a time, with small amount of water in a small bowl, stirring until smooth. Stir into soup. Simmer 30 minutes or until desired consistency. Makes 8 servings.

Note: Since this is a cream soup, never let the mixture come to a full boil or it will spill over or curdle. Remember that almost all soups taste even better if set aside (refrigerated 5 to 6 days) and reheated slowly before serving.

Celebrate Virginia!

Seven presidents are buried in Virginia: George Washington, Thomas Jefferson, James Madison, James Monroe, John Tyler, William Taft, and John F. Kennedy.

Bacon~Corn Chowder

1 pound bacon
2 (15-ounce) cans creamed corn
3 cups milk
**2 cups shredded sharp Cheddar
    cheese**

½ cup chopped green onions
1 teaspoon pepper

In a large saucepan, fry bacon until crisp. Drain, cool, and crumble. Pour drippings out of saucepan; add corn and milk. Cook over medium heat until mixture starts to bubble. Add cheese, green onions, bacon, and pepper, and bring to boiling point, but do not boil. Serves 6.

Virginia Cook Book

Cheddar Chowder

2 cups water
2 cups diced potatoes
½ cup diced carrots
½ cup diced celery
¼ cup chopped onion
1 teaspoon salt

¼ teaspoon pepper
¼ cup butter
¼ cup all-purpose flour
2 cups milk
2 cups grated Cheddar cheese
1 cup cubed ham

Combine water, potatoes, carrots, celery, onion, salt, and pepper in a large kettle. Boil 10–12 minutes. Meanwhile, in a small saucepan, make a white sauce by melting butter; add flour and stir until smooth. Slowly add milk and cook until thickened. Add grated cheese to white sauce; stir until melted. Add cheese sauce and cubed ham to vegetables that have not been drained. Heat thoroughly.

Berea's Home Cooking Favorites

Brunswick Stew Family Size

1 (2½- to 3-pound) chicken
2 stalks celery
1 small onion
Water
2 quarts tomatoes, fresh or
  canned
1 cup chopped onion
3 medium white potatoes, peeled but
  still whole

1 quart butter beans, drain if
  canned
1 quart whole-kernel corn, drain if
  canned
5 tablespoons sugar
Salt to taste
Red and black pepper to taste

Place chicken, celery, and small onion in a large kettle. Add about a quart of water. Simmer until meat is tender or begins to loosen from bones. Lift chicken from broth and discard celery and onion. Remove meat from bones and cut into small pieces. Add tomatoes, chopped onion, and whole potatoes to broth. Continue cooking over medium heat. Remove potatoes when tender, mash, and return to stew. (Some cooks omit this step and dice potatoes before adding to stew. It has been noted, however, that stew freezes better when potatoes have been mashed; otherwise, they're soggy.) Add cut-up chicken, butter beans, corn, and sugar. Add salt and peppers to taste. Bring to a boil while stirring. Cover; lower heat and simmer slowly 3–5 hours, stirring occasionally to prevent sticking, or until tomatoes have cooked to pieces. Makes about 6 quarts.

Recipe from Brunswick County/Lake Gasten Tourism Association, Inc.
Taste & See

Brunswick stew is a traditional dish from the southeastern United States. The origin of the dish is uncertain, and there are two competing claims as to the place in the South from which it hails. According to Brunswick County legend, the camp chef of a Virginia state legislator invented the recipe in 1828 on a hunting expedition and everyone was immediately hooked. Recipes for Brunswick stew vary greatly, but it is usually a tomato-based stew containing various types of lima beans/butter beans, corn, and other vegetables, and one or more types of meat.

Summer Corn and Tomato Stew

2 large onions, chopped
1 stick margarine
1 gallon fresh tomatoes, peeled,
  cored, quartered
2 tablespoons salt
¼ teaspoon black pepper

2 tablespoons sugar
2 teaspoons curry powder
12 ears fresh corn kernels,
  cut off cob
4 cups (16 ounces) grated
  Longhorn Cheddar cheese

In a stockpot, sauté onions in margarine until tender. Add tomatoes and next 4 ingredients. Cover and simmer 4 hours over low heat, stirring occasionally. Add corn and simmer 1 hour. Before serving, turn off heat and add grated cheese. Let cheese melt, stir once or twice, and serve immediately. Yields 8–10 servings.

Very Virginia

Mama Chrystal's Tender Beef Stew

1½ pounds ground chuck
1 cup chopped onion
4 cups diced cooked potatoes
1 (16-ounce) can stewed
  tomatoes

1 (16-ounce) can red kidney beans,
  drained
1 clove garlic, crushed
½ teaspoon sugar
Salt and pepper to taste

Form ground chuck into 1-inch meatballs. Fry meatballs in skillet until browned. Add onion and cook until soft. Add potatoes, tomatoes, beans, garlic, sugar, salt and pepper. Cook on low until flavors blend, about 30 minutes.

Celebrating Our Children Cookbook

5-Hour Beef Stew

1 envelope dry onion soup mix
1 (10¾-ounce) can cream of
   mushroom soup
1 (10¾-ounce) can cream of
   celery soup
3 pounds stew beef (or boneless
   chuck steak, cut up)

3 (15-ounce) cans potatoes,
   drained, or 3 potatoes, peeled,
   diced
4 stalks celery, cut up
2 large carrots, cut up
2 large onions, quartered

Mix together all soups. In large ovenproof casserole dish, place raw meat and remaining ingredients. Pour soups over all and mix well. Cover and bake in 250° oven for 5 hours. Go shopping, come home with a loaf of good bread, pour yourself a glass of wine, and enjoy supper.

A Laugh & A Glass of Wine

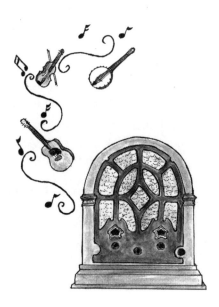

Five-Bean Chili

1 (16-ounce) can Great Northern beans, drained
1 (16-ounce) can pinto beans, drained
1 (16-ounce) can pork and beans, drained
1 (16-ounce) can dark red kidney beans, drained
1 (16-ounce) can navy beans, drained
1 (4-ounce) can sliced mushrooms, small pieces
1 (16-ounce) can stewed tomatoes

2 (28-ounce) cans tomato sauce
1 green bell pepper, chopped
2 or 3 large onions, chopped
4–6 stalks celery, chopped
3 pounds ground chuck
3 tablespoons sugar
3 tablespoons hot picante sauce
1 teaspoon salt
1 teaspoon pepper
1 tablespoon chili powder
2 tablespoons Worcestershire
1 teaspoon crushed garlic

Combine all beans, mushrooms, tomatoes, and tomato sauce in a large stockpot. In skillet, brown green pepper, onions, celery and ground chuck; drain if necessary. Add to bean mixture. Add remaining ingredients and bring to a boil. Let simmer, the longer the better. Makes about 8 quarts. Serve with crackers or cornbread.

Virginia Traditions

Virginia is known as the "Birthplace of Country Music," thanks to the Original Carter Family—A.P., Sara, and Maybelle—who were first recorded back in Bristol in 1927 at the RCA Bristol Sessions. "Will the Circle be Unbroken," "Wildwood Flower," "Keep on the Sunny Side," and "Wabash Cannonball" were all written by A.P. His wife, Sara, sang the soulful lyrics, and Sara's cousin Maybelle played lead guitar.

Gene's Chili

Quite possibly this is the best chili east of Texas.

2 tablespoons cooking oil or olive oil
1 medium onion, diced
1 medium green bell pepper, diced
3 pounds ground beef
Salt and pepper to taste
1 package McCormick Hot Chili Mix
1 package McCormick Regular Chili Mix

1–2 tablespoons chili powder
2 (15-ounce) cans stewed tomatoes
1 (10-ounce) can hot Ro-Tel tomatoes
1 (6-ounce) can tomato paste
1 (8-ounce) can tomato juice (optional)
½ cup water
1 (16-ounce) can pink or red kidney beans

Put oil in large pot. Sauté onion and green pepper 3–4 minutes. Add ground beef and salt and pepper to mixture; chop beef into small pieces as it browns; drain if needed. Combine remaining ingredients and pour into ground beef mixture. Simmer 1–2 hours; stir often.

The Hall Family Cookbook

Salads

The re-created Indian Village in Jamestown is representative of how the Powhatans were living at the time of the English colonization of Virginia. The legendary Pocahontas, daughter of Powhatan, powerful leader of more than 30 Indian tribes, lived in a village much like this. Historical interpreters demonstrate the daily life of the Powhatans.

Coleslaw

2 tablespoons mayonnaise
3 tablespoons sugar
2 tablespoons vinegar
3 tablespoons milk

Salt and pepper to taste
Pinch of celery salt (optional)
2–3 cups chopped cabbage

Mix all ingredients except cabbage. Pour over chopped cabbage and mix well.

Berea's Home Cooking Favorites

Pickled String Beans

2 pounds fresh string beans
1 small jar pimientos, slivered
1 medium onion, or several
   spring onions, thinly sliced
Vegetable oil to coat beans

Salt and pepper to taste
⅔ cup vinegar
1⅓ cups water, saved from
   cooking beans

Wash and French-cut beans. Cook in salted water until just tender. Drain, saving 1⅓ cups liquid. Put beans in mixing bowl. Add pimientos and onion. Pour in enough vegetable oil to coat beans. Toss together as a salad. Add salt and pepper. Combine vinegar and reserved water; pour over bean mixture. Serve warm, or store in covered container in refrigerator and serve cold on lettuce leaf with mayonnaise or cottage cheese. Garnish with hard-boiled eggs.

The Smithfield Cookbook

 In 2003, Archaeologists located what is believed to be the 17th-century village of Werowocomoco, headquarters for Chief Powhatan, along the York River in Gloucester County. Captain John Smith, who led the 1607 colonization of Jamestown, met with Chief Powhatan and, according to legend, his life was spared by Powhatan's daughter, Pocahontas.

Zucchini Relish

10 cups chopped zucchini
3 cups chopped green bell
  peppers
3 tablespoons salt
4 cups chopped onions
1 tablespoon hot pepper

3 tablespoons celery seed
1 tablespoon turmeric
5 cups sugar
3 tablespoons mustard seed
1 tablespoon black pepper
2½ cups vinegar

Mix first 5 ingredients and let stand overnight.

    Bring next 6 ingredients to a boil; add relish mixture and cook 25 minutes. Seal in sterilized jars.

The Riggs Family Cookbook

French Dressing

1 small onion, chopped
1 cup salad oil
¾ cup vinegar
1 cup ketchup
2 cups sugar

1 teaspoon dry mustard powder
1 teaspoon paprika
3 teaspoons salt
1 teaspoon Worcestershire
1 teaspoon garlic salt

Mix all ingredients together and blend in blender or food processor. Makes 1 quart salad dressing.

Kitty Caters

Spinach Salad

DRESSING:

¼ cup vinegar
½ cup sugar
1 cup oil

Dash of salt
Dash of Worcestershire
⅓ cup ketchup

Make Dressing one day before and refrigerate.

SALAD:

1 pound fresh spinach, broken
4 strips crisp bacon, crumbled
4 hard-boiled eggs, chopped
1 (15-ounce) can bean sprouts,
   chilled, drained

½ pound mushrooms, sliced
Croutons

Toss together Salad ingredients and Dressing. Toss again; add croutons. Serves 10.

Taste of the Town II

Bacon-Egg-Spinach Salad

½ cup oil
¼ cup sugar
2 tablespoons vinegar
1 teaspoon finely grated onion
½ teaspoon salt
¼ teaspoon dry mustard

1 pound fresh spinach
6 slices crisp bacon, crumbled
5 hard-cooked eggs, chopped
1 hard-cooked egg, sliced for
   garnish

Combine oil, sugar, vinegar, onion, salt, and mustard; set aside. Wash spinach, drain on paper towels, and tear into bite-size pieces. Place in large salad bowl. Add bacon and chopped eggs. Pour dressing over spinach, toss, and let stand ½ hour. Garnish with sliced egg. Serves 8.

The Fine Art of Dining

Greek Salad

The traditional Greek salad bowl consists of a variety of greens chopped or torn into bite-size pieces. The wooden bowl is rubbed with a clove of garlic, or a clove of garlic is marinated in the olive oil overnight.

1 head lettuce, mixed with a few stems of chicory, escarole, romaine, and endive
2 large tomatoes, cut in wedges
4 radishes, sliced
2 cucumbers, sliced
1 small green bell pepper, sliced in rings
1 Bermuda or red onion, sliced thinly in rings
Salt and pepper to taste
1 teaspoon oregano

Mix all ingredients in large wooden bowl and add seasoning. Toss lightly with Dressing. Garnish.

DRESSING:
2 tablespoons lemon juice or wine vinegar
6 tablespoons olive oil

Mix together well.

GARNISHES:
Black olives
Feta cheese
Anchovies

Garnish salad as desired.

Come Cook with Us

Warm Mushroom Salad

2 quarts mixed greens (spinach, arugula, and romaine)
3 tablespoons olive oil
1 (1-pound) package fresh mushrooms, cleaned, sliced
3 shallots, chopped
1 clove garlic, crushed
2 tablespoons chopped fresh chives
2 tablespoons lemon juice
2 tablespoons balsamic vinegar
1 teaspoon sugar
1 cup garlic croutons
Shavings of Parmesan cheese
Salt and pepper to taste

Tear greens into bite-size pieces and arrange in serving bowls. In medium skillet, heat olive oil over medium heat until hot. Add mushrooms, shallots, and garlic; cook and stir 3–5 minutes or until mushrooms are tender. Stir in chives, lemon juice, vinegar, and sugar; simmer 30 seconds. Spoon mixture over salad greens. Top with croutons and Parmesan cheese. Season with salt and pepper to taste.

Cooking with ARK Angels

Olive Salad

⅔ cup black olives
⅔ cup pimento-stuffed olives
½ small red bell pepper, diced
¼ small sweet onion, diced
1 garlic clove, minced
1 tablespoon olive oil
2 teaspoons red wine vinegar

Place olives in bowl. Coarsely crush olives with fork. Stir in remaining ingredients. Cover and chill up to 5 days. Makes about 1½ cups. Great on sub-type sandwiches.

From Chaney Creek to the Chesapeake

Cornbread Salad

6 cups crumbled baked
   cornbread
2 cups shredded Cheddar cheese
1 (15-ounce) can whole-kernel
   corn, drained
½ cup chopped green onions

1 pound bacon, cooked, drained,
   crumbled
2 large tomatoes, chopped
½ cup chopped green bell
   pepper
1 cup mayonnaise

Combine all ingredients in large bowl; cover and refrigerate until well
chilled. Makes about 12 servings.

The Riggs Family Cookbook

Wild Rice and Cranberry Salad

1 (6-ounce) package long-grain
   and wild rice mix
1 cup sweetened dried
   cranberries (craisins)
1 cup chopped fresh broccoli
   florets
4 green onions, chopped

3 celery ribs, thinly sliced
1 (2-ounce) jar diced pimento,
   drained
½ cup sweet and sour dressing
1 cup chopped dry roasted
   peanuts

Prepare rice mix according to package directions; cool. Combine rice,
cranberries, and next 4 ingredients; add dressing. Stir gently. Cover
and chill at least 2 hours. Stir in peanuts just before serving.

Recipes from Home

 How large is Virginia? Virginia's land area encompasses 39,594 square
miles, with an additional 3,180 square miles covered by water, mostly
in the Chesapeake Bay. Now ranked 37th among the states,
Virginia's area was once much larger. Prior to the American Revolution, the land that
is now West Virginia, Kentucky, and much of Ohio, Indiana, and Illinois was considered to be part of Virginia.

Wild Rice Chicken Salad

2 (6-ounce) packages long-grain
  and wild rice mix
2 (15-ounce) cans low-sodium
  chicken broth
3 (6-ounce) jars marinated
  artichoke quarters, undrained
4 cups chopped, cooked chicken
  (8 breasts)

1 medium red bell pepper,
  chopped
2 celery ribs, thinly sliced
5 green onions, chopped
1 (2¼-ounce) can sliced ripe black
  olives, drained
1 cup mayonnaise
1½ teaspoons curry powder

Cook rice according to package directions, using chicken broth instead
of water. Drain artichoke quarters, reserving ½ cup liquid. Stir
together rice, artichokes, chicken, and next 4 ingredients. In separate
bowl, stir together artichoke liquid, mayonnaise, and curry powder.
Toss with rice mixture. Cover and chill 8 hours. Serve on leaf lettuce.
Serves 8.

Cooking with Grace

Virginia Bicentennial Chicken Salad

¾ cup mayonnaise
1 teaspoon curry powder
2 teaspoons lemon juice
2 teaspoons soy sauce
2 cups cubed cooked chicken
  breasts
1 (8-ounce) can sliced water
  chestnuts, drained

½ pound seedless green grapes,
  halved
1 (8-ounce) can pineapple tidbits,
  drained
½ cup chopped celery
½ cup slivered almonds,
  toasted

Combine first 4 ingredients in a small bowl. Combine chicken and next 5 ingredients in a separate bowl; pour dressing over mixture, tossing to coat. Cover and chill overnight. Serves 4.

What Can I Bring?

Waldorf Chicken Salad— Mangus House

3 cups cubed cooked chicken
1 unpeeled red apple, diced
1 cup green or red grapes
1 cup sliced celery
6 pineapple rings, cut into pieces
  (or pineapple tidbits)

1 cup English walnut pieces
1 cup whipped cream
2 teaspoons lemon juice
Salt to taste
Mayonnaise to taste

Mix all ingredients together and chill before serving.

Vesuvius, Virginia: Then and Now

Fall Salad

DRESSING:
⅔ cup vegetable oil
½ cup vinegar
1 teaspoon sugar

½ teaspoon salt
⅛ teaspoon pepper

Combine ingredients in a jar and shake well; chill.

8 cups torn salad greens, chilled
1 cup diced red apples
1 cup diagonally sliced celery

¼ cup crumbled blue cheese
1 cup chopped nuts

Combine greens, apples, and celery. Shake Dressing and pour over salad. Add cheese and toss lightly. Garnish with nuts. Serves 6–8.

Tidewater on the Half Shell

Arugula, Pear and Gorgonzola Salad

3 tablespoons light olive oil
3 tablespoons balsamic vinegar
3 tablespoons crumbled Gorgonzola or blue cheese, divided
Salt and pepper to taste

¾ pound arugula or mixed baby greens
3 ripe pears (can use canned)
⅓ cup toasted pecans or walnuts

Whisk oil, vinegar, and 1½ tablespoons cheese in a bowl (or shake in a jar). Add salt and pepper to taste. Mix greens and dressing. Add peeled, cored pears, cut in ½-inch slices. Top with remaining cheese and pecans. Dressing can be made ahead and refrigerated. Return to room temperature before adding to salad. Serves 6.

Cooking with Grace

My Favorite Potato Salad

COOKED SALAD DRESSING:

1 egg, beaten	**¼ cup sugar**
¼ cup vinegar	**Salt and pepper to taste**

Combine all ingredients. Cook over medium heat until thick. Cool.

Tip: I like to pour Cooked Salad Dressing while hot over potatoes. Cool and add remaining ingredients.

Note: If I am serving potato salad with ham, I add more mustard.

4 cups diced cooked potatoes	**¾–1 cup mayonnaise**
½ cup diced celery	**1 tablespoon prepared mustard,**
¼ cup cut-up green onions or	**more or less**
white onion	**1 teaspoon celery seeds**
½ cup chopped sweet pickles	**½ teaspoon dried dill weed**
4 hard-boiled eggs, diced	**(optional)**
2 tablespoons chopped pimento	**Salt and pepper to taste**
¾ cup Cooked Salad Dressing	

Combine all ingredients and mix well. Chill.

Granny's Kitchen

Samuel Jackson "Sam" Snead (May 27, 1912–May 23, 2002), born in Ashwood, was one of the top golfers in the world for most of four decades. He won a record 82 PGA Tour events and about 70 others worldwide. He won seven majors: three Masters, three PGA Championships, and one British Open. Snead was inducted into the World Golf Hall of Fame in 1974, and won the PGA Tour Lifetime Achievement Award in 1998.

Dockside Potato Salad

5–6 medium red potatoes
¼ cup finely chopped onion
¼ cup finely chopped celery,
   including some leaves
1 dill pickle, chopped
2 tablespoons dried parsley
6 strips bacon, cooked crisp and
   crumbled

½–1 teaspoon salt
¼ teaspoon pepper
1½ tablespoons vinegar
4 tablespoons vegetable oil
1–1¼ cups mayonnaise

Cook potatoes in salted water until tender, 30–40 minutes; drain. Cool completely in refrigerator. Peel and cut into thin bite-size pieces. Place in large bowl. Add next 5 ingredients. Sprinkle salt, pepper, vinegar, and oil over all. Gently turn all ingredients over with wooden spoon until well mixed. Add mayonnaise and turn again until well moistened. Refrigerate several hours before serving. Serves 6–8.

Tidewater on the Half Shell

Taco Salad

1 medium-size bag nacho chips
   (cheese flavor if desired)
2 pounds hamburger meat
2 packages taco seasoning
1 (16-ounce) can refried beans
   (optional)
1 head lettuce, shredded

2 ripe tomatoes, cubed
2 cups cooked rice
2 cups shredded Cheddar cheese
Sour cream
Taco sauce (hot, medium, or
   mild)

Put nacho chips in zipper bag and slightly crush. Cook hamburger meat in skillet until browned, drain, and add taco seasoning mix.

Preheat oven to 325°. In a large glass lasagna pan or baking dish, pour a portion of the crushed nachos, just to cover bottom of pan. Add a layer of meat, sprinkling it evenly across the pan; add refried beans, if desired. Add a layer of shredded lettuce, tomatoes, rice, and shredded cheese. Continue to layer until all ingredients are used. Top layer should end with crushed nachos and shredded cheese. Heat in oven 15 minutes, or until warm and cheese is melted. Serve with sour cream and taco sauce. Enjoy!

All American Recipes

One of Virginia's nicknames is "Mother of Presidents" because no other state has produced more U.S. presidents than Virginia. The eight presidents who were born in Virginia are: George Washington (1789–1797), Thomas Jefferson (1801-1809), James Madison (1809–1817), James Monroe (1817–1825), William H. Harrison (1773–1841), John Tyler (1841–1845), Zachary Taylor (1849–1850), and Woodrow Wilson (1913–1921). This list includes six of the first ten presidents of the United States.

Day-Before Salad

1 (10-ounce) package frozen
  peas
1 large head lettuce, shredded or
  chopped
1 green bell pepper, chopped
1 cup chopped onion
3 stalks celery, thinly sliced
Mayonnaise

½ cup shredded Cheddar
  cheese
3 large tomatoes, diced
1 (16-ounce) jar red wine and
  vinegar salad dressing, divided
½ pound bacon
1 (4-ounce) can sliced black
  olives

Combine peas, lettuce, pepper, onion, and celery. Place in 9x13-inch glass dish. Spread a little (or a lot) of mayonnaise on top, however you choose. Sprinkle cheese over top. Cover, and refrigerate overnight. In separate container, combine tomatoes with ½ bottle of salad dressing. Refrigerate overnight. Stir occasionally.

Fry bacon, and crumble. Before serving, spoon tomatoes and remaining dressing over salad. Top with crumbled bacon and black olives. No other dressing is required.

Food, Family, and Friendships

King William III and Queen Mary II granted a charter to establish The College of William and Mary in Virginia. Founded in 1693 in Williamsburg, William and Mary is the second oldest educational institution in the United States. (Although Harvard began operation first, William and Mary's antecedents actually predate those of the Massachusetts institution.) Four presidents of the United States benefited from educational programs offered by the college: George Washington, Thomas Jefferson, James Monroe, and John Tyler. A succession of influential individuals—including President George Washington, President John Tyler, Chief Justice Warren Burger, former Prime Minister Margaret Thatcher, and former Secretary of State Henry A. Kissinger have held the post of Chancellor of The College of William and Mary. In 2006, Sandra Day O'Connor, former Associate Justice of the U.S. Supreme Court, was installed as the college's 23rd Chancellor.

Make-Ahead Oriental Salad

1 (15-ounce) can English peas,
  drained
1 (14-ounce) can shoepeg corn
1 (4-ounce) jar sliced mushrooms,
  drained
1 (4-ounce) jar chopped
  pimentos, drained
1 large green bell pepper, thinly
  sliced
1 cup sliced celery
1 (14-ounce) can bean sprouts,
  drained
1 (8-ounce) can sliced water
  chestnuts, drained

1 large onion, thinly sliced
1 cup vegetable oil
½ cup water
1 tablespoon soy sauce
½ teaspoon salt
¼ teaspoon pepper
1 cup sugar
½ cup vinegar
2 tablespoons red wine vinegar
1 teaspoon dry mustard
½ teaspoon paprika
⅛ teaspoon garlic powder

Combine vegetables in a large bowl and toss lightly. Combine remaining ingredients. Stir well. Pour marinade over vegetables, stirring gently. Cover and chill overnight. Drain vegetables or serve salad with a slotted spoon. Yields 12–15 servings.

Church Family Favorites

Oriental Salad

1 package chicken or vegetable
  ramen noodles
2 tablespoons sugar
1 teaspoon pepper
½ head Chinese cabbage,
  chopped

½ cup sunflower seeds
½ cup toasted slivered almonds
2–3 green onions, chopped

Mix seasoning packet from noodles, sugar, pepper, and oil. Mix with cabbage, sunflower seeds, almonds, and chopped onions. Crush noodles from packet and combine with above mixture.

Tasty Treasures from Johnson's Church

Tidewater Shrimp Salad

1 (16-ounce) package small shell
  pasta
2 pounds frozen salad shrimp,
  thawed, drained
1 cup chopped celery
6 green onions, chopped
1 cup mayonnaise

½ cup Russian salad dressing
2 tablespoons capers
1 tablespoon lemon juice
1 tablespoon celery seeds
¼ teaspoon salt
¼ teaspoon pepper
¼ teaspoon Old Bay Seasoning

Cook pasta using package directions (without adding fat or salt) until al dente; drain. Combine shrimp, celery, and green onions in a bowl and mix well. Combine mayonnaise, salad dressing, capers, lemon juice, celery seeds, salt, pepper, and Old Bay Seasoning in a bowl and mix well. Add mayonnaise mixture to the shrimp mixture and toss to coat. Stir in pasta. Chill, covered, until serving time. Yields 20 servings.

Vintage Virginia

Shrimp and Crabmeat Salad

1 pound fresh crabmeat
  (backfin)
1 pound shrimp, cooked, finely
  chopped
½ cup chopped green bell
  pepper

¼ cup finely chopped onion
1½ cups finely chopped celery
½ teaspoon salt
1 tablespoon Worcestershire
1 cup mayonnaise

Mix crabmeat, shrimp, green pepper, onion, and celery well. Stir salt and Worcestershire into mayonnaise. Mix all ingredients together well. Serve on lettuce or as desired.

The Smithfield Cookbook

Crab Mold

2 (6-ounce) cans crabmeat
1 (10¾-ounce) can cream of
   mushroom soup
1 package Knox gelatin
1 tablespoon lemon juice

¾ cup mayonnaise
3 drops hot sauce
¼ teaspoon paprika
½ cup chopped celery
6 small spring onions, chopped

Drain crabmeat well and pick over. Heat soup on low. Add gelatin and cool. Mix all ingredients. Spoon into an oiled mold and refrigerate 3 hours or overnight. Unmold onto leaf lettuce and garnish. Serve with crackers.

Church Family Favorites

Autumn Apple Salad

1 (20-ounce) can crushed
   pineapple, undrained
⅔ cup sugar
1 (3-ounce) package lemon-
   flavored gelatin
1 (8-ounce) package cream
   cheese, softened

1 cup diced, unpeeled apples
¾ cup chopped pecans
1 cup chopped celery
1 cup whipped topping
Lettuce leaves

In a saucepan, combine pineapple and sugar; bring to a boil and boil 3 minutes. Add gelatin; stir until dissolved. Add cream cheese; stir until mixture is thoroughly combined. Cool. Fold in apples, nuts, celery, and whipped topping. Pour into a 9-inch-square pan. Chill until firm. Cut into squares and serve on lettuce leaves. Yields 9–12 servings.

Joy in Serving

Taffy Apple Salad

1 (8-ounce) can crushed
  pineapple, drained, reserve
  juice
1 tablespoon flour
½ cup sugar
2 tablespoons cider vinegar

1 egg, beaten
6 cups coarsely diced, unpeeled
  apples
1 cup salted, shelled peanuts
1 (8-ounce) carton nondairy
  topping

Place reserved pineapple juice in a small saucepan. Add flour, sugar, vinegar, and egg. Cook on low heat, stirring constantly, until thick. Cool. Combine apples and pineapple. Pour cooled sauce over top. Fold in peanuts and topping. May sprinkle additional peanuts over top for garnish. Yields 12 servings.

Joy in Serving

Out of This World Snicker Salad

2 large Granny Smith apples
1 bag Snickers miniatures

1 (8-ounce) tub frozen Cool Whip,
  thawed

Chop apples and Snickers into small (fingertip-size) pieces. Mix with Cool Whip in a large bowl until evenly distributed.

Taste Trek!

Stuffed Pears

1 (8-ounce) package cream
  cheese, softened
½ cup powdered sugar
2–3 tablespoons pear juice

½ bag miniature marshmallows
½ cup chopped nuts
1 (15-ounce) can pear halves,
  drained

Mix cream cheese, sugar, and juice until creamy. Add marshmallows and nuts. Stuff pear halves.

From Chaney Creek to the Chesapeake

Spiced Peach Salad

1 (29-ounce) can spiced peaches
1 (16-ounce) can white grapes or
   Queen Anne cherries
¾ cup orange juice
1 (3-ounce) package lemon
   gelatin
1 (3-ounce) package orange
   gelatin
½ cup ginger preserves
½ cup pecan pieces

Drain peaches and grapes, reserving juice. Slice peaches and grapes.
Combine reserved juices with enough orange juice to measure 4 cups
and pour into a saucepan. Heat juices until hot. Remove from heat.
Combine hot juices, lemon gelatin and orange gelatin, in a heatproof
bowl, stirring until dissolved. Chill until partially set. Stir in peaches,
grapes, preserves, and pecans. Spoon into a 9x13-inch dish. Chill
until set. Serve on lettuce-lined salad plates. Yields 12 servings.

Vintage Virginia

Strawberry Salad

2 (3-ounce) packages strawberry
   Jell-O
1 (8-ounce) can crushed
   pineapple, drained
3 bananas, mashed
½ cup chopped pecans
2 (10-ounce) packages frozen
   strawberries
1 cup sour cream

Mix Jell-O with 1 cup boiling water. Add pineapple, bananas, nuts,
and berries. Pour half of mixture in a glass bowl or dish. Refrigerate.
Spread sour cream over cool mixture, then remaining half of fruit mixture over sour cream. Chill really well. Makes a very pretty dish.

Sharing Our Best

Virginia is the only state that does not allow the governor to run for
reelection. He serves a single four-year term, then a new governor
is elected.

Bing Cherry Salad

1 can Bing cherries, pitted,
  drained, reserve juice
1 (6-ounce) package dark cherry
  Jell-O

1 cup port wine
½–1 cup chopped nuts
1–2 tablespoons lemon juice

Add enough water to reserved cherry juice to make 1 cup. Heat this to boiling, and pour over Jell-O. Dissolve Jell-O thoroughly. Add cherries, port wine, nuts, and lemon juice. Pour into 4–6 individual molds, and refrigerate until set.

Food, Family, and Friendships

Heavenly White Fluff Salad

1 (6-ounce) package lemon
  Jell-O
2 cups boiling water
1 (8-ounce) package cream
  cheese, softened
1 (20-ounce) can crushed
  pineapple, drained, reserve juice

½ cup mayonnaise
1 cup whipping cream, whipped,
  or 1 (8-ounce) carton whipped
  topping
1 cup flaked coconut (optional)

Dissolve Jell-O in boiling water. Add cream cheese and beat until blended. Add reserved juice. Chill until partly set. Beat in mayonnaise. Add pineapple; fold in whipped cream and coconut, if desired. Pour into 9x13-inch dish. Chill until set. Heavenly!

Tip: Fold in 2 cups colored miniature marshmallows, especially pretty for spring and Easter. Or 1 cup maraschino cherries, red and green for Christmas. Gelatin "cut outs" on each square are pretty also; 3-ounce package red gelatin dissolved in 1½ cups hot water, poured into 9-inch square pan. Hearts for Valentines, and stars or bells for Christmas. Very festive!

Granny's Kitchen

Triple-Orange Ambrosial Salad

2 cups boiling liquid (water
  or fruit syrup)
1 (6-ounce) package orange
  Jell-O
1 pint orange sherbet
1 (11-ounce) can Mandarin orange
  segments, drained

Pour boiling liquid over Jell-O in bowl, stirring until gelatin is dissolved. Add orange sherbet; stir until melted. Stir in Mandarin orange segments. Pour into 6-cup ring mold; chill until firm.

TOPPING:

1 (11-ounce) can Mandarin
  orange segments, drained
1 (13½-ounce) can pineapple
  chunks, drained
1 cup flaked coconut
1 cup miniature marshmallows
1 cup dairy sour cream, or ½ cup
  whipping cream, whipped

Combine Mandarin orange segments, pineapple, coconut, and marshmallows. Fold in sour cream. Chill at least 3 hours. Fill center of unmolded salad with fruit mixture.

Cooking with ARK Angels

Banana Split Salad

1 (12-ounce) container Cool
  Whip, thawed
1 (14-ounce) can sweetened
  condensed milk
1 (21-ounce) can cherry pie
  filling
1 (8½-ounce) can crushed
  pineapple, drained
2–4 medium-size bananas, peeled,
  cubed
½ cup chopped nuts
Flaked coconut (optional)

Thoroughly mix Cool Whip and condensed milk. Add pie filling, pineapple, bananas, and nuts. Mix well. Pour into 3-quart bowl and chill several hours. Spread a little coconut on top, if desired.

Favorite Recipes: Barbara's Best Volume II

Blueberry Salad Mold

2 (3-ounce) packages strawberry
   Jell-O
2 cups boiling water

1 (21-ounce) can blueberry pie
   filling
1 cup sour cream

Dissolve Jell-O in boiling water. Cool. Add blueberry filling and sour cream; mix thoroughly. Pour into mold and chill.

DRESSING:
1 cup sour cream
1 teaspoon sugar

½ teaspoon ground ginger

Mix together and serve on chilled salad mold.

Thought for Food

Christmas Salad

2 (3-ounce) boxes cherry Jell-O
1 cup boiling water
1 (16-ounce) can whole
   cranberry sauce
2 cups cold water

½ cup chopped celery
1 (15-ounce) can crushed pineapple
   with juice
¾ cup chopped pecans

Mix Jell-O and hot water. Add cranberry sauce and mix well. Add cold water, celery, pineapple, and nuts. Put in 9x13-inch glass casserole and refrigerate.

A Taste of Tradition

Vegetables

Surveyed by George Washington and once owned by Thomas Jefferson, Natural Bridge in Rockbridge County is a limestone arch 215 feet high with a span of 90 feet, formed by Cedar Creek. Natural Bridge is designated as both a Virginia Historical Landmark and a National Historical Landmark.

Scalloped Potatoes

8–10 potatoes
1 (10¾-ounce) can cream of
  chicken soup
½ soup can milk
¼ stick butter
1 small onion, chopped

1 cup shredded Cheddar cheese
Salt and pepper to taste
½ teaspoon parsley flakes
Additional cheese for topping
  (optional)

Peel and slice enough potatoes for a 2-quart baking dish. Cook in salted water to cover until tender, but firm; drain. In saucepan, cook remaining ingredients over low heat until butter and 1 cup cheese melts. Stir often to keep from sticking. Place ½ potatoes in greased baking dish. Add ½ soup mixture. Add remaining potatoes and remaining soup mixture. If desired, add additional cheese on top. Bake in 350° oven 30 minutes.

Garden Gate Recipes

Fast and Easy Scalloped Potatoes

4 cups thinly sliced potatoes
2 cups milk, divided
2 teaspoons salt

2 tablespoons flour
¼ cup chopped onion

Cook potatoes in boiling salted water to cover 5 minutes. Blend ½ cup milk with salt and flour until smooth. Add to remaining milk in saucepan over low heat, stirring constantly until thickened (about 5 minutes). Arrange potatoes, onion, and heated milk sauce alternately in 1½-quart oven-safe buttered casserole dish. Bake at 350° for 35 minutes. Makes 4 servings.

Variation: For Cheese Scallop, add ½ cup grated cheese to milk sauce before pouring over partially cooked potatoes.

Country Home Favorites

Gratin of Potatoes with White Cheddar and Tarragon

3 pounds Yukon Gold potatoes
2 teaspoons salt
1 teaspoon ground black pepper
2½ teaspoons dried tarragon
1½ cups grated sharp white
   Cheddar cheese (about 6 ounces)

1 cup whipping cream
1 cup dry white wine or
   vermouth

Preheat oven to 400°. Butter a 9x13-inch glass baking dish. Peel potatoes and cut into ⅛-inch thick rounds. Layer ⅓ of potatoes in prepared dish, overlapping slightly. Sprinkle with ⅓ of salt, ⅓ of pepper, ⅓ of tarragon, and ⅓ of cheese. Repeat layering twice more with remaining potatoes, salt, pepper, tarragon, and cheese. Whisk cream and wine in medium bowl to blend. Pour over potatoes; bake uncovered until potatoes are tender when pierced with knife and top is golden, about 1 hour. Let gratin stand 5 minutes before serving.

A Taste of Prince William County Cookbook

Thomas Jefferson brought the first French chef to Virginia, and is credited with bringing to the New World what the French call "pommes frites," or french fries.

Hash Brown Casserole

1 stick margarine
1 (30-ounce) package shredded
  hash brown potatoes
½ onion, chopped
1 (10¾-ounce) can cream of
  chicken soup
1 (8-ounce) carton sour cream
2 cups shredded Cheddar cheese,
  divided
Salt and pepper to taste

Melt margarine in large bowl. Add thawed hash brown potatoes, onion, soup, and sour cream. Mix well. Add 1½ cups Cheddar cheese, salt and pepper. Mix well. Pour into greased 9x13-inch dish and top with remaining Cheddar cheese. Bake at 325° for 1 hour. Serve warm.

Sharing Our Best

Slow Cooker Hash Brown Casserole

½ cup plus 1 tablespoon
  margarine, melted, divided
3 tablespoons minced dried
  onion
½ teaspoon salt
⅛ teaspoon pepper
1 (10¾-ounce) can cream of
  chicken soup
1½ cups milk
1 cup shredded Cheddar cheese
1 (26-ounce) package frozen
  shredded hash brown potatoes
¾ cup crushed cornflakes

In a large bowl, combine ½ cup margarine, onion, salt, pepper, soup, and milk. Add cheese and hash browns. Mix well. Pour into a greased 5-quart slow cooker. Cover and cook on LOW for 4½–5 hours or until potatoes are tender. Just before serving, combine cornflake crumbs with remaining 1 tablespoon margarine in a pie plate. Bake at 350° for 4–6 minutes or until golden brown. Stir potatoes and sprinkle with crumb topping.

Joy in Serving

Pizza Potatoes

1 (7½-ounce) package scalloped
   potatoes
1 (14½-ounce) can tomatoes
1½ cups water
¼ teaspoon crushed oregano
   leaves

1 (4-ounce) package sliced
   pepperoni
1 (4-ounce) package shredded
   mozzarella cheese

Heat oven to 400°. Empty potato slices and packet of seasoned sauce mix into ungreased 2-quart casserole. Heat tomatoes, water, and oregano to boiling; stir into potatoes. Arrange pepperoni on top and sprinkle with cheese. Bake uncovered 30 minutes. Serves 4.

Note: May substitute ½ pound beef, browned and drained, for pepperoni; stir into potato mixture.

Recipe submitted by Cindy Shifflet Lee (Miss Virginia Farm Bureau 1978)
Country Treasures

Glazed Sweet Potato Casserole

6 medium sweet potatoes (about
  3½ pounds)
¼ cup firmly packed brown
  sugar
¼ cup honey
1 tablespoon cornstarch
½ teaspoon cinnamon

¼ teaspoon ground nutmeg
2 tablespoons orange rind
2 tablespoons butter or
  margarine
½ cup pineapple juice
¼ cup chopped walnuts

Cook sweet potatoes in boiling water to cover 20–25 minutes, or until fork-tender. Let cool to touch; peel and cut into ½-inch slices. Arrange slices in a lightly greased 9x13-inch baking dish; set aside.

Combine brown sugar, honey, cornstarch, cinnamon, nutmeg, orange rind, butter, and pineapple juice in a saucepan. Cook over medium heat, stirring constantly, until mixture begins to boil; boil 1 minute, stirring constantly, until mixture is thickened and bubbly. Pour over sweet potatoes; sprinkle with chopped walnuts. Cover and refrigerate 8 hours.

Remove dish from refrigerator; let stand 30 minutes. Uncover and bake at 350° for 30 minutes or until thoroughly heated. Makes 8 servings.

The Riggs Family Cookbook

The American Revolution refers to the period during the last half of the 18th century in which the thirteen colonies that became the United States of America gained independence from the British Empire. The thirteen colonies were British colonies in North America founded between 1607 (Virginia) and 1732 (Georgia). Although Britain held a dozen additional colonies in North America and the West Indies, the colonies referred to as the "thirteen" are those that rebelled against British rule in 1775 and proclaimed their independence as the United States of America on July 4, 1776. The majority of the fighting ended with the surrender of Britain's General Cornwallis in Yorktown on October 19, 1781. However, minor battles continued for another two years. The Treaty of Paris was finally signed on September 3, 1783, officially ending the American Revolution.

Sweet Potato Crunch

1 cup granulated sugar
½ stick margarine
½ cup milk
2 eggs, beaten

1 teaspoon ground cinnamon
3 cups mashed sweet potatoes
2 egg whites, stiffly beaten

Combine sugar, margarine, milk, eggs, and cinnamon. Add to sweet potato mixture. Fold egg whites into sweet potatoes.

TOPPING:

2 cups regular oatmeal
½ stick margarine, melted

1 cup packed brown sugar
Chopped nuts

Combine ingredients; place on top of sweet potato mixture. Bake at 350° for 30–40 minutes.

Favorite Recipes: Bayside Baptist Church

Stuffed Green Peppers

6 medium green bell peppers
1 pound ground beef
⅓ cup chopped celery
⅓ cup chopped onions
1 teaspoon salt
1 teaspoon mustard
¼ cup ketchup

1 egg, beaten
1 teaspoon hot sauce
1 teaspoon A-1 sauce
1 teaspoon Worcestershire
1 teaspoon white pepper
½ cup bread crumbs
½ teaspoon garlic salt

Cut off tops of peppers and remove seeds. Parboil pepper cups in small amount of salted water for 5 minutes; drain. Mix remaining ingredients together; divide into 6 portions and stuff peppers. Prepare Sauce. Pour approximately ¼ cup of Sauce into a baking dish which has been sprayed with vegetable spray. Place stuffed peppers in dish. Pour 1–1½ cups Sauce on top. Bake in preheated 375° oven for 45–50 minutes. Spoon on additional Sauce, if needed.

SAUCE:

½ cup sugar
1 tablespoon hot sauce
1 tablespoon A-1 sauce
1 tablespoon Worcestershire
1 (42-ounce) can tomato juice

1 tablespoon salt
2 teaspoons white pepper
½ cup ketchup
2 tablespoons cornstarch
1 (4-ounce) can tomato juice

Mix first 8 ingredients together and heat. Mix cornstarch and tomato juice; add to mixture, stirring constantly. Simmer until thickened. Makes enough Sauce for 12 peppers.

Mrs. Rowe's Favorite Recipes

Ratatouille-Stuffed Pepper Halves

The three pepper colors render a beautiful presentation on dinner plates or a buffet.

1 each: large red, yellow, green
  bell pepper
¼ cup olive oil
1 small eggplant
1 small onion, thinly sliced
1 clove garlic, minced
1 large tomato, coarsely chopped

1 cup sliced fresh mushrooms
½ teaspoon each: dried basil,
  oregano leaves, and salt
Dash of black and red pepper
1 zucchini, sliced lengthwise, cut
  into ½-inch chunks

Cut peppers in half lengthwise. Remove seeds and membranes without cutting through shell. Place pepper halves in a 2-quart rectangular glass dish, cover with vented plastic wrap, and microwave on HIGH 4–5 minutes, or until peppers are crisp-tender. Cover with cold water to stop cooking; drain and set aside with cut sides up.

Heat oil in a large skillet over medium heat. Sauté eggplant and onion until soft, stirring occasionally, about 10 minutes. Add garlic, tomato, mushrooms, basil, oregano, salt, black and red pepper. Bring to a boil over medium-high heat; reduce heat to medium-low and simmer about 5 minutes. Add zucchini; simmer 5 minutes longer, stirring occasionally. Spoon ratatouille mixture into prepared pepper halves. Heat 15 minutes in a 350° oven until mixture is steaming. Makes 6 servings.

The Best of Virginia Farms Cookbook

Owen Wister's 1902 novel, *The Virginian*, the "granddaddy of all cowboy yarns," has spawned many stage and film adaptations. But to viewers who made *The Virginian* one of the longest-running Westerns in TV history (1962-71), James Drury is the one true Virginian, against whom all others must be measured. It's ironic that James Drury made a name for himself by playing a man with no name. For nine seasons, the actor played the foreman of Shiloh Ranch, Wyoming, known only as "The Virginian," a role that took him from obscurity to TV stardom.

Spinach-Stuffed Tomatoes for Eight

2 pounds fresh spinach
6 slices bacon
½ cup chopped onion
1 cup sour cream

8 tomatoes
Salt to taste
1 cup shredded mozzarella cheese

Rinse spinach well and pat dry. Tear into bite-size pieces and set aside. Cook bacon in a large skillet until crisp. Remove bacon from skillet; reserve ¼ cup drippings in skillet. Drain bacon on paper towels and crumble. Add onion to bacon drippings in skillet. Cook until onion is tender, stirring occasionally. Stir in spinach. Cook, covered, 3–5 minutes. Remove skillet from heat and stir in sour cream and crumbled bacon.

Cut tops off tomatoes. Scoop out pulp and discard. Drain tomato shells and season lightly with salt. Spoon spinach mixture into tomato shells and place in a shallow baking pan. Bake at 350° for 20 minutes. Sprinkle with mozzarella cheese. Bake 10 minutes longer. Serves 8.

In Good Company

Tomato Cheese Strata

1 large onion, diced
1 large green bell pepper, diced
3 cloves garlic, pressed
6 tablespoons butter
2 teaspoons sugar
1 teaspoon salt and pepper

1 teaspoon oregano
1 loaf Italian bread, cubed,
   toasted
8 medium tomatoes, sliced
   thickly
1 pound mozzarella, cut in strips

Sauté onion, pepper, and garlic in butter. Add sugar and spices. Stir 3 minutes. In 9x13-inch casserole, layer ½ of toasted bread, ½ of onion mixture, ½ of tomato slices, overlapping, and ½ of cheese. Repeat layers. Cover with foil and bake at 400° for 20–30 minutes.

Cooking with ARK Angels

Smithfield Inn Stewed Tomatoes

One of the renowned dishes of the Smithfield Inn.

1 pint tomatoes, slightly mashed
2 (day-old) biscuits
¼ cup or less sugar
½ teaspoon vanilla

½ teaspoon lemon extract
1 teaspoon flour
1 tablespoon butter

Combine ingredients. Pour into greased casserole dish and bake at 350° for 30–40 minutes.

The Smithfield Cookbook

 Born about 1595 near Jamestown, Pocahontas was an Indian princess, daughter of Powhatan, the powerful chief of the Algonquian Indians. Between 1608–1609, she was a frequent and welcome visitor to the new settlement of Jamestown, bringing food and gifts from her father. As the English expanded their territory, however, conflicts arose. In April 1613, Pocahontas was brought to Jamestown as a hostage (to be exchanged for Powhatan's English hostages). Although at first discontent, she later converted to Christianity. During this time, she took an English name, Rebecca, and married John Rolfe. The marriage helped to establish peaceful relations between the Indians and the English, and therefore played a significant role in American history.

Cabbage Casserole

1 stick margarine
1½ cups crushed cornflakes,
  divided
4 cups chopped cabbage
¾ pound sausage, fried,
  crumbled
½ cup mayonnaise
1 (10¾-ounce) can cream of
  celery soup
1 cup milk
1 cup shredded Cheddar cheese

Melt margarine in a 9x13-inch baking dish. Add ½ cup crushed corn-flakes. Layer cabbage and sausage. Combine mayonnaise, soup, and milk; mix well. Pour over cabbage and sausage. Top with cheese. Sprinkle remaining cornflakes on top and bake at 350° for 30 minutes.

Just Like Mama's

Country Greens

1 (5-pound) package fresh
  greens (your choice)
1 pound salt pork
4 quarts water
½ teaspoon ground black
  pepper

Remove and discard stems and discolored spots from greens. Wash thoroughly through several waters and drain. Cut large leaves into strips. Set aside. Slice salt pork into ¼-inch strips, cutting to, but not through skin. Combine salt pork, water, and pepper in large pot. Bring to a boil on high, then simmer on reduced heat 1 hour. Add greens and cook uncovered 25–30 minutes or until tender.

A Taste of Tradition

Collards with Virginia Ham

Serve this vegetable in a bowl with its "potlikker."

**1 meaty bone from a Virginia
  ham, or 1 pound smoked
  ham hocks**
1 cup chopped onion
2 large cloves garlic, minced

**½ teaspoon Tabasco or hot
  pepper sauce**
2 pounds collard greens
2 cups dry white wine
2 tablespoons soy sauce

In a very large soup or pasta pot, place ham bone, onion, garlic, and Tabasco. Add enough water to barely cover bone. Cover and bring to a boil. Uncover pot and boil 5 minutes. Cut tough stems from center of each collard leaf. Rinse leaves very well in cold water, then chop very coarsely. Add collards to pot along with wine and soy sauce. Bring liquid to a simmer, then cover and lower heat. If necessary during cooking, add more water so greens don't stick to the pot. Stirring occasionally, cook 1½–2 hours, or until collards are very tender. Remove ham bones and meat from pot; cool, chop meat, and return to pot. Makes 6 servings.

The Best of Virginia Farms Cookbook

Pamela's Zucchini Squash Casserole

5 medium zucchini squash
  (1½ inches in diameter by
  about 7 inches long)
3 large fresh tomatoes, chopped
2 medium onions, chopped
1 teaspoon salt
¼ teaspoon pepper
1 pound sweet Italian sausage
  (optional)
2 tablespoons butter, melted
1 box flavored croutons

Cut squash into thirds and parboil 7 minutes, just to soften. Drain, and chop into small chunks. Place chunks into colander and drain again. Mix tomatoes, onions, salt, and pepper and let sit while preparing squash. Drain before mixing with remaining ingredients.

Remove casings and brown sausage about 15 minutes, breaking it apart with fork as it cooks. Mix butter and croutons with squash, tomato mixture, and sausage, and pour into a 9x13-inch baking dish or casserole. Bake in 350° oven 40 minutes to heat through.

CHEESE SAUCE:
2 pounds Velveeta cheese, cubed
2 or 3 tablespoons milk
6 slices bacon, fried crisp,
  crumbled

About 10 minutes before casserole is cooked, in a double-boiler, melt cheese and add milk as needed to thin to a consistency that will pour. Add crumbled bacon to Cheese Sauce. Dish up casserole and spoon Cheese Sauce over.

The Hall Family Cookbook

 Following a battle in 1862, while camped at Berkley Plantation, Union General Daniel Butterfield composed the bugle call "Taps." The haunting melody, once played to signal "lights out" at military bases, is now usually played at military burials.

Zucchini Pizza

4 cups thinly sliced zucchini
1 cup coarsely chopped onion
¼–½ cup margarine or
   butter
2 tablespoons parsley flakes
½ teaspoon salt
½ teaspoon black pepper
¼ teaspoon garlic powder

¼ teaspoon sweet basil leaves
¼ teaspoon oregano leaves
2 eggs, well beaten
1 (8-ounce) package shredded
   mozzarella cheese
1 (8-ounce) can crescent dinner
   rolls or pizza crust

Combine all ingredients, except eggs, cheese, and crust in skillet. Cook over medium heat until tender; set aside. Preheat oven to 375°. In large bowl, mix eggs and cheese together; add zucchini mixture and mix well. Place crescent rolls, pinched together, or pizza crust in pizza pan. Cover with zucchini mixture. Cook 15–20 minutes or until bottom crust is brown. Set oven to broil and brown top.

The Westwood Clubhouse Cookbook

Julie's Zukes

1 medium onion, chopped
¼ cup olive oil
2 medium zucchini, sliced
   ¼ inch thick
3–4 medium ripe tomatoes,
   chopped

¼ cup white wine
Pinch of oregano
Pinch of basil
Salt, pepper, and garlic to taste

Sauté onion in olive oil. Add zucchini slices and cook over medium heat until tender. Add chopped tomatoes, wine, and seasonings. Simmer until liquids reduce. Makes 4 servings.

Country Cookbook

Squash Casserole

2 (16-ounce) packages frozen
  sliced yellow squash, or fresh
  if available
1 cup chopped onion
½ cup chopped green bell
  pepper (optional)
1 cup mayonnaise
3 large eggs, slightly beaten

½ cup crushed, unsalted saltine
  crackers
1 (0.4-ounce) envelope buttermilk
  ranch-style salad dressing mix
1 cup shredded sharp Cheddar
  cheese
1 cup soft bread crumbs
4–5 tablespoons butter, melted

Sauté squash, onion, and bell pepper, if desired, in a little butter. Drain well. Combine squash mixture with next 5 ingredients. Pour into a lightly greased 2-quart shallow casserole. Combine bread crumbs and butter and spread on top. Bake at 350° for 30–45 minutes.

Our Best to You!

Middleburg Medley

1 medium onion, sliced
1 red bell pepper, sliced
2 tablespoons vegetable oil
3 garlic cloves, minced
2 small to medium zucchini,
  sliced
2 small to medium yellow
  squash, sliced
1 cup frozen whole-kernel corn

1 large tomato, peeled, chopped
2 jalapeño peppers, seeded,
  chopped
2–3 teaspoons chopped fresh
  basil
½ teaspoon dried Italian
  seasoning
½ teaspoon salt
½ cup grated Parmesan cheese

Sauté onion and bell pepper in hot oil in a large skillet over medium heat, stirring often, 4 minutes. Add garlic and cook 1–2 minutes or until vegetables are tender. Add zucchini and yellow squash, and cook, stirring often, 7 minutes.

Add corn and next 5 ingredients; reduce heat and simmer, stirring often, 7–10 minutes. Sprinkle vegetable medley with Parmesan cheese. Serve immediately with cooked pasta or as a side dish. Serves 2–4.

What Can I Bring?

Green Bean Casserole

2 (15-ounce) cans green beans,
   drained
1 (10¾-ounce) can cream of
   mushroom soup
¾ cup milk

2 (8-ounce) cans French-fried onion
   rings, divided
1 (3-ounce) jar real bacon bits,
   divided
⅛ teaspoon pepper

Heat oven to 350°. In bowl, combine beans, soup, milk, ½ of onions, ½ of bacon bits, and pepper. Pour into 1½-quart casserole dish. Bake 30 minutes. Top with remaining onions and bacon bits. Bake 5 minutes longer.

A Taste of Tradition

Green Bean Bundles

8 ounces small fresh green
   beans
1 fresh yellow straight neck
   squash

½ stick butter
½ cup lemon juice
Salad dressing of choice
   (optional)

Wash beans and squash. Snap stem end only from each bean. Cut ¾-inch thick slices from squash. Remove center from squash. Fill cavity with bundles of green beans. Place steamer basket in pan; add green bean bundles. Steam 4 minutes or until beans are bright green and crisp-tender. Drizzle with butter and lemon juice or your favorite dressing.

Celebrating Our Children Cookbook

Ralph Stanley is a living legend in Virginia. An American bluegrass musician, Stanley was born in Big Spraddle Creek near Stratton. Ralph's career received a big boost with his prominent role on the phenomenally successful soundtrack recording of the 2000 film, "O Brother, Where Art Thou?" The Ralph Stanley Museum in Clintwood displays instruments, awards, and other Stanley memorabilia.

Sassy Baked Beans

2 (28-ounce) cans Bush's baked
  beans
1 cup diced onion
1 cup diced green bell pepper
¼ cup dark corn syrup
½ teaspoon red pepper
1 teaspoon oregano
½ teaspoon celery seed
½ teaspoon fresh basil

½ cup BBQ sauce
1 tablespoon bacon bits
½ cup brown sugar
½ teaspoon garlic powder
½ teaspoon salt
½ teaspoon chili powder
1 tablespoon Worcestershire
¼ cup hot mustard
Sliced bacon

Mix all ingredients except bacon slices in a large casserole dish and marinate in refrigerator at least 4 hours or overnight.

Top casserole with bacon slices and bake uncovered at 375° for 45 minutes.

Vesuvius, Virginia: Then and Now

Mur's Peas

½ cup half-and-half
1 teaspoon sugar
1 teaspoon butter
⅛ teaspoon nutmeg

½ teaspoon salt
1 (10-ounce) package frozen green
  peas, defrosted

Cook all ingredients except peas over low heat. Simmer until mixture has reduced by about half. A film will form and it will appear slightly clotted—that's normal. Preparation to this point may be done in advance and reheated just before serving. Stir in peas. Heat until peas are thoroughly hot, but don't cook further. Serves 4.

Food to Die For

Sandra's Carrot Soufflé

1 pound carrots, cleaned, cut up
1 stick butter or margarine
3 eggs
¾ cup sugar

1 tablespoon baking powder
3 tablespoons flour
1½ teaspoons vanilla

Cook carrots; drain and add butter. Blend in processor along with eggs, sugar, baking powder, flour, and vanilla. Beat until creamy. Pour into greased casserole. Bake at 350° for 45 minutes.

Favorite Recipes: Bayside Baptist Church

Apple Glazed Carrots

1 tablespoon butter
1 (16-ounce) package peeled,
   trimmed baby carrots
1 cup unsweetened apple juice,
   or 2 small jars baby food
   apple juice

1 teaspoon honey
Salt and pepper to taste
1 tablespoon minced green
   onions

Melt butter in large skillet over medium-high heat. Add carrots. Sauté until carrots begin to brown, about 8 minutes. Add apple juice and honey and bring to a boil. Reduce heat. Simmer until carrots are tender and liquid is reduced to a glaze, stirring occasionally (about 15 minutes). Season to taste with salt and pepper. Transfer to a bowl. Sprinkle with green onions and serve.

Gather 'Round Our Table

 A marker in Amelia County honors Marion Virginia Hawes Terhune (pen name Marion Harland). Born in 1830 in Dennisville, Marion was the Betty Crocker of the 19th century, renowned for the best-selling cookbook in America, *Common Sense in the Household*, published in 1871.

Broccoli Casserole

2 (10-ounce) packages frozen
   broccoli, partially thawed
1 (10¾-ounce) can cream of
   mushroom soup
½ cup mayonnaise

2 eggs, well beaten
1 cup grated sharp cheese
1 medium onion, chopped
Salt and pepper to taste

Mix all ingredients together. Pour into a 9x13-inch casserole dish. Bake at 300° for 25–30 minutes.

TOPPING:

⅓ (8-ounce) package Pepperidge
   Farm Stuffing Mix

⅓ cup margarine

Top baked casserole with stuffing mix. Cut margarine and sprinkle pieces over top. Return to oven and bake at 350° for an additional 30–35 minutes.

Vesuvius, Virginia: Then and Now

Pineapple Soufflé

1½ sticks butter
6 slices white bread, cubed
2 eggs, beaten
1 cup sugar
¼ cup all-purpose flour
1 (29-ounce) can unsweetened
   crushed pineapple

Melt butter in skillet; add bread cubes and toast to a golden brown; set aside. Mix together eggs, sugar, flour, and pineapple (including juice). Grease a 1½-quart casserole dish. Layer egg mixture then bread into dish and repeat. Bake at 350° for 1 hour. Serve slightly warm.

G.W. Carver Family Recipes

Scalloped Pineapple

Serve with ham, chicken, or an oriental meal.

1 (20-ounce) can pineapple
   chunks
⅓ cup sugar
3 tablespoons all-purpose flour
1 cup grated Cheddar cheese
½ cup crumbled buttery
   crackers
¼ cup butter, melted

Preheat oven to 350°. Drain pineapple, reserving 3 tablespoons juice. Combine pineapple juice with sugar and flour. Pour pineapple into a greased 1-quart casserole dish, and cover with juice mixture. Top with grated cheese. Combine cracker crumbs with melted butter. Sprinkle on top of casserole. Bake 20 minutes, or until bubbly. Yields 4 servings.

Virginia Fare

In colonial times, pineapples were recognized as a symbol for hospitality. Sea captains would bring this exotic fruit home from their journeys and mount it on the fence post to indicate they were at home and available to receive visitors.

Hot Apples and Cranberries

1 (21-ounce) can apple pie filling

1 (16-ounce) can whole cranberry sauce

Preheat oven to 350°. Grease a 2-quart casserole. Put in half apple pie filling, half whole cranberry sauce, then remaining pie filling. Top with remaining whole cranberry sauce. Bake to boiling hot, 20–30 minutes. Serve with ham, pork, chicken, or turkey. Yields 6–8 servings.

Loving, Caring and Sharing

Pasta, Rice, Etc.

PHOTO ©VIRGINIA HISTORICAL SOCIETY / VIRGINIA TOURISM CORPORATION

The White House of the Confederacy is a neoclassical mansion built in 1818 in Richmond by John Brockenborough, who was president of the Bank of Virginia. From 1861 to 1865, the house was not only the official residence of President Jefferson Davis, it was also the social, political, and military center of the Confederacy.

Crockpot Macaroni and Cheese

1 (8-ounce) package dry elbow
  macaroni
1 (12-ounce) can evaporated
  milk
1½ cups whole milk
2 eggs

¼ cup butter, melted
1 teaspoon salt
½ teaspoon pepper
3 cups shredded sharp Cheddar
  cheese, divided

Cook macaroni in boiling, salted water 5 minutes. Drain; pour into crockpot. Mix all other ingredients, except 1 cup cheese. Add to macaroni; stir well. Put remaining cup of cheese on top of macaroni. Do not stir. Cook in covered crockpot on HIGH 2 hours.

Favorite Recipes: Barbara's Best Volume II

Don's Secret Recipe for Spaghetti

1¼ pounds ground beef
Oil
1 onion, chopped fine
½ can water
1 (14½-ounce) can diced
  tomatoes
4 tablespoons brown sugar
1 tablespoon salt

¼ teaspoon red pepper
½ teaspoon chili powder
2 dashes hot sauce
2 tablespoons tomato paste
½ (15½-ounce) can Manwich
  sauce
½ pint hot chow chow
Cooked spaghetti

Brown ground beef in a little oil until it loses its pink color. Drain; reserve oil, and put meat in heavy kettle. Then cook onion in oil drained from beef until it changes color; drain and add to ground beef in kettle. Add water, tomatoes, brown sugar, salt, red pepper, chili powder, hot sauce, tomato paste, Manwich sauce, and chow chow. Cook over low heat 1½ hours. Stir often to keep from sticking. Serve over spaghetti.

Grandma's Cookbook

Baked Spaghetti

1 pound ground beef
1 tablespoon oil
½ cup chopped onion
½ teaspoon crushed basil
   leaves
¼ teaspoon crushed thyme
   leaves
1 large garlic clove, minced
2 (10¾-ounce) cans condensed
   tomato soup
1 (6-ounce) can tomato paste

2 soup cans water
½ cup grated Parmesan cheese,
   divided
2 teaspoons salt
¼ teaspoon ground black
   pepper
1 medium bay leaf
½ pound spaghetti, cooked until
   just tender
Additional Parmesan cheese for
   garnish

In large saucepan, brown beef in oil. Add onion, basil, thyme, and garlic. Cook until tender. Stir in soup, tomato paste, water, ¼ cup cheese, salt, pepper, and bay leaf. Cook over low heat 15 minutes. Stir occasionally.

Remove bay leaf from sauce. Combine sauce with drained spaghetti. Pour into 2-quart shallow baking dish, 8x12x2 inches. Sprinkle with remaining cheese. Bake at 350° for 25 minutes or until hot. Stir before serving. Serve with additional Parmesan cheese.

Mrs. Rowe's Favorite Recipes

Mark's Baked Pepperoni Spaghetti

1 (6-ounce) package spaghetti
2 tablespoons butter
⅓ cup Parmesan cheese
2 eggs, well beaten
1 pound lean ground beef
1 (26-ounce) jar spaghetti sauce
　with mushrooms

1 cup ricotta cheese
1 package pepperoni slices
½ cup grated mozzarella
　cheese

Cook spaghetti according to package directions; drain. Stir butter, Parmesan cheese, and eggs into cooked spaghetti. Spray a 9x13-inch baking pan with vegetable spray. Put spaghetti in bottom of pan. Spread Parmesan mixture on top. Brown ground beef; drain well. Add spaghetti sauce and simmer 10 minutes. Spread ricotta cheese over noodles and Parmesan mixture. Spread meat mixture on top of ricotta cheese mixture. Top with pepperoni and mozzarella cheese. Cover and bake at 350° for 30–40 minutes. Uncover and continue baking until cheese begins to brown.

The Westwood Clubhouse Cookbook

Although the first feast of thanksgiving took place at Plymouth Rock in 1622, a collective prayer of thanksgiving was held in the Virginia Colony on December 4, 1619, near the current site of Berkeley Plantation, marking the first Thanksgiving in North America. Thanksgiving Day is now an annual one-day holiday to give thanks, traditionally to God, for the things one has at the end of the harvest season. In 1939, President Roosevelt set the date for Thanksgiving to the fourth Thursday of November (approved by Congress in 1941).

Pasta with Savory Sausage and Cream

1 tablespoon olive oil
¼ cup sun-dried tomatoes in oil, drained, oil reserved
1 tablespoon oil from sun-dried tomatoes
½ cup diced yellow onion
3 medium cloves garlic, minced
1 pound sweet Italian sausage, casings removed
½ teaspoon crushed red pepper

1 (28-ounce) can Italian-style plum tomatoes, drained, chopped
1½ cups whipping cream
½ teaspoon salt
1 (8-ounce) package bowtie pasta
¼ cup minced fresh wide-leaf parsley or basil
½ cup pine nuts, toasted
Feta or Gorgonzola cheese

Heat olive oil and reserved sun-dried tomato oil in a large skillet; mix in onion and garlic and cook until tender. Stir sausage, sun-dried tomatoes, and red pepper into olive and onion mixture. Cook 7 minutes, breaking up sausage until no longer pink. Stir in tomatoes, whipping cream, and salt. Lower heat and simmer until mixture thickens, approximately 4 minutes.

Cook bowtie pasta in boiling water with salt, approximately 10 minutes or until al dente. Drain water; stir bowtie pasta into sauce. Simmer an additional 2 minutes. Stir in parsley or basil. Serve with toasted pine nuts and the cheese of your choice. Serves 4.

Toast to Tidewater

Pasta with Greens and Feta

6 tablespoons olive oil
4 cups chopped onions
8 cups mixed greens, washed,
   dried, coarsely chopped kale,
   (spinach, etc.)
Salt to taste

1 (16-ounce) package pasta (fusilli,
   shells, etc.)
½ pound feta cheese
Grated Parmesan to taste
   (optional)
Freshly ground black pepper

Heat olive oil in a large skillet. Add onions and cook 10 minutes or so, over medium heat, stirring occasionally. Meanwhile, put water for pasta on to boil. Add chopped greens to skillet, salt lightly, and stir until greens begin to wilt. Cover and cook 10–15 minutes on medium-low heat. Cook pasta al dente. Just as it becomes ready, add crumbled feta cheese to greens—this is the sauce. When pasta is cooked, drain and add to sauce. Mix thoroughly. Cook completed dish until heated through, and add Parmesan, if desired. Add freshly ground pepper. The greens become mild and sweet cooked this way.

G.W. Carver Family Recipes

Lasagna

1 large onion, chopped
1 large garlic clove, minced
3 tablespoons olive oil
1 pound Italian sausage
1 pound ground beef
8 ounces pepperoni
1 (32-ounce) jar spaghetti sauce
1 tablespoon oregano
1 tablespoon basil

1 (8-ounce) package lasagna
  noodles
1 (16-ounce) carton cottage
  cheese
3 ounces grated Parmesan
  cheese
1 large egg, beaten
1 (12-ounce) package shredded
  mozzarella cheese

Sauté onion and garlic in oil until onion is tender; do not burn garlic. Break sausage into chunks and add to pan. When sausage is partially cooked, add hamburger and continue to cook. Cut pepperoni into small chunks and add when meat is done. Cook about 5 minutes. Add sauce, oregano, and basil; reduce heat, and simmer while preparing remaining ingredients.

Preheat oven to 350°. Cook noodles in large pot of water. Mix cottage cheese, Parmesan cheese, and egg in separate bowl. When noodles are done, lay 3 noodles in bottom of pan; layer ¼ cheese mixture, then ¼ meat mixture, and ¼ sauce mixture. Then add layer of mozzarella cheese. Continue process until pan is full. Make sure top layer covers noodles so they will not harden in oven. Bake at 350° for approximately 30 minutes or until mixture boils around edges.

A Taste of Tradition

Bill "Bojangles" Robinson (May 25, 1878–November 25, 1949) was a pioneer and preeminent African-American tap dance performer. Born in Richmond, "Bojangles" started dancing at age six on street corners to earn nickels and dimes. He later became a Vaudeville star and appeared in fourteen movies. His birthday is commemorated as National Tap Dance Day.

Everyone's Favorite Lasagna

4 tablespoons margarine
1 pound ground beef
½ cup chopped onion
1½ teaspoons garlic salad
   dressing mix
½ cup dry bread crumbs
¼ cup milk
2 eggs, slightly beaten
½ cup grated Parmesan cheese,
   divided
½ cup parsley flakes (scant),
   divided
2½ teaspoons salt, divided
¼ teaspoon pepper, divided

2 (6-ounce) cans tomato paste
3 (14½-ounce) cans tomatoes,
   cut up
2 tablespoons sugar
1 teaspoon fennel seed
   (optional)
1½ teaspoons dried basil
½ pound lasagna noodles
1 (8-ounce) package grated
   mozzarella cheese
1 (8-ounce) package grated
   Cheddar cheese
1 (16-ounce) container cottage
   cheese

Melt margarine in Dutch oven or very large skillet. Combine ground beef, onion, dressing mix, bread crumbs, milk, eggs, ¼ cup Parmesan, scant ¼ cup parsley flakes, 1 teaspoon salt, and ⅛ teaspoon pepper. Mix well; brown in melted margarine. Drain fat. Add tomato paste, tomatoes (with juice), sugar, fennel seed, if desired, basil, remaining ¼ cup Parmesan, remaining ¼ cup parsley flakes, remaining 1½ teaspoons salt, and remaining ⅛ teaspoon pepper. Simmer 1–2 hours, stirring occasionally to prevent sticking. Cook noodles until tender; drain.

Put ½ cup sauce in lasagna pan or 9x13-inch casserole dish. Layer cooked noodles, sauce, cottage cheese, mozzarella, Cheddar, and Parmesan, if desired. Repeat with noodles, sauce, mozzarella, and Cheddar. Bake 30 minutes at 350°. Let sit 5 minutes for easier serving.

Note: This makes for a very large recipe of sauce which freezes extremely well. It is better to freeze the sauce separately and to make each casserole fresh, than to freeze the entire casserole.

Recipe submitted by Mrs. John Love, Luenburg
Country Treasures

Famous Virginians

A Sampling of Famous People from Virginia

PRESIDENTS

William Henry Harrison (Charles City)
Thomas Jefferson (Edge Hill)
James Madison (Port Conway)
James Monroe
   (Westmoreland County)

Zachary Taylor (Montebello)
John Tyler (Greenway)
George Washington
   (Westmoreland County)
Woodrow Wilson (Staunton)

POLITICAL / LITERARY

Stephen Austin (Austinville)
Henry Clay (Hanover County)
Patrick Henry (Hanover County)
Sam Houston (Timber Ridge)

"Stonewall" Jackson (Clarksburg)
Robert E. Lee (Stratford)
George Mason (Mason Neck)
Booker T. Washington (Hale's Ford)

ENTERTAINMENT

Pearl Bailey (Newport News)
Warren Beatty (Richmond)
Sandra Bullock (Arlington)
Maybelle Carter (Nicklesville)
June Carter Cash (Maces Springs)
Roy Clark (Lunenburg)
Patsy Cline (Winchester)
Joseph Cotten (Petersburg)
Spencer Christian (Charles City)
Katie Couric (Arlington)
Missy Elliott (Portsmouth)

Ella Fitzgerald (Newport News)
Bruce Hornsby (Williamsburg)
Dave Matthews Band (Charlottesville)
Shirley MacLaine (Richmond)
Wayne Newton (Roanoke)
Tim Reid (Norfolk)
Bill "Bojangles" Robinson (Richmond)
George C. Scott (Alexandria)
Willard Scott (Alexandria)
Ralph Stanley (Big Straddle Creek)
Statler Brothers (Staunton)

SPORTS

Arthur Ashe (Richmond)
Jeff Burton (South Boston)
Ward Burton (South Boston)
Willie Lanier (Clover)
Moses Malone (Petersburg)
Alonzo Mourning (Chesapeake)
Ricky Rudd (Chesapeake)
Elliott Sadler (Emporia)

Ralph Sampson (Harrisonburg)
Bruce Smith (Norfolk)
Sam Snead (Hot Springs)
Curtis Strange (Norfolk)
Fran Tarkenton (Richmond)
Lawrence Taylor (Williamsburg)
Lanny Wadkins (Williamsburg)
Pernell Whitaker (Norfolk)

Vermicelli with Scallops

1 pound bay scallops
2 tablespoons fresh lemon juice
2 tablespoons chopped parsley
1 onion, chopped
1 clove garlic, minced
2 tablespoons olive oil
2 tablespoons butter, divided
1½ cups canned Italian
  tomatoes, undrained, cut up
2 tablespoons chopped fresh
  basil, or ½ teaspoon dried,
  crushed basil

½ teaspoon dried oregano
½ teaspoon dried, crushed thyme
  leaves
1 (12-ounce) package vermicelli,
  cooked
2 tablespoons heavy cream
Dash of ground nutmeg

Rinse scallops and place in glass dish; sprinkle with lemon juice and chopped parsley. Cover and marinate in refrigerator while preparing sauce.

Cook and stir onion and garlic in oil and 1 tablespoon butter in large skillet over medium-high heat until onion is tender. Add tomatoes with juice, basil, oregano, and thyme. Reduce heat to low. Cover; simmer 30 minutes, stirring occasionally. Meanwhile, cook vermicelli; drain. Keep sauce and vermicelli warm in their own utensils.

Drain scallops. In another large skillet, add remaining 1 tablespoon butter and scallops. Cook and stir over medium heat until scallops are cooked through and light golden brown on each side (about 10 minutes total), adding more butter if necessary. Add cream, nutmeg, and tomato sauce mixture. Place warm vermicelli in a large bowl and pour scallops and sauce over it. Toss gently to coat. Serves 4.

It's Delicious!

Risotto with Tomato, Corn and Basil

2½ cups water
2 cups milk (whole or low fat)
2 tablespoons butter
1 cup minced onion
1 garlic clove, minced
¾ cup uncooked Arborio rice
3 tablespoons white wine
1½ cups corn kernels

1 ripe tomato, seeded, chopped
  fine
½ cup grated Parmesan cheese
½ cup thinly sliced basil,
  divided
½ teaspoon salt
Pepper to taste

Heat water and milk to a simmer. Keep heat low. Melt butter in a separate pan and sauté onion 3–4 minutes. Add garlic and rice. Stir constantly for 1 minute. Add wine. Stir until absorbed. Begin to add milk/water mixture ½ cup at a time. Wait until each addition is absorbed before adding the next amount. When rice has cooked 15 minutes and most of the liquid has absorbed, add corn, tomato, and remaining milk/water mixture. Cook, stirring frequently, until rice is tender, but still slightly chewy. Risotto should take 18–20 minutes to cook.

    Stir in cheese, ½ the basil, salt, and pepper. Spoon onto plates and top with remaining basil. Serves 4.

Cooking with Grace

The Chesapeake Bay Bridge Tunnel is the world's largest bridge-tunnel complex. The Bridge-Tunnel Project is a four-lane, twenty-mile-long vehicular toll crossing of the lower Chesapeake Bay, providing the only direct link between Virginia's Eastern Shore and south Hampton Roads.

Fried Rice

3 cups boiled or steamed plain
  rice, cold, preferably day old,
  refrigerated
1 tablespoon soy sauce
½ teaspoon Ac'cent or MSG
Salt and pepper to taste
3 tablespoons oil
2 garlic cloves, minced
1 cup frozen green peas

½ cup finely sliced, cooked ham,
  roast pork, beef, chicken, or
  bacon (or a combination)
2 eggs, slightly beaten,
  scrambled
3 tablespoons finely cut
  scallions
Parsley for garnish

Mix rice, soy sauce, Ac'cent, salt and pepper. Set aside. In hot oil, brown garlic; add peas and meat. Stir-fry a minute or 2. Add rice mixture and stir-cook 5 minutes. Mix in scrambled eggs and scallions. Transfer to platter. Garnish with strips of scrambled eggs and sprinkle more scallions on top. Surround with sprigs of parsley. Serves 4–6.

Philippine Cooking in America

Paella

1½ pounds chicken, cut into
serving pieces
1 pound boneless pork, cut into
1½-inch cubes
2 teaspoons salt, divided
5 cups water
12–15 fresh clams, in shell,
washed to remove sand
2 garlic cloves, crushed
1 medium onion, finely sliced
1 pound large shrimp, shelled,
deveined

1 (6-ounce) can tomato paste
1 teaspoon MSG
2 cups uncooked rice, washed,
drained
1 cup frozen green peas
¼ cup pimentos, sliced into thin
strips (optional)
3 crabs in shell, boiled, halved (if
available)

Wash chicken and pork and pat dry, then sprinkle with 1 teaspoon salt. Fry meats in a big (5-quart capacity) pot until golden brown. Transfer meats to dish and set aside.

In another pot, boil water with remaining 1 teaspoon salt. When water is rapidly boiling, add clams. Let it boil once more, then shut off heat. Set aside. Save clam broth. Sauté garlic and onion in hot oil where meats were fried, until garlic is light brown. Add shrimp, fried chicken, and pork; sauté 2 minutes. Add tomato paste, MSG, and rice. Stir and cook 3 minutes. Add clam broth. Cover, let boil rapidly a minute, stir once, reduce heat to low, and simmer, covered, until mixture is almost dry and rice is almost cooked. Season to taste. Carefully stir in peas, pimentos, and clams. Arrange crabs on top. Cover and continue cooking over low heat until rice is cooked. Serves 10–12.

Philippine Cooking in America

Spinach-Mushroom Quiche

CUSTARD MIXTURE:

3 eggs
1½ cups heavy cream
¼ teaspoon pepper

⅛ teaspoon salt
Pinch of nutmeg
1½ cups grated Swiss cheese

Beat eggs and cream in mixing bowl. Stir in remaining ingredients.

SPINACH-MUSHROOM MIXTURE:

1 (10-ounce) package frozen
   chopped spinach, cooked,
   drained
¼ cup diced onion
½ cup sliced mushrooms

2 tablespoons butter, melted
1 (9-inch) unbaked pie crust
2 tablespoons parsley
2 tablespoons grated Parmesan
   cheese

Sauté spinach, onion, and mushrooms in melted butter 10 minutes. Stir into Custard Mixture. Pour into pie crust and top with parsley and Parmesan cheese. Bake 30–35 minutes at 375°, until golden and fluffy.

Tasty Treasures from Johnson's Church

Crustless Quiche

10 eggs
½ cup all-purpose flour
½ teaspoon salt
1 teaspoon baking powder
¼ cup butter, melted

3 (4-ounce) cans chopped green
   chiles, drained
1 (1-pound) package shredded
   Monterey Jack
2 cups low-fat cottage cheese

Beat eggs; add flour, salt, and baking powder. Mix in butter, chiles, and cheeses. Pour into a sprayed 9x13-inch baking pan and bake at 400° for 15 minutes, then 350° for 40 minutes. Knife should come out clean.

First Family Favorites

Crustless Crab Quiche

½ pound fresh mushrooms,
   thinly sliced
2 tablespoons butter
4 eggs
1 cup sour cream
1 cup small-curd cottage cheese
½ cup grated Parmesan cheese
4 tablespoons flour

1 teaspoon onion powder
¼ teaspoon salt
4 drops Tabasco
2 cups shredded Monterey Jack
   cheese
16 ounces fresh backfin
   crabmeat

Preheat oven to 350°. Sauté mushrooms in butter. Drain on paper towels. In blender, combine remaining ingredients except Monterey Jack cheese and crabmeat. Blend until thoroughly mixed. Pour mixture into large bowl. Stir in mushrooms, cheese, and crabmeat. Pour into a greased 9- or 10-inch quiche dish or 10-inch pie plate. Bake at 350° for 45 minutes or until knife comes out clean. Let stand 5 minutes before cutting. Serves 6–8.

Note: May be prepared ahead and brought to room temperature before baking. One-half pound slivered ham may be substituted for crab.

Tidewater on the Half Shell

Arlington County was ceded to the District of Columbia in 1789, then returned to Virginia by Congress in 1846. At twenty-six square miles, it's the fourth smallest county in the nation, but is home to both Arlington National Cemetery and the Pentagon.

Taco Pizza

1 pound ground beef
1 (1½-ounce) package taco
  seasoning mix
1 cup mild salsa
  or 1 cup pizza sauce
1 large Boboli Original Pizza
  Crust

1–1½ cups grated Cheddar
  cheese
1–1½ cups grated Monterey Jack
  cheese

Brown ground beef and add taco seasoning mix according to directions. Spread salsa or pizza sauce on crust; spread on ground beef mixture. Sprinkle cheeses on top and bake at 350° for 10 minutes or until cheese melts.

Favorite Recipes: Barbara's Best Volume II

Quick 2-Cheese Pizza Snacks

1 (10-count) can refrigerated
  flaky biscuits
¼ cup grated Parmesan cheese
1½ cups spaghetti or pizza
  sauce

1 cup assorted toppings (onions,
  pepperoni, sautéed mushrooms,
  peppers, etc.)
1½ cups shredded mozzarella
  cheese

Heat oven to 400°. Separate biscuits. Divide each biscuit in half crosswise for a thin, crisp crust. On an ungreased baking sheet, flatten each biscuit and crimp edge to form a small ridge for crust. Sprinkle Parmesan cheese over each biscuit. Spread sauce and toppings over Parmesan cheese. Top with mozzarella. Bake 10 minutes on lowest rack until biscuits are lightly browned. Serve.

Variation: Instead of biscuit crust, make pizza snacks using prepared mini-pizza crusts, pita or mini-pita bread, sliced mini-bagels, or English muffins.

For Men Who Like to Cook, Want to Cook (or HAVE to!)

Meats

PHOTO BY CODY RAY

Often viewed by tourists in horse-drawn wagons, Colonial Williamsburg is an example of a living history museum, an open-air assemblage of buildings populated with historical reenactors who explain and demonstrate aspects of daily life in Virginia's colonial times. The historic district of Williamsburg is open any hour of the day, free of charge.

Pork Tenderloin with Mustard Cream Sauce

1 (1-pound) pork tenderloin
⅓ cup flour
½ teaspoon each salt and
  pepper
3 tablespoons butter or
  margarine

4 green onions
⅓ cup dry white wine
1 cup heavy cream
¼ cup Dijon mustard
Salt and pepper to taste

Cut pork tenderloin into ½-inch slices. Place between pieces of wax paper and pound to ¼-inch thickness with a meat mallet. Mix flour, salt, and pepper together and coat pork medallions with mixture, shaking off excess. Sauté pork medallions ⅓ at a time in butter in a skillet for 2 minutes on each side; remove to a warm platter, reserving the drippings.

Slice green onions, keeping white and green parts separate. Reserve green portions. Add white portions to drippings in skillet and sauté 1 minute or until tender. Stir in wine and cook 3 minutes or until reduced to 2 tablespoons. Add cream and simmer 5 minutes or until thickened to desired consistency. Whisk in Dijon mustard and season with additional salt and pepper to taste. Spoon over pork medallions and sprinkle with reserved green onion tops. Serve immediately. Serves 4.

Oh My Stars! Recipes that Shine

Virginia has had three capital cities: Jamestown (1619–1699), Williamsburg (1699–1780), and Richmond (1780–present). Richmond was also the capital of the Confederacy during the Civil War.

Pork Tenderloin with Cinnamon

1 (2-pound) pork tenderloin
4 tablespoons sugar
¼ teaspoon salt
4 tablespoons soy sauce
1½ teaspoons cinnamon
2 tablespoons sherry
1 teaspoon powdered ginger
2 teaspoons dry mustard
2 teaspoons lemon juice

Preheat oven to 325°. Place pork in roasting pan. Combine remaining ingredients and pour over pork. Bake 1 hour, basting frequently with sauce. Yields 4–6 servings.

Virginia Fare

Peanut-Crusted Pork with Bourbon Mushroom Cream

1 pound pork loin, cut into
  ¼-inch slices
2 cups chopped salted peanuts
¼ cup canola oil
1½ cups sliced button
  mushrooms
1½ cups sliced shiitake
  mushrooms
1 tablespoon chopped garlic
3 tablespoons–¼ cup sugar (to
  taste)
½ cup bourbon
2 cups heavy cream

Preheat oven to 350°. Coat one side of pork with peanuts, and place, peanut side up, in an oiled baking pan. Bake about 5 minutes, or until done. Heat oil in a medium saucepan over medium heat; add mushrooms and garlic. Cook about 4 minutes. Stir in sugar, and remove from heat. Add bourbon, and cook 3 minutes. Stir in heavy cream; reduce heat. Cook until sauce thickens, stirring frequently. Spoon over pork. Makes 4–6 servings.

Celebrate Virginia!

Baked Stuffed Pork Chops

DRESSING:

3 cups bread crumbs
1 small onion, minced
2 stalks celery, finely chopped
½ teaspoon salt

White pepper to taste
1 teaspoon sage
Broth, any kind

Mix together and add only enough broth to hold crumbs together. Do not make Dressing too wet.

4 (1½-inch-thick) pork chops
1 cup all-purpose flour
1 teaspoon salt
⅓ teaspoon white pepper
1 egg, well beaten

1 tablespoon prepared mustard
¾ cup milk
1 cup Dressing, divided
1 cup cooking oil

Prepare pork chops by cutting slit along fat side and into chop to form a pocket. Combine flour, salt, and pepper. Prepare egg wash by mixing egg, mustard, and milk. Using ¼ cup Dressing, stuff tightly into each pocket and press fatty edges together to close. Dip each chop into egg wash, then flour. In very hot oil, fry until golden brown. Remove; drain and place in large casserole dish. Cover with thin gravy. Cover with foil and bake uncovered an additional 30 minutes.

Mrs. Rowe's Favorite Recipes

Two Charlottesville places designed by Thomas Jefferson (Monticello and the University of Virginia) appear on the World Heritage Foundation list, ranking them with the Great Pyramids of Egypt. The World Heritage List includes 830 properties forming part of the cultural and natural heritage that the World Heritage Committee considers as having outstanding universal value.

Pork Chop Casserole

6 pork chops (preferably without bone)
Flour for dredging
2 tablespoons vegetable oil
Salt and pepper to taste
2 (10¾-ounce) cans cream of mushroom soup

1 cup grated Cheddar cheese
3 medium baking potatoes
1 (15-ounce) can green beans or shelley beans, drained

If necessary, remove bones from pork chops. Dredge in flour. Brown in oil in frying pan. Remove chops. To oil and bits remaining in pan, add salt and pepper, soup, and grated cheese. Heat until warm, cheese is melted, and mixture is blended.

Prepare a 9x13-inch baking dish by spraying it with Pam. Peel and thinly slice potatoes. Place in layers in prepared pan. Top with beans. Place chops on top of beans. Pour sauce mixture over chops. Cover with foil and bake at 350° for 1½ hours or more. Uncover for last 10–15 minutes to slightly brown. Serves 3.

Note: Chicken breasts or turkey medallions may be substituted for pork chops.

It's Delicious!

Ham and Cauliflower Brooks

1 head cauliflower
2 cups chopped, cooked country
　ham
2 tablespoons butter
1½ cups sour cream
¼ cup chopped onion

2 egg yolks, slightly beaten
⅛ teaspoon nutmeg
⅛ teaspoon mace
1½ teaspoons paprika
¼ teaspoon pepper
¾ cup grated Cheddar cheese

Cook cauliflower in salted boiling water to cover until almost done, about 15 minutes. Drain, run cold water on cauliflower, then break into flowerets. In bottom of a greased casserole, alternate layers of flowerets with layers of ham. Dot top with butter.

Preheat oven to 375°. Combine sour cream, onion, eggs, and spices; mix well, and pour over casserole. Cover and bake 25–30 minutes. Remove cover; top with cheese. Brown slightly and serve. Serves 6.

Note: Fresh mushrooms may be added to this recipe. Sauté them in butter first, then add between layers of cauliflower and ham. This casserole can be made the day before and baked just before serving.

The Ham Book

Sunday Dinner Steaks

6–8 beef cubed steaks
¾ cup all-purpose flour
¾ teaspoon black pepper
Oil
1 envelope onion mushroom
　soup mix

1 (8-ounce) can mushrooms,
　undrained
1 medium onion, sliced thin
2 (10-ounce) cans beef gravy
2 cans water

Dredge steaks in flour/pepper mixture. Brown lightly on both sides in hot oil. Put steaks in 9x13-inch pan. Sprinkle with onion soup mix. Cover with mushrooms. Layer onion slices on top. Mix gravy and water together and pour over steaks and onion. Do not stir. Cover tightly with foil. Bake at 250° for 3–4 hours.

Favorite Recipes: Bayside Baptist Church

Salisbury Steak and Gravy

1 pound ground beef
¾ teaspoon salt
½ teaspoon sage (optional)
1 tablespoon finely chopped
**   onion**

¼ cup cracker crumbs
¼ teaspoon pepper
1 egg

Combine ground beef, salt, sage, onion, crumbs, pepper, and egg. Mix well; form into 4 patties. Fry in lightly oiled frying pan until done and brown on both sides. Remove from skillet and set aside.

GRAVY:

3 tablespoons flour
2 cups hot water

2 beef bouillon cubes
Kitchen Bouquet (optional)

Stir flour in oil (3 tablespoons) left from frying patties. Stir in water in which bouillon has been dissolved. Stir and cook until thick. Put meat patties back in skillet with gravy, and simmer over low heat until heated through. Add a few drops of Kitchen Bouquet to brown gravy, if desired.

Not By Bread Alone Cookbook

The famous slogan and bumper sticker, "Virginia is for Lovers," was adopted in 1969 by the state travel service (now the Virginia Tourism Corporation). The phrase came from a $100-a-week copywriter who worked for the state's advertising agency at the time. The phrase, considered bold and provocative in those days, created a new image for a more exciting Virginia.

Pamela's Flank Steak and Noodles

2 tablespoons flour
Salt and pepper to taste
1 (1½- to 2½-pound) flank
  steak
2 tablespoons cooking oil
1 cup tomato or V8 juice
1 (16-ounce) can whole tomatoes,
  chopped
1 medium onion, diced
1 medium green bell pepper,
  diced

¼ cup ketchup (regular or
  spicy)
2 teaspoons Worcestershire
¼ cup dry red wine
1 (8-ounce) can sliced
  mushrooms
1 (12-ounce) package broad egg
  noodles, cooked

Put flour, salt and pepper in a plastic bag. Add steak to bag and shake to coat. Heat oil in large pot. Brown meat on both sides in hot oil. Add juice, tomatoes, onion, pepper, ketchup, and Worcestershire; cover and simmer 2 hours or until meat is tender.

Remove flank steak; slice across grain at an angle into thin slices. Return meat to pot and mix well. Add mushrooms and wine. Simmer, uncovered, until heated through and sauce thickens. Remove from heat and serve over noodles.

The Hall Family Cookbook

 Mount Vernon, home of George Washington, was depicted on a one-cent U.S. stamp of 1936. Mount Vernon is also the subject of a 1.5-cent stamp, which was first available at Mount Vernon, Virginia, on February 22, 1956. Both stamps features a view of Washington's home facing the Potomac River.

Betty's Beef Stroganoff

2 pounds round steak or sirloin,
cut in ½-inch strips
⅓ cup flour
1 teaspoon salt
¾ teaspoon Ac'cent
⅓ cup plus 3 tablespoons butter,
divided
½ cup finely chopped onion

1 small clove garlic, crushed
1 cup beef broth
1 tablespoon sherry
½ pound mushrooms, sliced
1 cup sour cream
1 teaspoon Worcestershire
Rice or noodles, cooked

Trim meat and coat evenly with a mixture of flour, salt, and Ac'cent. Heat ⅓ cup butter in a heavy 10-inch skillet over low heat. Add meat strips, onion, and garlic. Brown over medium heat, turning frequently.

When meat is browned, slowly add broth and sherry. Bring liquid rapidly to boiling, reduce heat, cover, and simmer until meat is tender. While meat is cooking, sauté mushrooms in remaining 3 tablespoons butter. Blend sour cream and Worcestershire sauce and add to meat in small amounts along with mushrooms. Return to heat and continue cooking 3–5 minutes. Do not boil at this point. Serve immediately over rice or noodles.

Thought for Food

Easy Beef Sirloin Over Pasta

1 (8-ounce) package penne pasta,
  uncooked
1 pound beef sirloin, boneless,
  cut into 4-inch pieces
½ cup balsamic vinaigrette
  dressing, divided
1 (14½-ounce) can diced
  tomatoes, undrained
1 onion, sliced, divided
1 (4-ounce) jar sliced mushrooms,
  drained
½ (1-pound) block Velveeta, cut
  into cubes

Cook pasta as directed on package. Meanwhile, cook meat in 2 table-spoons dressing in large skillet 5 minutes or until meat is brown on both sides, turning after 3 minutes. Stir in diced tomatoes, onion, and mushrooms along with remaining dressing. Bring to a boil. Reduce heat to medium; simmer 10 minutes or until meat is cooked through and onions are tender. Add cheese and gently stir until melted. Let stand 2–3 minutes. Serve over hot pasta.

Delightfully Seasoned Recipes

The Atlantic headquarters of the North Atlantic Treaty Organization (NATO) is located in Norfolk. NATO is an alliance of twenty-six countries from North America and Europe committed to fulfilling the goals of the North Atlantic Treaty signed on April 4, 1949. The parties to this treaty reaffirm their faith in the purposes and principles of the Charter of the United Nations and their desire to live in peace with all peoples and all governments. Norfolk is also the home base for the U.S. Navy's Atlantic Fleet. The U.S. Atlantic Fleet provides fully trained, combat-ready forces to support U.S. and NATO commanders in regions of conflict throughout the world.

Baked Macaroni and Meat in Cream Sauce

2 medium onions, chopped
1 stick butter
2 pounds ground beef
1 (8-ounce) can tomato sauce
½ (6-ounce) can tomato paste
½ teaspoon garlic powder
Salt and pepper to taste
1 (16-ounce) package macaroni
1 cup grated Romano cheese

In skillet, sauté onions in butter. Add ground beef and brown. Add tomato sauce, paste, and seasonings, and simmer for 1 hour. Boil macaroni for 10 minutes. Drain. Add grated cheese and mix.

CREAM SAUCE:
7 heaping tablespoons flour
2 quarts milk, divided
1 stick butter
6–8 eggs, beaten well
½ cup grated Romano cheese
Salt to taste

Dissolve flour in 1 cup cold milk. Heat remaining milk with butter and add flour-milk mixture. Cook until thick, stirring constantly. Remove from heat; add eggs gradually and stir well. Return to heat and cook 3 minutes more. Add grated cheese. Season to taste. Remove from heat.

In a large bowl, mix ¼ of Cream Sauce with macaroni. Add meat sauce and mix all together. Top with remaining Cream Sauce. Bake 1 hour at 350° or until nicely browned. Cut into squares. Makes 25–30 servings.

Come Cook with Us

Coca-Cola Brisket

1 (3- to 4-pound) brisket of beef
1 (10- or 12-ounce) can or bottle
  Coca-Cola Classic
Oil

2 large onions, chopped
1 tablespoon paprika
2 envelopes dry onion soup mix
Water

In a plastic or crockery bowl, place brisket and cover with Coca-Cola (use more, if needed). Refrigerate covered for 24 hours.

Remove meat from marinade. Discard marinade. In Dutch oven large enough for brisket to lie flat, pour a thin coating of vegetable oil. Over very high heat, sear meat on both sides on the stove top. Remove pan from heat and remove meat from pan. Add onions to pan. Sprinkle paprika and both envelopes of dry soup mix over onions and mix. Lay brisket on top. Add enough water to come up sides of brisket. Cover with lid. Bake at 325° for 2–2½ hours. Check occasionally to make sure liquid is not drying out too much. Slice and serve with onion mixture as gravy.

My Table at Brightwood

Cabbage Rolls

1 large head cabbage
1 pound ground beef
2 cups tomato juice, divided
¼ cup uncooked rice
¼ cup sauerkraut
1 small clove garlic, chopped
½ teaspoon salt
¼ teaspoon pepper

Cut stalk from cabbage head. Place cabbage in a large pot of boiling water to loosen leaves. Remove 12 leaves. Mix remaining ingredients, using 1 cup tomato juice; save the other cup for broth. Put a ball of beef mixture on each leaf. Roll cabbage around ball and fasten with toothpicks, if necessary. Place rolls in a large, heavy pot no more than 2 layers deep. Put remaining cup of tomato juice on top of rolls. Bring to a boil. Reduce heat and cover. Cook for 1 hour; salt and pepper to taste while cooking.

Variation: May be made in layers and baked; it saves time and is just as tasty, although rolls are prettier. Rolls may also be baked in a heavy, covered pan in oven at 375°–400° for 1½ hours; uncover last 15 minutes of baking.

From Chaney Creek to the Chesapeake

Invented in 1885 by Charles Addison, Dr Pepper is the oldest soft drink in the United States. It was named for Dr. Charles Pepper of Rural Retreat. (Coca-Cola was invented in 1886.)

Best of British Shepherd's Pie

1 pound lean ground beef	Salt and pepper to taste
1 large onion, diced	5–6 large potatoes, peeled,
3–4 carrots, sliced	quartered
1 (1-ounce) package brown gravy	Milk
mix	Butter
8–10 tablespoons Worcestershire,	Pinch of white pepper
divided	Shredded Cheddar cheese

Brown beef in a skillet; drain fat. Add diced onion, sliced carrots, gravy mix, and 4–5 tablespoons Worcestershire. Mix together until boiling; add salt and pepper, and 4–5 tablespoons more Worcestershire.

Boil potatoes until fairly soft when poked with a knife. Smash them up, adding some milk and butter and a little white pepper to desired consistency. Transfer meat mixture to a medium-size casserole dish; top with potatoes until all meat is completely covered. Run a fork over top of potatoes and sprinkle with Cheddar cheese. Broil pie on low shelf in oven about 15 minutes.

All American Recipes

Fiesta Casserole

1 pound hamburger meat	1 (15-ounce) can corn, drained
1 onion, diced	1 bag instant rice
1 green bell pepper, diced	Salt and pepper to taste
1 (14½-ounce) can diced	1 cup water
tomatoes, undrained	

In skillet, brown hamburger with onion and green pepper; drain. Add tomatoes with liquid and corn. Stir. Add instant rice, salt, pepper, and water; stir. Cover and let cook on medium heat 30 minutes or until rice is done.

Kids in the Kitchen

Big Ol' Mess

1 pound smoked sausage, cut
  into chunks
3 jalapeño peppers, sliced
1 green bell pepper, cut into
  bite-size chunks
1 sweet onion, cut into bite-size
  chunks
¼ cup Tabasco
1 (10-ounce) bottle sweet and sour
  sauce

Place sausage, peppers, and onion in foil bag. Mix Tabasco and sweet
and sour sauce and pour over mixture in foil bag. Seal bag and place
on grill or in oven at 350°; cook 45 minutes, turning bag about every
15 minutes. Slit bag open and serve from bag.

Delightfully Seasoned Recipes

Chili Pie with Cornbread Topping

1½ cups white cornmeal
½ cup all-purpose flour
1 teaspoon salt
3 teaspoons baking powder
2 eggs
1 cup buttermilk
½ cup margarine, softened
2 tablespoons chopped parsley
1 large pot chili, prepared
  according to your favorite recipe,
  kept hot

Mix cornmeal, flour, salt, and baking powder. Add eggs, buttermilk,
and margarine. Beat about 1 minute until smooth. Do not overbeat.
Stir in parsley. Place hot chili in large rectangular baking dish. Spoon
topping around edges of chili. Bake at 425° for 15–19 minutes.

My Table at Brightwood

Spanish Rice

1 pound ground chuck or round
½–¾ cup chopped onion
¼ cup chopped green bell
  pepper
2 tablespoons olive oil
½ cup uncooked rice
2¼ cups water

1 beef bouillon cube
1 (8-ounce) can tomato sauce
1 teaspoon chili powder
Salt and pepper to taste
1 (8-ounce) package shredded
  cheese

Brown beef, onion, and bell pepper in oil. Drain grease, if any. Add rice, water, bouillon cube, tomato sauce, chili powder, salt and pepper. Cover and simmer 20–25 minutes until rice is cooked. Uncover and add cheese. Stir and serve immediately.

Vesuvius, Virginia: Then and Now

Hamburger Pie

1¼ pounds ground beef
⅓ cup chopped onion
½ cup chopped green bell
  pepper
1 (8-ounce) can sliced
  mushrooms
¼ teaspoon garlic powder
½ teaspoon salt

1 (8-ounce) can tomato sauce
1 (8-ounce) can green beans
1 (8-ounce) can crescent rolls
1 egg, slightly beaten
2 cups shredded Monterey Jack
  cheese, divided
Paprika

Preheat oven to 375°. Brown meat, onion, green pepper, mushrooms, garlic powder, and salt. Drain fat. Add tomato sauce and green beans. Simmer while preparing crust.

Separate crescent rolls into 8 triangles and place in ungreased 9-inch pie plate. Press over bottom and up sides to form crust. Combine egg and 1 cup cheese; spread over crust. Spoon hot mixture into crust. Sprinkle with remaining cheese and paprika. Bake 20– 25 minutes. Cool 10 minutes before serving. Serves 4–6.

Tried and True Recipes

Meatballs

MEATBALLS:

3 pounds lean ground beef
1 (5-ounce) can evaporated milk
2 cups old-fashioned oats
2 eggs
3 teaspoons salt

½ teaspoon pepper
2 teaspoons chili powder
½ teaspoon garlic powder
½ cup chopped onion

Combine ingredients in a large bowl. Mix well. Shape into 1-inch diameter balls. Place meatballs in a single layer on wax paper-lined cookie sheets. Freeze until solid. Store frozen meatballs in freezer bags until ready to cook.

SAUCE:

2 cups ketchup
1 cup brown sugar
½ teaspoon liquid smoke

½ teaspoon garlic powder
½ cup chopped onion

Combine ingredients and stir well until sugar is dissolved.

To assemble, place frozen meatballs into a 9x13-inch baking dish (2 dishes will be needed for whole recipe). Pour Sauce evenly over meatballs. Bake at 350° for 1 hour. Yields 8 dozen meatballs.

Joy in Serving

Sweet-Sour Meatballs on Rice

¾ pound ground chuck
3 tablespoons minced green
  onions
1 egg
¼ teaspoon salt
¼ teaspoon ground ginger
4 tablespoons soy sauce, divided
2 tablespoons vegetable oil
1 green bell pepper, cut in strips

1 (8¼-ounce) can sliced
  pineapple
1 cup frozen sliced carrots, cooked,
  drained, liquid reserved
¼ cup sliced water chestnuts
1½ tablespoons sugar
1½ tablespoons white vinegar
1 tablespoon cornstarch
2 servings hot cooked rice

Combine first 5 ingredients with 2 tablespoons soy sauce. Mix well and shape in balls, using 2 measuring tablespoons for each. (Balls hold shape best when chilled before cooking.) Sauté in oil in skillet until done; remove and keep warm.

Add green pepper to skillet and sauté 2 minutes. Drain pineapple, reserving syrup. Cut pineapple in chunks and add to skillet with carrots and water chestnuts. Sauté 3 minutes, then add meatballs. In small saucepan, mix remaining soy sauce, reserved liquids (add water to make 1 cup), sugar, vinegar, and cornstarch. Bring to a boil, stirring, until thickened and clear. Pour over contents of skillet and simmer 5 minutes. Serve on rice. Makes 2 servings.

Recipe submitted by Joy N. Starkey, Charles City, James City, New Kent
Country Treasures

 Materials falling from space that survive entry into the earth's atmosphere are called bolides. The largest known bolide impact occurred approximately 33 million years ago in the southern part of Chesapeake Bay. It made a crater twice the size of Rhode Island and as deep as the Grand Canyon.

Mom's Best Ever Hot Dog Sauce

This is the best hot dog chili I have ever eaten! You will love it at your next cookout!

1 pound ground beef
1 large onion, finely chopped
2 (6-ounce) cans tomato paste
1 (24-ounce) bottle ketchup
2 teaspoons chili powder
2 tablespoons brown sugar
1 teaspoon Worcestershire
   sauce
1½ cups water

In a medium skillet over medium-high heat, brown ground beef and onion; drain. In a large kettle, place all ingredients; add water; cover and cook slowly for 2 hours until thick. This can be made ahead and frozen.

Country Home Favorites

Don't Peek Casserole

2 pounds stew meat
2 (10¾-ounce) cans cream of
   mushroom soup
2 (4-ounce) cans button
   mushrooms, drained
1 package Lipton onion soup mix
1 cup water
Cooked noodles or rice

Mix all ingredients except noodles in casserole dish with lid. Cover, and bake at 325° for 3 hours. Serve over noodles or rice. Do not uncover while baking.

Just Like Mama's

Venison Swiss Steak

2–3 pounds venison round
   steak, trimmed
¼ cup flour
½ teaspoon salt
Dash of pepper
Dash of cayenne pepper
Dash of thyme
Dash of nutmeg
Dash of ground cloves
2 tablespoons butter

2 large onions, sliced
1 (28-ounce) can crushed
   tomatoes
1 (28-ounce) can diced tomatoes
1½ cups burgundy wine
1½ tablespoons
   Worcestershire
½ garlic clove
1 (4-ounce) can sliced
   mushrooms

Preheat oven to 375°. Place steaks between wax paper to pound; pound on both sides with mallet. Combine flour and seasonings; pound flour into venison a little at a time. Melt butter in a large iron skillet; add steaks and brown on both sides. Add sliced onions to meat and cook until browned. Add tomatoes, wine, and Worcestershire, then garlic. Cover and bake about 2½ hours or until venison is tender. Remove from oven, and add mushrooms; bring to a boil on top of stove and let simmer, covered, for 5 minutes. Serve over white steamed rice.

Cookin' for the Cure

Poultry

PHOTO ©TIM THOMPSON / VIRGINIA TOURISM CORPORATION

When Edwin Boston Mabry built his water-powered grist mill in 1905 in Virginia's Blue Ridge Mountains, he had no idea it would become one of the most photographed places in the United States. Located on the Blue Ridge Parkway, the mill is now run by the National Park Service.

Creamed Chicken and Biscuits

1½ teaspoons margarine
½ large onion, chopped
4 cups chopped cooked chicken
1 (10¾-ounce) can cream of
  chicken soup (undiluted)
1 cup sour cream
½ cup milk
1 cup shredded mild Cheddar
  cheese, divided
6 frozen biscuits, thawed

Preheat oven to 350°. Grease bottom and sides of 7x11-inch baking dish. Heat margarine in a small nonstick skillet over medium-high heat until melted. Stir in onion; sauté until tender. Combine onion, chicken, soup, sour cream, and milk in a medium bowl; mix well. Spoon mixture into prepared baking dish. Bake 15 minutes. Remove from oven. Sprinkle baked layer with ¾ cup Cheddar cheese. Arrange biscuits in a single layer over top. Sprinkle with remaining Cheddar cheese. Bake until biscuits are golden brown and the sauce is bubbly, about 20 minutes. Serve immediately. Yields 6 servings.

Loving, Caring and Sharing

Chicken Spectacula

3 cups chopped cooked chicken
1 (6-ounce) box Uncle Ben's
  combination white and wild
  rice, cooked
1 (10¾-ounce) can cream of
  celery soup
1 (4-ounce) jar chopped
  pimentos
1 medium onion, chopped
1 (16-ounce) can French-style
  green beans, drained
1 cup mayonnaise
1 (8-ounce) can water chestnuts,
  sliced, drained
Salt and pepper to taste

Mix all ingredients. Pour into greased 3-quart casserole dish. Bake 25–30 minutes at 350°.

Grandma's Cookbook

Chicken Paprika

½ cup flour
3 teaspoons paprika, divided
¼ teaspoon salt
¼ teaspoon pepper
1½–2 pounds boneless chicken breasts

3 tablespoons margarine
1 cup chopped onion
1½ cups chicken broth
1 tablespoon cornstarch
½ cup sour cream, divided

In large plastic bag, place flour, 1 teaspoon paprika, salt, and pepper. Add chicken, a few pieces at a time; shake to coat well. In large skillet, melt margarine over medium heat. Add chicken; brown on all sides, about 10 minutes. Remove chicken. Add onion. Cook, stirring 1 minute. Stir in chicken broth and rest of paprika. Return chicken. Bring to a boil. Reduce heat; cover and simmer 25 minutes. Remove chicken. Stir together cornstarch and 2 tablespoons sour cream. Stir into pan juices. Stirring constantly, bring to a boil over medium heat; boil 1 minute. Stir in remaining sour cream and chicken. Freezes well; reheat at 350° for 20 minutes.

Gather 'Round Our Table

Coq a Vin Simplified

A great dish to take to a convention for a first night dinner.

3 medium potatoes, peeled, cut in chunks
3 carrots, peeled, cut into pieces same size as potatoes
2 medium onions, also cut into same size chunks

4 chicken breasts or thighs
2 cups wine
Salt and pepper to taste
Water to cover

Place all ingredients in a crockpot. Use enough water to cover. Cook on HIGH overnight or about 8 hours.

Taste Trek!

Virginia Brann's Poppy Seed Chicken Casserole

4 boneless, skinless chicken breasts
1 (8-ounce) container fat-free sour cream
½ cup chicken stock from boiled chicken

1 (10¾-ounce) can fat-free cream of chicken soup
½ stick butter
1 sleeve Ritz Crackers
1 tablespoon poppy seeds

Preheat oven to 350°. Boil chicken breasts until fully done; reserve broth. Chop chicken into chunks or shred and place into a greased casserole dish. In separate bowl, mix sour cream, chicken stock, and cream of chicken soup together. Spread soup mixture over chicken, completely covering it. In the same bowl as soup mixture, melt butter in microwave. Crumble package of crackers into small pieces. Add cracker crumbs and poppy seeds to melted butter. Stir so that all crackers are covered in butter and poppy seeds. Add crackers to top of casserole. Bake 30 minutes, until crackers are golden brown.

Kids in the Kitchen

Feta-Stuffed Chicken Breasts

1 (10-ounce) package frozen
   chopped spinach, thawed
8 ounces feta cheese
½ cup mayonnaise
1 garlic clove, minced
6 large boneless, skinless
   chicken breasts

Salt and pepper to taste
¼ cup flour
½ teaspoon paprika
12 strips bacon

Drain spinach and squeeze dry. Place spinach in a medium bowl. Crumble feta cheese into bowl. Add mayonnaise and garlic and mix well.

Cut a pocket in each chicken breast. Sprinkle with salt and pepper to taste. Spoon spinach mixture into pockets. Press pockets to close or secure with wooden picks. Mix flour with paprika on wax paper. Roll stuffed chicken breasts in flour mixture to lightly coat. Wrap 2 pieces of bacon around each stuffed chicken breast.

Place a greased rack in a baking dish. Arrange stuffed chicken breasts on the rack. Do not allow chicken to touch. Bake, uncovered, at 325° for one hour or until chicken is tender. Serves 6.

In Good Company

Born in 1909 in Greenville, singer Kate Smith made Irving Berlin's "God Bless America" an overnight sensation when she sang the song for the first time on November 11, 1938, on her weekly radio show. Berlin wrote the anthem in 1918 and revised it in 1938 as a "peace" song in the face of spreading war in Europe.

Chicken Stuffed with Spinach and Feta Cheese

10 (6-ounce) boneless, skinless
chicken breasts
½ (10-ounce) package frozen
chopped spinach, thawed,
drained
1½ cups cottage cheese
8 ounces feta cheese, crumbled
1¼ cups seasoned bread
crumbs, divided

1 ounce grated Parmesan
cheese
2 eggs, beaten
1 teaspoon oregano
½ teaspoon garlic powder
½ teaspoon pepper
¼ teaspoon nutmeg
6 tablespoons margarine, melted

Pound chicken between sheets of wax paper with a meat mallet until flattened. Press spinach to remove excess moisture. Combine spinach, cottage cheese, feta cheese, half the bread crumbs, Parmesan cheese, eggs, oregano, garlic powder, pepper, and nutmeg in a bowl and mix well. Spoon 3 ounces of spinach mixture in the center of each chicken breast. Fold chicken over to enclose filling.

Arrange chicken on a nonstick baking sheet. Brush with margarine. Sprinkle with remaining bread crumbs. Chill, covered, for 1 hour or longer. Bake at 325° for 30–40 minutes or until chicken is cooked through. Yields 10 servings.

Vintage Virginia

Chicken Wreath

1 (12-ounce) can chicken
1 (10¾-ounce) can cream of
  chicken soup
¼ cup chopped onion

1 cup shredded Cheddar cheese
Salt and pepper to taste
2 (8-count) cans crescent rolls

Drain chicken and mix well. Add soup, onion, cheese, salt, and pepper; mix well. Should be consistency of chicken salad.

Open crescent rolls and pull apart. Place on pizza pan with pointed side to outside of pan. Spoon chicken mixture evenly around ring. Fold crescent roll tips back over chicken mixture and tuck under ring. Bake at 375° for 15–20 minutes or until golden brown. Cut into serving portions.

Sharing Our Best

Mary Ann's Formal Yardbirds

This is an easy-to-prepare recipe because the chicken mix can be made a day ahead and refrigerated.

2 cups chopped cooked chicken
1 (3-ounce) package cream
  cheese, softened
2 tablespoons butter, softened
½ teaspoon salt
½ teaspoon pepper
2 tablespoons milk
1 tablespoon onion

1 tablespoon diced pimento
1 tablespoon Italian salad
  dressing
2 (8-ounce) packages crescent
  rolls
Melted butter
Crushed croutons
Paprika

Mix chicken, cream cheese, butter, salt, pepper, milk, onion, pimento, and salad dressing together; set aside. Press 2 crescent roll triangles at seam to form a rectangle; add ½ cup chicken mixture to center of each and pull up ends and twist. This will look similar to a giant candy kiss. Top with a spoonful melted butter, crushed croutons, and a sprinkle of paprika. Bake at 350° for 20–25 minutes. Yields 8 servings.

Virginia Traditions

The Greenbrier's Chicken Saltimbocca

4 (4-ounce) boneless, skinless
chicken breasts
4 (½-ounce) thick prosciutto
slices
4 (½-ounce) slices provolone
cheese, Havarti cheese, or
fontina cheese
2 teaspoons minced fresh sage
½ cup flour
Salt and pepper to taste
2 teaspoons olive oil
1 garlic clove, crushed
⅓ cup white wine
1 cup chicken stock
½ teaspoon cornstarch
1 tablespoon cold water
Fresh sage for garnish

Place chicken breasts on a work surface and pound lightly. Layer 1 slice of prosciutto and 1 slice of cheese on 1 side of each piece of chicken; sprinkle with sage. Fold the other side over to enclose the filling. Mix flour with salt and pepper. Coat both sides of chicken lightly with flour mixture.

Heat a large nonstick sauté pan over medium heat. Add olive oil and heat. Add garlic and sauté just until garlic begins to brown. Remove and discard garlic. Increase heat to medium-high.

Add chicken to sauté pan and sauté until brown on both sides. Add wine and chicken stock. Reduce heat, and simmer 3 minutes; do not boil. Remove chicken to a heated platter and tent with foil to keep warm.

Blend cornstarch with cold water in a small bowl. Scrape up browned bits from bottom of skillet with a wooden spoon. Add cornstarch mixture. Cook until thickened, stirring constantly. Spoon over chicken. Garnish with fresh sage and serve immediately. Serves 4.

Oh My Stars! Recipes that Shine

 Virginia became the tenth state to join the Union on June 25, 1788.

Sour Cream Marinated Chicken Breasts

Savory and moist.

1 pint sour cream
¼ cup lemon juice
2 tablespoons Worcestershire
1 tablespoon celery salt
1 teaspoon garlic salt
1 tablespoon paprika

½ teaspoon pepper
12 boneless, skinless chicken
   breasts
1½–2 cups cracker crumbs
½ cup margarine, melted

Combine sour cream, lemon juice, Worcestershire sauce, celery salt, garlic salt, paprika, and pepper. Pour over chicken breasts and marinate overnight in refrigerator.

Remove chicken breasts from marinade and roll in crumbs. Place in single layer in buttered 9x13-inch pan. Drizzle melted margarine over chicken. Bake at 350°, uncovered, 1 hour or until browned and tender.

Not By Bread Alone Cookbook

Chicken Casserole

3 cups chopped cooked chicken
   breasts (or turkey)
4 hard-boiled eggs, chopped
   medium-fine
2 cups cooked rice
1½ cups finely diced celery
1 small onion, finely diced
1 cup mayonnaise

2 (10¾-ounce) cans cream of
   mushroom soup
1 (3-ounce) package slivered
   almonds
1 teaspoon salt
2 tablespoons lemon juice
1 cup bread crumbs

Mix all ingredients except bread crumbs. Place in greased 9x13-inch casserole dish. Top with bread crumbs. Spray with butter cooking spray and bake at 350° for 40–45 minutes. This can be made a day ahead and refrigerated overnight. Serves 10–12.

Taste & See

Pamela's Chicken and Wild Rice Casserole

2 whole chicken breasts, split
1 cup water
1 cup sherry
½ teaspoon salt
½–1 tablespoon curry (to your taste)
1 medium onion, diced
½ cup diced celery
2 (6-ounce) packages Uncle Ben's Long Grain Wild Rice

1 (8-ounce) can mushrooms, drained, reserve liquid
1 (8-ounce) carton sour cream
1 (10¾-ounce) can cream of mushroom soup
½ cup dried currants, slivered almonds, or flaked coconut (optional)

In large pot, combine chicken, water, sherry, salt, curry, onion, and celery; simmer 1 hour. Remove chicken. Strain vegetables, reserving broth. Pull chicken off bone into bite-size pieces. Put chicken and strained veggies in large, deep casserole dish.

Cook rice as directed on package using broth, mushroom liquid, and enough water to accommodate instructions for liquid. Add cooked rice to casserole dish. Add mushrooms, sour cream, and soup to casserole dish. Mix well. Bake at 350° for 50 minutes, covered. Remove cover and bake 10 more minutes. Allow to cool a few minutes and serve. Add currants, almonds, or flaked coconut, if desired.

The Hall Family Cookbook

Blue Cheese Vinaigrette Chicken

¼ cup butter
½ medium red onion
6 boneless chicken breast
  halves

1 (6-ounce) bottle blue cheese
  vinaigrette dressing
Fresh Parmesan cheese, grated

Preheat oven to 350°. Melt butter in a 9x13-inch casserole dish. Place chopped or sliced red onion in butter. Put in chicken breasts and pour blue cheese vinaigrette dressing over chicken. Cover with fresh Parmesan cheese. Bake uncovered 45 minutes.

Taste of the Town II

Adobo
(Chicken and Pork)

1 (2-pound) chicken, cut into
  serving pieces
1 (1-pound) pork butt, cut into
  1½-inch cubes or pork chops
½ cup vinegar

3 garlic cloves, crushed
½ laurel leaf (optional)
½ cup soy sauce
½ teaspoon whole peppercorns

Mix all ingredients in a pot. Let stand an hour or even overnight. Cook covered on medium-high heat until mixture boils. Reduce heat to medium; turn meat and cook, covered, for one hour or until meat is tender and only a small amount of liquid is left. Serve with plain boiled rice. Serves 6.

Note: After meat is cooked, it may be browned by heating a tablespoon of oil until hot, then browning the drained meat. Pour over remaining liquid where meat was cooked, before serving. Chicken or pork may be used individually.

Philippine Cooking in America

Hot Chicken Salad

2–2½ cups diced cooked
  chicken
½–2 cups diced celery
½–1 cup mayonnaise
Dash of salt
½ teaspoon prepared mustard
½ (10¾-ounce) can cream of
  mushroom soup
2 tablespoons lemon juice

1 tablespoon grated onion
1 (15-ounce) can green peas,
  drained
2 eggs, hard-boiled, sliced
½–1½ cups almonds or
  croutons
½ cup grated cheese
1 cup crushed potato chips

Mix together all ingredients except cheese and potato chips. Bake in 350° oven 30–45 minutes, or at 400° for 20–25 minutes until it bubbles. Serves 8–10.

Discovery Tour 2006 Cookbook

Gourmet Cornish Hens

½ cup butter, divided
1 cup sliced fresh mushrooms,
  (or canned, drained)
¼ cup slivered almonds
¼ cup diced celery
1 (6-ounce) package long-grain
  wild rice

6 thin slices country ham
3 Rock Cornish hens, halved (or 6
  chicken breasts)
¼ cup dry white wine

In ¼ cup butter, sauté mushrooms, almonds, and celery. Prepare wild rice according to package directions. Add sautéed celery mixture to rice. In shallow pan or 3-quart casserole, arrange ham slices in single layer; spoon a mound of rice mixture in center of each ham slice. Season hens to taste, and put on top of rice, skin side up. Bake in 350° oven 1 hour, basting frequently with mixture of remaining ¼ cup melted butter and wine.

Pungo Strawberry Festival Cookbook

Seafood

Designed by sculptor Paul DiPasquale to commemorate Virginia Beach's annual Neptune Festival, Neptune is a 12.5-ton, bronze sculpture that includes 12 fish, an 8-foot octopus, two 17-foot dolphins, a 5-foot lobster, and an 11-foot sea turtle that is held in Neptune's hand. The Festival commemorates the city's unique position as the "City by the Sea."

PHOTO © M.P. PRUCHA

Scalloped Oysters

1½ pints oysters
¾ teaspoon salt
¼ teaspoon pepper
⅓ cup butter or margarine,
   melted

3 cups coarse soda cracker crumbs
   (Waverly or Keebler are good)
¾ cup milk

Remove any bits of shell from oysters. Strain oyster liquid through cheesecloth; reserve liquid. Add salt and pepper to oysters. Mix butter or margarine and crackers. Alternate layers of oysters and cracker mixture in greased baking dish. Combine milk and oyster liquid; pour into baking dish. Bake in 350° oven 30 minutes. Serves 4.

For Men Who Like to Cook, Want to Cook (or HAVE to!)

Native Americans created great mounds of leftover oyster shells, feeding heavily upon them for centuries without destroying the oyster bars in the Chesapeake Bay. Early English settlers were also able to harvest oysters in great quantities without reducing the ability of the species to recover. The Constitution of Virginia states that the natural oyster beds, rocks, and shoals in the waters of the Commonwealth shall not be leased, rented, or sold but shall be held in trust for the benefit of the people of the Commonwealth. America's only oyster museum is on Chincoteague Island, where the Oyster and Maritime Museum documents the island's oystering and seafood history.

Mammaw's Steamed Crabs

First of all, the best crabs in the world are the ones you catch yourself. That's a whole 'nother story though, about catching crabs. But now that you have the crabs, about a bushel, fill the bathtub half full of water and dump them in. Now you can see what you have. Don't take too long to get the pot and stove ready or the crabs will drown for lack of oxygen.

1 (12-ounce) can beer	**A bushel of fresh crabs**
2 tablespoons Old Bay	**Old Bay Seasoning for additional**
Seasoning	**seasoning**
6 ounces vinegar	**Butter, melted**
Water	

Get a big pot with a tray inside the bottom to keep crabs out of the fluids. Remember you're steaming them, not boiling them. Into the pot, pour a can of beer, 2 tablespoons Old Bay Seasoning, and vinegar, and fill to the bottom of the raised tray with water. (Somehow my grandmother always had a can of beer around, although I never saw her drink one.)

Fill the pot to the top with crabs; be careful, they'll cut your fingers with their sharp claws. Maybe use some tongs or heavy gloves. Pour some more Old Bay on top of crabs (but don't let them jump out of the pot). Turn on the heat and steam 'em up. Stay close by because when it starts getting hot in the pot, the crabs may try to push the top off and jump out. When they've just turned red, they're done.

Spread out some newspapers on the table and pour crabs (not the sauce) out. Have some large-handled butter knives or small wooden mallets to help (with breaking the shells). Maybe some melted butter in bowls and a few piles of Old Bay Seasoning out on the table. Some people like crackers to go with their Coca-Colas or beer. Now, picking and eating them crabs is another story, too....

Celebrate Virginia!

Soft-Shell Crabs

Soft-shell crabs are abundant and cheap almost all summer long. Most people don't cook them at home because they don't know how to clean the crabs. It is real easy to do right in your kitchen sink. Crabs must be alive when you clean them. You can wrap them in plastic and freeze them in a zip-lock bag if you want to have some crabs in the winter.

TO CLEAN CRABS:

Lift each side of crab's shell and pull off "dead man" (gills). Remove crab's apron. Squeeze crab firmly in middle to force out all innards. Do not leave any yellow or green stuff as it can be bitter. Rinse cavity. Drain on paper towels.

1 egg
¼ cup water
Peanut oil for frying
Seafood breading mix (any brand you like)

2 teaspoons Old Bay Seasoning
Soft-shell crabs (2 per person)

Mix egg with water. Beat until frothy. Heat 2–3 inches of peanut oil in big iron frying pan. Mix generous amount of seafood breading mix with Old Bay Seasoning in a big zip-lock bag. Dip each crab in egg/water, drop into breading mix, and shake until thoroughly coated. Fry until golden brown. Don't let your oil get too hot or coating will burn. When you drop crabs in pan, put cover on pan immediately as they will spatter and pop at first.

Note: If you cook a lot of crabs, of course you will have to increase quantities of ingredients accordingly.

Our Best to You!

Hampton Roads Crab Imperial

Everyone loves this!

1 pound crabmeat
1 egg
2 eggs, hard-boiled, chopped
⅔ cup chopped pimentos or
    green bell pepper (or ⅓ each)
1 teaspoon dry mustard

1 teaspoon prepared mustard
¼ teaspoon curry powder
3 tablespoons mayonnaise
Sprinkle of garlic salt
Paprika for garnish
Small handful bread crumbs

Preheat oven to 425°. Mix all ingredients lightly except paprika and bread crumbs; spoon into individual shells or 1-quart casserole. Sprinkle paprika and fine bread crumbs on top of each crab mixture. Bake 15–20 minutes. Serves 4.

Virginia Hospitality

Deviled Crabs

1 pound crabmeat
½ cup Ritz Cracker crumbs
2 tablespoons Worcestershire
1 tablespoon parsley flakes
1 tablespoon celery seeds
2 eggs, beaten

4 tablespoons mayonnaise
2 tablespoons mustard
¼ cup butter, melted
Dash of hot sauce
Paprika

In a large bowl, mix all ingredients except paprika, until well-blended. Spoon into greased, oven-proof serving dishes or shells and sprinkle with paprika. Bake 1 hour at 350°. Serve hot.

Virginia Cook Book

Crab Cakes

1 pound crabmeat
3 teaspoons mayonnaise
2 tablespoons dry mustard
2 slices bread, crumbled
1 egg, beaten

¼ teaspoon salt
1 tablespoon Worcestershire
¼ teaspoon white pepper
½ teaspoon red and hot sauce

Mix all ingredients together and shape into cakes. Fry in Crisco until brown. Makes 8 small or 6 large cakes.

Garden Gate Recipes

Tina's Easy Crab Cakes

1 cup boiling water
1 (6-ounce) package stove-top
   cornbread stuffing mix
3 eggs
2 (6-ounce) cans crabmeat,
   drained, flaked

½ stick butter or margarine
1 medium lemon, cut into 6
   servings

Add boiling water to stuffing mix; mix just until moist. Let stand 5 minutes. Beat eggs lightly in large bowl. Add crabmeat; mix lightly. Add prepared stuffing; mix well; shape into 6 patties. Melt butter in large skillet on medium heat. Add patties; cook 5 minutes on each side, or until heated through and lightly browned on both sides. Serve with lemon wedges.

The Westwood Clubhouse Cookbook

 At twenty-eight miles long, Virginia Beach is the world's longest resort beach. In terms of population, Virginia Beach is the largest city in Virginia.

Crab Melt

1 pound crabmeat
¼ cup diced celery
¼ cup diced red onion
4 hard-boiled eggs, diced
½ teaspoon Old Bay Seasoning
¼ teaspoon dill weed

½ cup mayonnaise
¼ cup sour cream
4 English muffins
8 slices tomato
8 slices Cheddar cheese

Combine first 8 ingredients in a medium bowl. Separate muffins. Top each muffin half with 1 slice of tomato, crab mixture, and 1 slice of Cheddar. Broil in oven just until cheese melts. Serves 4.

Recipe from The Main Street Mill Pub & Grill, Fort Royal
A Taste of Virginia History

Crab Florentine

6 tablespoons butter
¼ cup flour
1⅓ cups milk
2 chicken bouillon cubes
1 cup shredded Cheddar cheese
7 ounces crabmeat, rinsed,
    drained, flaked

⅔ cup white wine
½ cup crumbled cheese
    crackers
2 tablespoons butter, melted
2 (10-ounce) packages frozen
    chopped spinach, cooked,
    drained

Heat 6 tablespoons butter in a skillet until melted. Add flour, stirring until blended. Stir in milk and bouillon cubes. Cook until thickened, stirring constantly. Stir in cheese, crabmeat, and white wine. Toss cracker crumbs and 2 tablespoons butter in a bowl until coated. Spread equal portions of spinach in each of 8 greased, individual baking shells. Spoon crabmeat mixture over spinach. Sprinkle with cracker crumbs. Bake at 425° for 15–20 minutes or until bubbly. Yields 8 servings.

Vintage Virginia

Neptune's Delight

Versatile as well as delicious–any combination of seafood may be used.

1 stick butter	**½ pound lobster chunks, cooked**
½ cup all-purpose flour	**½ pound crabmeat**
1 quart milk, scalded	**½ pound shrimp, cooked**
½ teaspoon salt	**½ cup grated Parmesan cheese**
½ teaspoon dry mustard	**½ cup cracker meal**
2 teaspoons Worcestershire	**½ teaspoon paprika**
½ cup sherry	

Preheat oven to 400°. Combine butter and flour in a saucepan; brown over low heat, stirring constantly. Add scalded milk and let come to a boil; whip with a beater until all lumps disappear. Add spices and sherry. Put shellfish in a 2-quart casserole and cover with sauce. Sprinkle with cheese mixed with cracker meal and paprika. Brown lightly in oven 15 minutes. Serves 6–8.

Virginia Hospitality

Baked Stuffed Shrimp

Great company dish! Can be prepared earlier in the day and refrigerated. Large shrimp do just as well as jumbo.

**24 raw jumbo shrimp, shelled,
  deveined**
**2 tablespoons plus 1 stick butter,
  divided**
1 small onion, minced
¼ cup minced celery
½ green bell pepper, minced
1 tablespoon chopped parsley
1 pound backfin crabmeat

1 teaspoon salt
¼ teaspoon thyme
Dash of Tabasco
1 tablespoon Worcestershire
½ cup seasoned bread crumbs
1 egg, beaten
1 cup light cream or milk
1 stick butter
Paprika

Split shrimp lengthwise so they can be opened flat, but do not cut all the way through. Spread flat in buttered shallow baking dish, and set aside. In 2 tablespoons butter, sauté onion, celery, and green pepper until onion is just transparent. Remove from heat. Add parsley. Toss vegetable mixture with crabmeat. Add seasonings, bread crumbs, egg, and cream. Toss gently. Mound crab mixture on shrimp. Melt stick of butter, and pour over shrimp. Sprinkle with paprika, and bake at 400° for 15 minutes. This can be prepared early in the day. If so, pour butter over shrimp just before baking. Makes 6 servings.

Food, Family, and Friendships

The Neptune Festival sends off summer with a bang. The month-long celebration of Virginia Beach's seafaring heritage culminates in the fabulous Boardwalk Weekend each September. Taking place along thirty blocks of the oceanfront, the festival features the North American Sand Sculpting Championship, numerous sporting events, fireworks, food, an open-air art show along the Boardwalk, an air show, and the Neptune Parade. The festival is ranked among the top ten festivals in the Southeast by the Southeast Tourism Association.

Drunken Shrimp Overboard

12 ounces St. George Porter (ale)
⅓ cup toasted sesame oil
1 tablespoon frozen lime juice concentrate
2 tablespoons Thai fish sauce
5 cloves garlic, crushed
1 teaspoon powdered cardamom
1 teaspoon Chinese red chili paste
1½ pounds large shrimp (30 count), heads off but in shells
Wooden skewers soaked in water for several hours

Mix St. George Porter, sesame oil, lime juice, fish sauce, garlic, cardamom, and chili paste; pour into a large plastic bag. Place shrimp in plastic bag; marinate in refrigerator overnight.

Prepare hot grill. Place shrimp on soaked bamboo skewers, 3 per skewer. Grill about 40–60 seconds per side or until shells just turn orange-pink, do not over cook. Serve immediately. Serves 6.

Note: If you are not able to grill, reserve marinade and sauté shrimp over medium-high heat on stove until pink.

Toast to Tidewater

Southern Shrimp and Grits

1 pound shrimp, peeled
6 slices bacon
Peanut oil
2 cups sliced fresh mushrooms
1 cup sliced green onions
1 garlic clove, crushed

4 teaspoons fresh lemon juice
Salt and pepper to taste
Hot sauce to taste
Chopped fresh parsley to taste
Cheesy Grits

Rinse shrimp, pat dry, and set aside. Chop bacon into small pieces. Cook bacon in large heavy skillet until browned at the edges. Remove bacon from skillet; set aside. Add enough peanut oil to bacon drippings in skillet to cover bottom of pan. Heat mixture over medium-high heat. Add shrimp. Sauté until shrimp begin to turn pink. Add mushrooms, green onions, garlic, and bacon. Cook until shrimp are pink and bacon is crisp. Add lemon juice, salt and pepper, hot sauce, and parsley and mix well.

Divide Cheesy Grits among 4 warm plates. Spoon shrimp mixture over grits and serve immediately.

CHEESY GRITS:

4 cups cooked grits
1 cup shredded sharp Cheddar
  cheese
½ cup grated Parmesan cheese

White pepper to taste
Nutmeg to taste
Hot sauce to taste

Prepare enough grits according to package directions to yield 4 cups. Add Cheddar and Parmesan cheeses to hot grits and stir until cheeses melt. Season with white pepper, nutmeg, and hot sauce, mix well, and set aside. Keep grits warm.

In Good Company

Shrimp-Tarpley Curried

¼ pound butter
1–1½ pounds uncooked shrimp, peeled

1 tablespoon curry powder
Cooked rice

Melt butter in small saucepan. Add shrimp and curry. Cook until shrimp are done, stirring occasionally. Serve over rice. Serves 2.

The Smithfield Cookbook

Camaron Rebosado
(Fried Shrimp)

1 pound large, raw shrimp, with with shells
1 teaspoon salt
1 teaspoon MSG
1 large egg
½ cup cornstarch or flour

1½ teaspoons baking powder
Dash of black pepper
2–3 tablespoons water (optional)
1 cup vegetable oil for deep frying

When shelling shrimp, keep shell at tail intact. Cut a deep slit in the back of each shrimp and devein. Mix salt and MSG; dip wet finger in mixture and rub between slits in each shrimp.

In a bowl, beat egg, cornstarch, baking powder, and pepper. Mix until smooth. If mixture is too thick, add 2–3 tablespoons water. Coat each shrimp with mixture, leaving tail uncoated, and fry in hot oil, a few at a time until golden brown. Drain on paper towels. Serve hot with ketchup or sweet and sour sauce. Serves 6.

Philippine Cooking in America

Kung Pao Lobster

1 teaspoon chopped garlic
½ teaspoon chopped ginger
1½ tablespoons cornstarch
¼ teaspoon baking soda
¼ teaspoon sugar
Salt and pepper to taste
1 pound cooked lobster meat, sliced

¼ cup oil
1 small onion, diced
2 small zucchini, cut in ½-inch cubes
1 red bell pepper, cut in ½-inch cubes
2 ounces cashews or peanuts

Combine garlic, ginger, cornstarch, baking soda, sugar, salt and pepper. Add lobster, mix, and let stand 20 minutes. Heat oil in wok. Add lobster and stir-fry over high heat about 20 minutes. Remove. Add onion, zucchini, and pepper to same oil and stir-fry about 30 seconds. Mix Sauce ingredients together and add to wok. Cook, stirring, until Sauce is thickened. Add lobster and nuts and heat through completely.

SAUCE:

1 cup chicken stock
1 tablespoon Chinese rice wine or dry sherry
1 tablespoon cornstarch

2 teaspoons chili sauce
2 teaspoons Chinese bean paste (optional)
2 teaspoons sesame oil

Combine ingredients and mix well.

A Taste of Prince William County Cookbook

Pan-Seared Yellowfin Tuna

Kosher salt and cracked black   **¼ cup peanut oil**
peppercorns to taste

Preheat a heavy cast-iron skillet. Season tuna generously with kosher salt and peppercorns. Add peanut oil to skillet and sear fish on one side for approximately 2 minutes. Reduce heat to medium, flip tuna, and continue cooking one minute. Place tuna in the middle of each of 4 plates on a bed of Eastern Shore Blue Crab Succotash. Serves 4.

EASTERN SHORE BLUE CRAB SUCCOTASH:

¼ cup unsalted butter	**1 teaspoon minced garlic**
1 tablespoon minced shallots	**2 teaspoons Old Bay Seasoning**
2 cups sweet corn	**½ pound jumbo lump crabmeat**
1 cup frozen lima beans	**¼ cup heavy cream**
½ red bell pepper, diced	**Salt and white pepper to taste**

Melt butter in a large sauté pan. Add shallots and cook about one minute. Add corn, lima beans, and red pepper. Cook one minute over medium-high heat. Add garlic and Old Bay and stir until well mixed. Add crabmeat and cream and toss until heated through, being careful not to break up lumps of crabmeat. Season to taste and divide among 4 heated plates.

Recipe from The Wharf, Alexandria
A Taste of Virginia History

Norfolk is the home base for the U.S. Navy's Atlantic Fleet. The U.S. Atlantic Fleet provides fully trained, combat-ready forces to support U.S. and NATO commanders in regions of conflict throughout the world.

Potato Chip-Encrusted Flounder

1 cup all-purpose flour
2 large eggs
1 cup milk
3 cups crumbled potato chips

2 pounds medium flounder
  fillets
½ cup vegetable oil

Preheat oven to 350°. Place flour in a shallow container. Beat eggs and milk together in another shallow container. Place potato chips in a third shallow container. Dredge fillets in flour, then dip in egg mixture. Place fillets in potato chips and press into both sides.

Place oil in a large sauté pan over medium heat. Add flounder and cook until golden brown on both sides. Finish in oven for 6–7 minutes. Serve immediately. Serves 4.

A Taste of Virginia History

Baked Fish

2 or 3 large fillets of fish (trout,
  rock, or flounder)
2 tablespoons mayonnaise,
  divided
1–1½ cups cracker crumbs

2 or 3 slices bacon
1 small onion, sliced
Juice of 1 lemon, divided
Salt and pepper to taste
Old Bay Seasoning to taste

Rinse and dry fillets; spread small amount of mayonnaise on each side of each fillet. Roll fillets in cracker crumbs. Place fillets on aluminum foil sheet large enough to enclose fillets. Lay strips of bacon and onion slices on each and sprinkle with lemon juice. Salt and pepper lightly and sprinkle with seafood seasoning. Close foil and place in preheated 375° oven and bake for 20 minutes. After 20 minutes, open foil carefully and let fish brown approximately 5 minutes. Remove from oven and enjoy!

Our Best to You!

Bluefish Greek Style

The acidic tomatoes are the perfect foil for this relatively fatty, flavorful fish.

2 tablespoons olive oil
1 medium onion, chopped
2 medium carrots, peeled, thinly
  sliced
2 cloves garlic, minced
½ cup dry white wine
1 (14½-ounce) can chopped
  tomatoes, including liquid
2 tablespoons chopped fresh
  parsley

½ teaspoon salt
¼ teaspoon pepper
4 (6-ounce) skinless bluefish
  fillets, rinsed, patted dry
¼ cup kalamata or black Greek
  olives
¼ cup crumbled feta cheese

Preheat oven to 400°. Heat oil in medium skillet over medium-high heat. Add onion, carrots, and garlic. Cook, stirring frequently, until vegetables are tender. Add wine and scrape any brown bits from bottom of skillet. Add tomatoes to skillet along with parsley, salt, and pepper. Simmer on low heat 15 minutes.

Spread half of tomato mixture in bottom of a 2-quart rectangular baking dish. Place fish on top and spread remaining tomato mixture over top. Bake 10–15 minutes, or until fish flakes easily when tested with a fork. Top with olives and cheese; serve immediately. Makes 4 servings.

The Best of Virginia Farms Cookbook

 Native son and Confederate General Thomas Jackson got his nickname "Stonewall" in Manassass, where he fought in the first Battle of Bull Run and won the nickname for his calm demeanor and stout defense of Henry Hill. Thomas "Stonewall" Jackson was one of the most honored generals of the American Civil War. (He is also remembered for teaching slaves to read the Bible in the 1850s, contrary to Virginia law at the time.)

Baked Salmon with Pecan-Crunch Coating

4 (4- to 6-ounce) salmon fillets
⅛ teaspoon salt
⅛ teaspoon pepper
2 tablespoons Dijon mustard
2 tablespoons butter, melted
1½ tablespoons honey

¼ cup soft bread crumbs
¼ cup finely chopped pecans
2 teaspoons chopped parsley
Fresh parsley sprigs and lemon
    wedges for garnish

Sprinkle salmon with salt and pepper. Place skin-side down on lightly greased 9x13-inch baking pan. Combine mustard, butter, and honey. Brush on fillets. Combine bread crumbs, pecans, and parsley. Spoon mixture evenly over fillets. Bake in a 450° oven for 10 minutes or until fish flakes easily when tested with a fork. Garnish, if desired. Serves 4.

The Fine Art of Dining

Marinated Grilled Salmon

½ cup unsalted butter
⅓ cup honey
⅓ cup packed brown sugar
2 tablespoons fresh lemon juice

¾ teaspoon crushed dried red
    pepper flakes
1 (2-pound) center-cut salmon
    fillet, skin on

Combine butter, honey, brown sugar, lemon juice, and red pepper flakes in saucepan. Cook over medium heat, stirring until smooth (5–7 minutes). Cool. Arrange salmon in dish and add marinade. Let stand 30 minutes, turning once. Prepare grill, oil surface, and use fish holder. Cook salmon skin side up over medium coals 5–7 minutes. Turn over; cook another 5–7 minutes until fish flakes easily. Serves 4.

Cooking with Grace

Honey Grilled Salmon

¾ cup honey
⅓ cup soy sauce
¼ cup packed dark brown
  sugar
¼ cup pineapple juice
2 tablespoons lemon juice
2 tablespoons white distilled
  vinegar

2 teaspoons olive oil
1 teaspoon ground black pepper
½ teaspoon cayenne pepper
½ teaspoon paprika
¼ teaspoon minced garlic
4 (8-ounce) salmon fillets (without
  skin)

Make the sauce by combining all ingredients, except salmon, in a medium saucepan over medium-low heat. Stir occasionally until sauce begins to boil, then simmer uncovered 15 minutes, or until sauce is syrupy. Watch it closely to make sure it doesn't boil over.

Preheat grill to medium. Rub each salmon fillet with vegetable oil, then sprinkle with salt and pepper. Grill for 4–7 minutes per side or until done. Serve salmon with a small cup of sauce on the side.

A Taste of Heaven

Grilled Salmon with Five-Roasted Pepper Salsa

The Omega-3 fatty acids in salmon have received praise from the scientific community for their possible role in the reduction of cholesterol. Teamed here with an easy-to-prepare, low-fat, very colorful salsa, the result is a healthy meal.

4 (6-ounce) salmon fillets
Olive oil vegetable spray
1 (6-ounce) red bell pepper
1 (6-ounce) yellow bell pepper
1 (6-ounce) green bell pepper
2 tablespoons chopped red
   onion

1 tablespoon chopped opal basil
1 teaspoon extra virgin olive oil
   (or V8 juice)
1 shallot, chopped
Juice of 1 lime
Salt and cracked black pepper to
   taste

Grill salmon over hot coals using nonstick olive oil vegetable spray on grill. Roast peppers until black on all sides. Cover with plastic wrap for 5 minutes. Rinse off charred skin and remove seeds. Dice. Mix with remaining ingredients and season salsa to taste. Yields 4 servings.

Chef's Note: Salmon should be removed from the grill when the middle is still reddish. It will continue to cook somewhat and will remain moist.

Recipe by Jim Makinson, Kingsmill Resort, Williamsburg
Culinary Secrets of Great Virginia Chefs

Pocahontas' life has formed the basis of many legends. Because she never learned to write, the thoughts, feelings, and motives of the historical Pocahontas remain largely unknown. Her story became the source of much romantic myth-making in the centuries following her death. The Walt Disney Company's 1995 animated feature *Pocahontas* presents a highly-romanticized and fictional view of a love affair between Pocahontas and John Smith, in which Pocahontas teaches Smith the value of respect for nature. However, the records of the Jamestown settlers indicate that Pocahontas had only a friendship with Captain John Smith (having saved his life more than once), and actually married John Rolfe.

Chowning's Tavern Salmon Cakes

SALMON CAKES:

1 (1-pound) fresh salmon fillet, steamed or poached, flaked
2 large eggs, lightly beaten
2 tablespoons milk
½ cup fresh bread crumbs

1 small onion, finely chopped
1 celery rib, finely chopped
Salt and freshly ground black pepper to taste

In a large bowl, mix together salmon, eggs, milk, bread crumbs, onion, celery, and salt and pepper. Divide mixture into 12 small cakes and place on a plate or platter. Cover with plastic wrap and chill at least 1 hour. (Cakes can be made up to 4 hours in advance.)

½ cup flour
½ teaspoon salt
¼ teaspoon freshly ground black pepper
2 large eggs

2 tablespoons water
2 cups fresh bread crumbs
2 tablespoons unsalted butter
2 tablespoons vegetable oil

In a shallow bowl, mix flour with salt and pepper. In a separate bowl, beat eggs with water. In a third bowl, place bread crumbs. In a large skillet over medium-high heat, melt butter with oil. Roll each cake in seasoned flour to coat thoroughly. Shake off any excess flour and dip in beaten egg mixture. Drain off any excess egg and transfer to bread crumbs. Turn cakes in crumbs until completely coated. Cook cakes in hot butter and oil mixture until lightly browned, 2–3 minutes on each side. Drain on paper towels and serve at once with herbed tomato sauce, if desired. Serves 4.

The Colonial Williamsburg Tavern Cookbook

Cakes

PHOTO ©BOB KRIST / VIRGINIA TOURISM CORPORATION

On April 9, 1865, General Robert E. Lee (Confederate) surrendered to Lt. General Ulysses S. Grant (Union) at the home of Wilmer McLean in the village of Appomattox Court House, Virginia, bringing an end to the Civil War.

Williamsburg Orange Cake

2½ cups all-purpose flour
1½ cups granulated sugar
¾ teaspoon salt
1½ cups buttermilk
½ cup shortening
3 eggs
1½ teaspoons vanilla
1 cup golden raisins, cut up

½ cup finely chopped walnuts
2 tablespoons grated orange peel, divided
½ cup butter, softened
4½ cups powdered sugar
4–5 tablespoons orange-flavored liqueur or orange juice

Preheat oven to 350°. Flour and grease 3 (8-inch) cake pans. Beat flour, sugar, salt, buttermilk, shortening, eggs, vanilla, raisins, walnuts, and 1 tablespoon grated orange peel in large mixer bowl on low speed for 30 seconds. Beat on high speed, scraping bowl occasionally, for 3 minutes. Pour into pans. Bake 30 minutes or until wooden toothpick comes out clean. Cool. To make frosting, mix butter and powdered sugar until fluffy. Beat in liqueur and remaining tablespoon orange peel. Frost layers.

Cooking with ARK Angels

Appalachian Blackberry Cake

½ cup shortening
2 cups sugar
3 egg yolks (reserve 2 whites)
½ teaspoon allspice
2½ cups sifted all-purpose
 flour
1 teaspoon baking soda
1 teaspoon cinnamon
½ teaspoon nutmeg
2 cups blackberries, drained, juice
 reserved

Cream together shortening, sugar, and egg yolks until smooth. Add dry ingredients, then blackberries. Mix well. (Add a little reserved juice, if needed.) Pour into a greased 9x13-inch pan. Bake at 350° for 30–35 minutes.

SEVEN MINUTE ICING:
1½ cups sugar
2 egg whites
6 tablespoons water
½ teaspoon vanilla

Combine sugar, egg whites, and water in top of double boiler. Boil constantly 7 minutes, beating with electric mixer until icing stands in peaks. Add vanilla. Spread on cooled cake.

Discovery Tour 2006 Cookbook

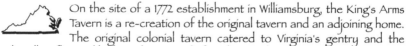

On the site of a 1772 establishment in Williamsburg, the King's Arms Tavern is a re-creation of the original tavern and an adjoining home. The original colonial tavern catered to Virginia's gentry and the politically influential before, during, and after the Revolution.

Blackberry Wine Cake

½ cup chopped pecans
1 (18¼-ounce) package white
  cake mix
1 (3-ounce) package blackberry
  gelatin

4 eggs
½ cup vegetable oil
1 cup blackberry wine

Preheat oven to 325°. Grease and flour a 9- or 10-inch tube pan. Put chopped pecans in bottom of pan. Combine cake mix, blackberry gelatin, eggs, oil, and blackberry wine. Beat 2 minutes, then pour batter over top of pecans. Bake 40–45 minutes or until cake tests done. Pour ½ of Blackberry Glaze over top of cake while still warm. Let sit 10 minutes, then remove cake from pan. Allow cake to cool fully before pouring remaining glaze on top.

BLACKBERRY GLAZE:
1 cup confectioners' sugar
½ cup blackberry wine

½ cup butter, softened

Combine ingredients; beat until smooth.

Taste Trek!

The Emancipation Proclamation was an executive order in 1863 by U.S. President Abraham Lincoln during the American Civil War, which declared the freedom of all slaves in those areas of the rebellious Confederate States of America that had not already returned to Union control. In 1863 in Hampton, an oak tree served as the site of the first southern reading of the Emancipation Proclamation. The Emancipation Oak is 98 feet in diameter, with branches that extend upward as well as laterally, as if offering refuge. It is designated one of the 10 Great Trees of the World by the National Geographic Society and is a National Historic Landmark.

Whiskey Cake

1½ cups seedless dark raisins
1½ cups water
3 tablespoons bourbon
½ cup butter, softened
1 cup sugar
3 eggs, separated

2 cups sifted all-purpose flour
1 teaspoon baking powder
1 teaspoon baking soda
1 teaspoon salt
1 cup chopped nuts
1 teaspoon vanilla

The day before making cake, combine raisins and water in a saucepan. Bring to a boil and cook 10 minutes. Cool, add whiskey, and allow to stand overnight.

Cream butter and sugar, beating until fluffy. Add egg yolks one at a time, beating well after each addition. Sift together flour, baking powder, baking soda, and salt. Drain liquid from raisins, saving 1 cup (if not sufficient amount, add whiskey to fill cup). To creamed mixture, alternately blend in dry ingredients and liquid, a third of each at a time. Stir in nuts, vanilla, and raisins. Beat egg whites until stiff. Fold into batter. Pour into 2 (9-inch) greased pans. Bake at 350° about 25 minutes. Cool and frost.

BUTTER CREAM FROSTING:
½ cup soft butter or margarine
1 (1-pound) box powdered
   sugar, sifted

1 cup chopped walnuts or pecans
1 teaspoon vanilla
3–5 tablespoons whiskey

Cream butter with powdered sugar until light and fluffy. Add rest of ingredients and beat until of spreading consistency. Fills and frosts 2 (9-inch) layers.

The Smithfield Cookbook

Fresh Apple Cake

2 cups sugar
1 cup oil
2 eggs
1 cup flaked coconut
4 fresh apples, peeled, chopped

2¼ cups all-purpose flour
1 (16-ounce) package butterscotch
　chips
1 cup chopped pecans
1 cup raisins

Mix together sugar, oil, and eggs; add remaining ingredients. Pour into greased Bundt pan and bake at 350° for 45–50 minutes.

GLAZE:
½ cup butter
1 cup brown sugar

¼ cup evaporated milk
1 teaspoon vanilla

Place butter and sugar in saucepan; let melt and add milk, bringing to a full boil. Cool and add vanilla, then pour over cake.

Discovery Tour 2006 Cookbook

Apple Pie Cake

¼ cup butter, softened
1 cup sugar
1 teaspoon baking soda
2 tablespoons hot water
1 egg
1 cup all-purpose flour

1 teaspoon cinnamon
1 teaspoon vanilla
¼ teaspoon nutmeg
½ cup chopped nuts
2 cups diced apples

Cream together butter and sugar. Dissolve baking soda in hot water and add to creamed mixture. Stir in all other ingredients. Pour into greased 9-inch pie pan. Bake at 350° for 35–40 minutes. Serve warm with ice cream or sweetened whipped cream.

Variation: For an easy/lazy brunch, double recipe and bake in a 9x13-inch pan; cut into squares for easy serving. Serve with slices of Cheddar cheese and tiny sausage links. Fresh yogurt or whipped cream cheese is good with it, too.

Vesuvius, Virginia: Then and Now

The Best Carrot Cake Ever

2 cups sugar
1 cup vegetable oil
4 eggs
2 (4-ounce) jars strained baby
  food carrots
1 teaspoon vanilla

2 cups all-purpose flour
½ teaspoon salt
1½ teaspoons baking soda
2 teaspoons ground cinnamon
¼ teaspoon nutmeg
¼ teaspoon cloves

Combine sugar and oil; beat well. Add eggs, carrots, and vanilla; beat mixture until smooth. Combine remaining dry ingredients. Add to creamed mixture, beating well. Pour batter into 2 greased and floured 9-inch round cake pans. Bake at 350° for 30 minutes or until a wooden toothpick comes out clean. Cool in pans for 10 minutes. Remove layers from pans. Cool completely on wire racks before icing.

CREAM CHEESE FROSTING:

1 (8-ounce) package cream cheese,
  softened
½ cup margarine, softened
1 tablespoon vanilla

4 cups confectioners' sugar,
  sifted
1½ cups chopped pecans

Cream together cream cheese and margarine. Add vanilla and powdered sugar, 1 cup at a time. Mix well and add pecans. Spread between layers and all over cake.

G.W. Carver Family Recipes

Virginia's first successful commercial tobacco crop was cultivated in 1612 by Englishman John Rolfe, who later married Indian princess Pocahontas. In Virginia, tobacco once reigned supreme, but government employment, especially the federal government and military, has since replaced tobacco as the state's largest industry.

Four Day Coconut Cake

This is a delicious moist cake.

2 cups sugar
1 (16-ounce) container sour
  cream
2 (6-ounce) packages frozen
  flaked coconut

1 (18¼-ounce) package yellow
  cake mix

The night before baking the cake, combine sugar, sour cream, and coconut. Store in refrigerator.

The next morning, prepare cake and bake in 2 layers according to package directions. Turn out layers. Cool. Split each layer to make 2 layers for a total of 4. Frost each layer with sour cream mixture; assemble. Cover and store in airtight container in refrigerator, and do not cut for 4 days.

Country Home Favorites

Mountain Dew Cake

1 (18¼-ounce) box orange cake
    mix
1 (3-ounce) box instant coconut
    cream pie filling

1 cup vegetable oil
4 eggs
1 cup Mountain Dew beverage

Mix ingredients and pour into 3 floured and greased layer pans. Bake at 350° for 30 minutes. Test at 25 minutes.

FILLING AND FROSTING:

1 (16-ounce) can crushed
    pineapple
1½ cups sugar

1 stick margarine
2 tablespoons flour
1 (7-ounce) can flaked coconut

Bring ingredients, except coconut, to a boil over medium heat. Remove from heat and stir in coconut. Let cool 15 minutes. Spread between layers and on top of cake.

Recipes from Home

Black Russian Cake

1 (18¼-ounce) package yellow
    cake mix
1 (5.9-ounce) package chocolate
    instant pudding mix
4 large eggs
1 cup vegetable oil

½ cup vodka
½ cup water
½ cup sugar
½ cup Kahlúa, divided
½ cup powdered sugar

Beat first 7 ingredients and ¼ cup Kahlúa at medium speed with an electric mixer until smooth; pour into a greased and floured Bundt pan. Bake at 350° for 50 minutes.

Combine remaining ¼ cup Kahlúa and powdered sugar, stirring until smooth. Let cake cool slightly. Remove cake from pan. Puncture cake surface with a large wooden pick and brush with glaze. Let harden. Serves 16.

What Can I Bring?

German Chocolate Upside Down Cake

1 cup flaked coconut
1 cup chopped pecans
1 (18¼-ounce) box German
  chocolate cake mix
1 stick margarine

1 (8-ounce) package cream
  cheese
1 (1-pound) box confectioners'
  sugar

Mix coconut and pecans together and put in a greased 9x13-inch pan. Mix cake mix according to package directions and pour on top of coconut mixture. In a saucepan, heat margarine and cream cheese until mixture is warm enough to stir in confectioners' sugar. Spoon mixture over top of cake mix. Bake at 350° for 35–45 minutes.

Joy in Serving

Anne's Chocolate Cake

1 (18¼-ounce) package fudge
  cake mix
2 eggs, beaten

1 teaspoon almond extract
1 (21-ounce) can cherry pie
  filling

Grease bottom of 9x13-inch pan with solid shortening or margarine. Combine cake mix, eggs, and flavoring. Stir by hand until well mixed. Blend in pie filling. Pour into prepared pan. Bake in 350° oven 25–30 minutes or until toothpick comes out clean.

FROSTING:
1 cup sugar
5 tablespoons butter or
  margarine

⅓ cup milk
1 (6-ounce) package semisweet
  chocolate chips

Prepare Frosting while cake is baking. In a small saucepan, combine sugar, butter, and milk. Boil 1 minute, stirring constantly. Remove from heat, and stir in chocolate chips until smooth. Pour over partially cooled cake.

Food, Family, and Friendships

The Pentagon

The Pentagon building is the headquarters of the United States Department of Defense. Even though the building is located in Arlington, the United States Postal Service requires that "Washington, DC" be used in conjunction with the six zip codes assigned to it: 20301–Secretary of Defense; 20310–Army; 20330–Air Force; 20350–Navy; 20380–Marines; 20318–Joint Chiefs of Staff.

Construction of the Pentagon began September 11, 1941, and was completed on January 15, 1943. Housing approximately 23,000 military and civilian employees and about 3,000 nondefense support personnel, it is the highest-capacity office building in the world, as well as one of the world's largest buildings in terms of floor area. It has five sides, five floors above ground (plus two basement levels), and five ring corridors per floor with a total of 17.5 miles of corridors.

At five acres, the central plaza in the Pentagon is the world's largest "no-salute, no-cover" area (an area exempt from the normal rule that, when out of doors, U.S. military personnel must wear hats and salute superior officers).

Other Pentagon Facts:

Stairways: 131
Escalators: 19
Elevators: 13
Windows: 7,754
Restrooms: 284
Drinking fountains: 691
Clocks installed: 4,200
Light fixtures: 16,250

Daily lamp replacements: 250
Total glass area: 7.1 acres
   (309,276 square feet)
Telephone cable: 100,000 miles
Internal telephone lines: 68,000 miles
Telephone calls made daily: 200,000
Pieces of mail handled monthly by the
   Defense Post Office: 1,200,000

Chocolate Chip Pound Cake

1 (18¼-ounce) package yellow
  cake mix
1 (3-ounce) package vanilla
  instant pudding
⅔ cup oil
⅔ cup water

4 eggs
1 (6-ounce) package semisweet
  chocolate chips
½ square German chocolate,
  grated

Beat cake mix, pudding, oil, water, and eggs until well blended. Stir in by hand the chocolate chips and German chocolate. Bake in greased tube pan 1 hour at 300°. Test for doneness at end of 1 hour. May need cooking 10–15 minutes longer. Cool in pan 15 minutes.

Church Family Favorites

Cold Oven Pound Cake

2 sticks margarine, softened
½ cup oil
3 cups sugar
5 eggs
1⅓ cups milk

3 cups all-purpose flour
½ teaspoon baking powder
¼ teaspoon salt
1 tablespoon vanilla
2 teaspoons lemon extract

Cream margarine, oil, and sugar. Add eggs, milk, and dry ingredients. Add vanilla and lemon extract. Grease and flour Bundt pan. Place in a cold oven and set oven temperature on 350°. Bake 1 hour and 15 minutes.

Garden Gate Recipes

Orange Glaze Pound Cake

1½ sticks margarine, softened
2⅔ cups sugar
1 teaspoon orange flavoring
1 teaspoon butter flavoring
1 teaspoon vanilla flavoring
⅔ cup shortening

5 large eggs
1 cup milk
4⅔ cups all-purpose flour
1 teaspoon baking powder
1 teaspoon salt

Mix first 7 ingredients in order given. Add milk and flour with baking powder and salt, a little at a time until all is used. Spoon or pour into greased and floured tube pan, and bake at 300° for 35 minutes, then at 325° for 30 minutes or until done. Make glaze just as the cake is getting done, and spoon on hot cake when you take it from the oven. Cool in pan about 30 minutes and wrap in plastic wrap.

ORANGE GLAZE:
½ stick margarine
½ cup sugar

½ cup water (scant)
1 teaspoon orange flavoring

Boil until syrup-like, and pour or spoon on hot cake while still in pan. Cool 30–35 minutes. Take out of pan and wrap in plastic wrap.

Note: May use lemon or rum flavoring instead of orange.

Grandma's Cookbook

 The nation's largest Osage orange tree—55 feet tall and spanning 90 feet—grows at Red Hill at Brookneal, the last home of Virginia's first governor Patrick Henry.

Ever Moist Coconut Pound Cake

2 sticks butter, softened
½ cup Crisco
3 cups sugar
5 eggs
3 cups all-purpose flour

½ teaspoon salt
1 teaspoon baking powder
1 cup milk
2 teaspoons coconut flavoring
1 (7-ounce) bag coconut flakes

Beat butter and Crisco together; add sugar and beat until mixed. Add eggs, one at a time; beat until fluffy. Mix dry ingredients together and add alternately with milk, ending with flour mixture; beat well. Add flavoring and coconut. Pour into 10-inch greased tube pan and bake at 350° for 75 minutes, or until straw comes out clean.

SYRUP TOPPING:

⅔ cup sugar
⅓ cup water

1 teaspoon coconut flavoring
2 teaspoons butter

Boil sugar, water, flavoring, and butter for 1 minute. Pour boiling syrup on cake immediately upon removing from oven. Let sit 10 minutes before removing from pan. Wrap cake with plastic wrap while still hot.

Tangier Island Girl

Maryanne's Birthday Cake

7 tablespoons butter, melted
½ cup brown sugar

1⅔ cups crushed Oreo cookies

Mix ingredients and press in the bottom of a springform pan; set aside.

FILLING:

1 (18-ounce) jar creamy peanut butter
2½ (8-ounce) packages cream cheese, softened
2 cups sugar
2 tablespoons butter, melted

2 teaspoons vanilla
1½ cups heavy cream
1 cup semisweet chocolate pieces
Chocolate covered strawberries
Whipped cream

Blend together peanut butter, cream cheese, sugar, and butter; add vanilla. In a large bowl, beat heavy cream until peaks form. Add peanut butter mixture slowly and pour into springform pan. Refrigerate for 6 hours.

To serve, melt chocolate pieces in microwave and glaze over pie; top with chocolate covered strawberries and whipped cream.

A Laugh & A Glass of Wine

 Pasty Cline was born on September 8, 1932, in Winchester. She is best known for classic songs like "Walkin' After Midnight," "I Fall To Pieces," and "Crazy." She became one of the first country music singers to have major success on the pop charts. Since her death at the age of thirty in a 1963 plane crash during the height of her fame, she has been considered one of the most influential and successful female vocalists of the 20th century.

Second-Day Wedding Cake

In the late 18th century and the early part of the 19th century, the Second Day Wedding Cake was popular in Tennessee, Kentucky, and parts of Virginia. The wedding took place at the home of the bride with her nearest kin and closest friends present. A great feast was set out for the bride's dinner, and a dark wedding cake with fruits and nuts was served.

Another dinner was prepared at the groom's home on the second day of the marriage. The bride wore her second-day wedding dress, and guests who were more distant relatives and friends were invited. Each guest brought a thin layer of the cake, which was stacked as they arrived and spread with apple butter. The more guests, the higher the cake, thus the alternate name "Stack Cake." Real apple butter was made with sweet apples, no sugar or spices added. It was done when it was so thick it would not pour from a jar when turned upside down.

1 cup molasses
1 cup sugar
1 cup lard or solid vegetable
  shortening
1 tablespoon baking soda
1 tablespoon salt

1 tablespoon plus 1 teaspoon
  ginger
1 cup boiling water
7 cups all-purpose flour
Real apple butter

Preheat oven to 400°. Combine molasses, sugar, and lard or vegetable shortening in a large saucepan, and mix well. Bring to a boil. Remove from heat. Place baking soda, salt, and ginger in a measuring cup, fill with boiling water, and mix well. Stir into molasses mixture.

Add flour, stirring until dough is stiff enough to handle. Roll out dough thinly. Place a plate of desired size onto the dough, and cut into circles. The recipe will make enough dough for 7 layers. Place dough circles on baking sheets, and bake 12–15 minutes or until brown. Do not overcook. The layers will be very hard. Stack layers, spreading apple butter between each layer. The cake will improve if wrapped and stored in a cool place several days. Makes 16–20 servings.

Celebrate Virginia!

Strawberry Fluff Cake

1 angel food cake
1 cup milk
1 pint vanilla ice cream, softened
1 (3-ounce) package vanilla
  instant pudding
1 (3-ounce) package strawberry
  Jell-O
1½ cups hot water
1 pint strawberries
1 (8-ounce) carton Cool Whip

Line bottom of glass baking dish with cake, broken into bite-size pieces. Mix milk, ice cream, and instant pudding, and pour over cake. Let it set up in the refrigerator. Mix Jell-O, hot water, and strawberries; pour over cake. Let set up in refrigerator, then add Cool Whip on top.

Recipes from Home

Coffee Angel Food Cake

Here's my hands-down favorite dessert recipe. It's much too easy to be as good as it is.

1 tablespoon freeze-dried coffee
  (decaf, if desired)
1 (18¼-ounce) box Duncan Hines
  Angel Food Cake Mix

Dissolve coffee in water called for (per package directions) and make cake according to package directions. When cool, ice cake with Butter Icing.

BUTTER ICING:

2 tablespoons freeze-dried coffee
3–4 tablespoons milk
½ cup butter, softened
¼ teaspoon salt
2½ cups sifted confectioners'
  sugar
1 teaspoon vanilla
Slivered almonds, toasted

Dissolve coffee in milk. Cream butter with electric mixer. Add salt and sugar, a small amount at a time, beating all the while. Add milk mixture as needed. Add vanilla. Beat until light and fluffy. Just before serving, top cake with slivered, toasted almonds. The almonds are essential!

Food to Die For

Strawberry Cheesecake with Gingersnap Crust

GINGERSNAP CRUST:

3 cups crushed gingersnaps   **½ stick unsalted butter, melted**
¼ cup sugar

Process gingersnap crumbs, sugar, and butter in a food processor until well mixed. Press over bottom and halfway up side of a 9-inch spring-form pan with a 2½-inch side. Bake at 325° on center oven rack 10 minutes. Cool on wire rack.

FILLING:

3 (8-ounce) packages cream   **1 teaspoon vanilla extract**
 cheese, softened   **3 eggs**
¾ cup sugar   **2 cups fresh strawberry halves**

Beat cream cheese and sugar in mixing bowl until light and fluffy. Add vanilla and eggs, and beat just until blended. Spoon into prepared crust. Bake at 325° for 1 hour, or until side of cheesecake is slightly puffed and begins to crack, and center is almost set when gently shaken.

Cool on wire rack and chill, covered, 8 hours or longer. Place on a serving plate and remove side of pan. Arrange strawberries around outer edge. Cut into wedges to serve. Serves 10.

Oh My Stars! Recipes that Shine

Key Lime Cheesecake— Cheesecake Factory

CRUST:

1¾ cups graham cracker crumbs	5 tablespoons butter, melted
	1 tablespoon sugar

Combine crumbs, butter, and sugar in a bowl. Stir well to coat crumbs, keeping crumbly. Press crumbs onto bottom and half way up the side of an 8-inch springform pan. Bake 5 minutes and set aside.

3 (8-ounce) packages cream cheese, softened	½ cup fresh lime juice (about 5 limes)
1 cup sugar	3 eggs
1 teaspoon vanilla extract	Whipped cream

In a large bowl, combine cream cheese, sugar, and vanilla. Mix with electric mixer until smooth. Add lime juice and eggs, and continue to beat until smooth and creamy. Pour filling into Crust. Bake 60–70 minutes at 350° in a water bath. If top is turning light brown, it is done. Remove from oven and allow to cool at room temperature. With a knife, loosen edges around springform pan. Put in fridge. When chilled, remove pan sides and cut. Serve with whipped cream.

Delightfully Seasoned Recipes

During the 1930s, Earl Hamner, Jr. wrote about his youth in Nelson County during the Depression. His writings were the basis for the television series *The Waltons*. John-Boy's bedroom and Ike Godsey's store are re-created at Walton's Mountain Museum in Schuyler, home of Earl Hamner, Jr.

Pumpkin Cheesecake

3 (8-ounce) packages cream
  cheese, softened
½ cup sugar
1 (16-ounce) can pumpkin
3 eggs
1 teaspoon ground cinnamon
½ teaspoon ground ginger
¼ teaspoon nutmeg
1 teaspoon grated lemon peel
1 graham cracker crust, with ¼
  cup gingersnap crumbs
  sprinkled in bottom
Whipped topping for garnish
Lemon twists for garnish

Preheat oven to 300°. Beat cream cheese and sugar in bowl until fluffy. Beat in pumpkin and eggs. Mix in cinnamon, ginger, nutmeg, and lemon peel. Pour mixture into crust. Bake about 1¼ hours or until cheesecake is set in center. Cool to room temperature on wire rack. Refrigerate 3–4 hours. Garnish with whipped topping and lemon twists.

Celebrating Our Children Cookbook

Lemon Mousse Cake

1 yellow cake, baked in Bundt
  pan
1 envelope unflavored gelatin
¾ cup water
1 (14-ounce) can sweetened
  condensed milk
1 teaspoon grated lemon rind
½ cup lemon juice
2 cups stiffly whipped cream
Fresh blueberries for garnish
  (optional)

Line bottom and sides of an 8- or 9-inch springform pan with slices of baked cake. Trim edges neatly to fit pan, especially along the top; set aside. Sprinkle gelatin over water in a small saucepan. Let stand 1 minute. Cook over low heat, stirring constantly 1 minute or until dissolved. Set aside. Combine condensed milk, lemon rind, and lemon juice, stirring well. Add reserved gelatin mixture, stirring well. Fold in whipped cream. Pour mixture into prepared springform pan. Cover and refrigerate overnight or until set. Remove sides of springform pan when ready to serve. May garnish top with fresh blueberries, if desired.

My Table at Brightwood

18th Century Icing Recipe
from One of Martha Washington's Cookbooks

ORIGINAL RECIPE:

Take two Pound of double refin'd Sugar, beat and sift it very fine, and likewise beat and sift a little Starch and mix with it, then beat six Whites of Eggs to Froth, and put to it some Gum-Water, the Gum must be steep'd in Orange-flower-water, then mix and beat all these together two Hours, and put it on your Cake: when it is baked, set it in the Oven again to harden a quarter of a Hour, take great Care it is not discolour'd. When it is drawn, ice it over the Top and Sides, take two Pound of double refin'd Sugar beat and sifted, and the Whites of three Eggs beat to a Froth, with three or four Spoonfuls of Orange-flower-water, and three Grains of Musk and Amber-grease together; put all these in a Stone Mortar, and beat these till it is as white as Snow, and with a Brush or Bundle of Feathers, spread it all over the Cake, and put it in the Oven to dry; but take Care the Oven does not discolor it. When it is cold, paper it, and it will keep good five or six Weeks.

MODERN ADAPTATION:

3 egg whites
1–2 cups plus 2 tablespoons
   confectioners' sugar, divided

1 teaspoon grated lemon peel
2 tablespoons
   orange-flower water

Beat egg whites and 2 tablespoons confectioners' sugar in a large bowl 3 minutes. Add additional confectioners' sugar until 1–2 cups have been incorporated. Add lemon peel and orange-flower water. Beat until stiff enough to remain separated when cut through with a knife. Spread over top and sides of cake. Let it stand in a 200° oven 1 hour or until hardened. Makes approximately 2 cups.

Note: The icing will be brittle and shatter when the cake is sliced.

Celebrate Virginia!

Six presidents' wives were born in Virginia: Martha Washington, Martha Jefferson, Rachel Jackson, Letitia Tyler, Ellen Arthur, and Edith Wilson.

Nana's Jelly Roll

4 eggs
¾ cup sugar
¾ cup pancake mix
Confectioners' sugar

Jam, jelly, pudding, or whipped
**   topping**
Sliced fruits, such as bananas or
**   strawberries (optional)**

Preheat oven to 400°. Grease a 9x13-inch baking pan, and line with wax paper. Grease wax paper. (It is not necessary to line the baking pan if it is sufficiently greased.)

Place eggs in a blender. Add sugar and blend well. Blend in pancake mix. Pour batter into prepared pan. Bake 10 minutes in middle of oven. Invert cake onto a dishtowel sprinkled with confectioners' sugar. Remove wax paper, and roll cake in the dishtowel. Unroll cake when cool, and spread with jelly, pudding, or whipped topping. Add fruit to whipped topping, if desired. Roll up tightly. Refrigerate for at least 1 hour before slicing. Makes 10 servings.

Celebrate Virginia!

Glorified Gingerbread

2 cups all-purpose flour
1 cup sugar
½ teaspoon ginger
½ teaspoon cinnamon
½ cup shortening

1 egg, beaten
1 teaspoon baking soda
2 tablespoons molasses
½ teaspoon salt
1 cup sour milk

Sift flour and add sugar and spices. Rub shortening into dry ingredients to make fine crumbs. Take out ½ cup crumbs to sprinkle over top of mixture. To remaining crumbs, add egg, soda, molasses, salt, and sour milk. Beat well; pour into greased loaf pan and sprinkle with reserved crumbs. Bake at 350° for about 45 minutes.

For Men Who Like to Cook, Want to Cook (or HAVE to!)

Cookies and Candies

The Ralph Stanley Festival is a celebration of bluegrass music held annually at Hills of Home Park near Coeburn and McClure. Here a young banjo player shows off his prized banjo featuring a depiction of Virginia native, bluegrass legend, and Grand Ole Opry honoree Dr. Ralph Stanley.

3-C Cookies
(Chocolate, Cherries, and Coconut)

¾ cup butter, softened
1 cup packed brown sugar
1 egg
1 teaspoon vanilla
2¼ cups all-purpose flour
½ teaspoon salt

1 teaspoon baking powder
¾ cup chopped maraschino
   cherries
½ cup shredded, sweetened
   coconut
1 cup semisweet chocolate chips

Preheat oven to 350°. Cream butter and sugar together. Add egg and vanilla. Beat until fluffy. Blend in flour, salt, and baking powder. Add chopped cherries, coconut, and chocolate chips. Blend just until mixed. Drop onto ungreased cookie sheets and bake 9–11 minutes, depending on size of cookie and type of cookie sheet used. Remove to wire rack and cool.

Tried and True Recipes

Chinese Chews

¾ cup all-purpose flour
1 cup sugar
1 (8-ounce) box chopped dates

2 cups chopped pecans
2 eggs
Confectioners' sugar

Mix flour, sugar, dates, and nuts together. Add well-beaten eggs to mixture and mix well. Pat out in pan about 12 x 14 inches. Bake at 375° about 30 minutes or until golden brown. Cool. Cut into squares and coat with confectioners' sugar.

Gather 'Round Our Table

Booker T. Washington, born into slavery in 1856 in Hales Ford, was the first African-American depicted on a U.S. coin (a half-dollar minted from 1946–1951) and a U.S. postage stamp (issued in 1940).

Carmelitas

32 caramels, unwrapped
5 tablespoons cream
1 cup all-purpose flour
1 cup quick oatmeal
¾ cup packed brown sugar
½ teaspoon baking soda

¼ teaspoon salt
¾ cup butter, melted
1 (8-ounce) package semisweet
  chocolate chips
½ cup chopped pecans

Preheat oven to 350°. Melt caramels and cream in double boiler. Set aside. Combine flour, oatmeal, sugar, soda, salt, and butter. Press half of crumbs into a 9x13-inch pan. Bake at 350° for 10 minutes.

Spread caramel mixture over crust, then chips and pecans. Sprinkle with remaining crumb mixture. Bake another 15–20 minutes. Chill one hour. Cut into bars. Makes 24.

Tidewater on the Half Shell

Great Grandma Rogge's Washington Cookies

1½ cups all-purpose flour
1 teaspoon baking soda
1 teaspoon salt
2 sticks butter, softened
1 cup brown sugar
½ cup sugar
2 eggs, beaten

1 teaspoon vanilla
2 cups old-fashioned oatmeal
1 (6-ounce or 12-ounce) package
  Ghirardelli's semisweet
  chocolate chips
1 cup chopped walnuts (optional)

In large bowl, sift together flour, baking soda, and salt; set aside. In another bowl, cream together butter and sugars until fluffy. Add eggs and vanilla. Add sifted flour to mixture ⅓ at a time while stirring. Add oatmeal, chocolate chips, and nuts to mixture; stir well. Drop by spoonful onto ungreased cookie sheet at a dozen per sheet. Bake at 375° for 10 minutes.

The Hall Family Cookbook

Mookies

1 (1-pound, 15-ounce) bag Betty
   Crocker sugar cookie mix
1 stick butter or margarine,
   softened

1 egg
1 (16-ounce) can vanilla icing
Candy sprinkles

Prepare cookie dough as directed using butter and egg. Drop into greased mini-muffin pan. Bake at 375° for 9–11 minutes. Remove cookies from oven, and using a mini-tart press, press the mookies in (forming a muffin shaped cup). Cool and spoon icing into cups. Sprinkle top with candy sprinkles.

Note: May use any flavor cookie mix and icing you choose.

All American Recipes

Sweet Briar Cookies

1 large egg white, room
   temperature
1 cup dark brown sugar
⅛ teaspoon baking soda

⅛ teaspoon salt
2 teaspoons vanilla
2 cups pecan pieces

With an electric mixer, beat egg whites and sugar together. When light, add baking soda and salt. Stir in vanilla and pecan pieces. Drop onto greased cookie sheets and bake 15–20 minutes at 325°. Cool slightly before removing. Makes 28 cookies.

Food to Die For

More major Civil War battles were fought in Virginia from 1861 through 1865 than in any other state. Today, one-third of the nation's most important Civil War battlefields are in Virginia, and most are open to the public.

Baklava

1½ pounds walnuts, ground
1 pound almonds, ground
1 teaspoon cinnamon

½ teaspoon ground cloves
1 pound sweet butter, melted
1 pound filo pastry sheets

Mix together walnuts, almonds, and spices. Butter a 11x16½-inch baking pan and fit several pastry sheets on bottom, brushing each well with butter. Sprinkle with nut mixture. Continue this procedure until all ingredients are used, ending with 8–10 pastry sheets on top. With sharp knife, mark in diamond shapes; do not cut all the way through. Bake at 325° for 1½ hours. Makes 40 pieces.

SYRUP:
1 small jar honey
3 cups water
2 cups sugar

1 cinnamon stick
½ lemon

Bring to a boil and simmer 20–25 minutes. If using a candy thermometer, simmer until it reaches 225°. Strain, cool, and pour over hot baklava.

Come Cook with Us

Lace Cookies

1 cup oatmeal
2 tablespoons plus 1 teaspoon
   flour
¼ teaspoon baking powder
1 cup sugar

1 teaspoon salt
¼ cup margarine or butter,
   melted
1 egg, beaten well
2 teaspoons vanilla

Mix all dry ingredients. Pour warm butter, egg, and vanilla over dry ingredients. Mix and put in refrigerator to cool. Drop onto foil-lined baking sheets ¼–½ teaspoon at a time (they spread a lot, so drop small amounts). Bake at 325° for 8–10 minutes. Cool, then pull off foil. They are very thin and crisp.

Recipe submitted by Mrs. R. Turner Jones, Highland
Country Treasures

Oatmeal Cookies

Delicious!

2 eggs
1 cup brown sugar
1 cup white sugar
1 teaspoon vanilla
1 cup shortening, melted

2 cups all-purpose flour, sifted
1 teaspoon baking soda
½ teaspoon baking powder
½ teaspoon salt
2 cups oatmeal

Mix eggs, sugars, vanilla, and shortening. Add sifted flour and other ingredients, adding oatmeal last. Mix well and drop by spoonfuls on ungreased cookie sheet. Bake at 375° for 7–10 minutes. Match up cookies by size and use confectioners' sugar icing between them to make oatmeal cakes.

Cookin' for the Cure

 Virginia actually extends 95 miles farther west than West Virginia.

Sandies

1 cup butter, softened
1¼ cups confectioners' sugar, divided
2 teaspoons vanilla

1 tablespoon water
2 cups sifted all-purpose flour
1 cup chopped pecans

Preheat oven to 300°. Cream butter and ¼ cup confectioners' sugar together. Add vanilla and water. Add flour. Mix well and add chopped pecans. Form small balls, and place on ungreased cookie sheet. Bake at 300° for 20–25 minutes or until slightly brown. While still warm, roll in remaining confectioners' sugar. Makes 3 dozen.

Cooking with Grace

Karamu Cookies

½ cup butter, softened
½ cup peanut butter
½ cup firmly packed brown sugar
1 teaspoon vanilla

1 egg
1½ cups all-purpose flour
½ teaspoon baking soda
½ teaspoon salt

Blend butter and peanut butter together. Add sugar and vanilla; beat until smooth. Blend in egg. Sift flour, baking soda, and salt together. Add dry ingredients to peanut butter mixture and mix well. Divide dough into 2 portions. Shape each into a log. Cut in ¼-inch slices and place on greased baking sheet. Bake at 400° for 8–10 minutes. Cool cookies on wire rack.

FROSTING:

2 cups powdered sugar
3 tablespoons whipping cream, unwhipped

1 teaspoon vanilla
Food coloring

Combine all ingredients, except food coloring. Beat until smooth. Tint portions of frosting with food coloring. Decorate cookies with African designs. Makes 48.

Children's Party Book

Nannie White's Potato Chip Crunch Cookies

Delicious and crunchy. A dainty party cookie.

1 cup butter or margarine, softened	**1½ cups crushed potato chips**
½ cup sugar	**½ cup chopped pecans**
1 teaspoon vanilla	**2 cups sifted all-purpose flour**

Cream together butter or margarine, sugar, and vanilla. Add crushed potato chips and chopped pecans. Sift in flour. Form into small balls, using about 1 teaspoon dough for each. Place on ungreased cookie sheet. Press balls flat with bottom of a tumbler dipped in sugar. Bake at 350° for 16–18 minutes, or until cookies are lightly browned. If desired, sprinkle with colored sugar crystals and top each cookie with pecan half or candied cherry half. Makes 3½ dozen cookies.

Granny's Kitchen

Peggy's Special Chess Bars

Everyone will love these. All my friends do!

1 (18¼-ounce) box chocolate cake mix	**1 (8-ounce) package cream cheese, softened**
1 stick butter, softened	**1 (1-pound) box powdered sugar**
4 eggs, divided	**1 tablespoon vanilla**

Mix cake mix, butter, and 1 egg in large mixing bowl. Press into bottom of 10x15-inch baking pan.

In mixing bowl, combine cream cheese, remaining 3 eggs, powdered sugar, and vanilla, and mix with electric mixer 2 minutes until creamy. Pour over cake batter mixture. Bake in preheated 325° for 30–40 minutes or until golden brown on top. Place on wire rack and completely cool before cutting into squares.

Country Home Favorites

Peanut Butter Crunch Bars

1 stick butter
1 (16-ounce) jar peanut butter
3¾ cups powdered sugar
3 cups crispy cereal or
 cornflakes

1 (16-ounce) package semisweet
 chocolate chips

Melt butter over low heat in a saucepan. In mixing bowl, blend peanut butter and sugar. Add melted butter and continue to blend. Stir in cereal. Pile mixture into a lightly greased 9x13-inch pan and spread evenly over bottom of pan.

In a separate saucepan, melt chocolate chips over low heat. Spread melted chocolate evenly over cereal layer. Refrigerate to cool. Cut into bars. Makes approximately 30 bars.

Delightfully Seasoned Recipes

Care Package Almond Bars

1 (18¼-ounce) yellow cake mix
1 stick butter or margarine,
 melted
3 large eggs, divided
1 teaspoon vanilla extract

1 (8-ounce) package cream cheese,
 softened
1 (16-ounce) box confectioners'
 sugar
4 ounces sliced almonds

Preheat oven to 350°. In a large bowl, combine cake mix, butter, and 1 egg. Beat to a dough-like consistency. Spread on bottom of greased 9x13x2-inch baking pan. In a bowl, combine remaining 2 eggs, vanilla, cream cheese, and confectioners' sugar. Beat 3 minutes and spread over cake mixture. Bake 15 minutes, top with almonds, and bake an additional 30 minutes or until firm. Cut into bars while still warm. Yields 36–40 bite-size bars.

Very Virginia

Fresh Apple Blondies

Fresh apples add a special touch to these treats! Serve them with vanilla ice cream and Butterscotch Sauce.

2½ cups all-purpose flour
2 teaspoons baking powder
1 teaspoon baking soda
1 teaspoon cinnamon
1 teaspoon salt
2 cups sugar
1 cup vegetable oil

2 eggs
2 teaspoons vanilla extract
3 cups chopped apples
1 cup chopped nuts (optional)
1 (12-ounce) package (2 cups)
   butterscotch chips

Sift flour, baking powder, baking soda, cinnamon, and salt together. Combine sugar and oil in mixing bowl and beat until smooth. Add eggs and beat until thickened. Add dry ingredients and vanilla and mix well. Fold in apples and nuts, if desired.

Spoon into a 9x13-inch baking pan sprayed with nonstick cooking spray. Sprinkle with butterscotch chips and press chips down lightly with a spatula. Bake at 350° for 50–60 minutes or until a wooden pick inserted into center comes out clean. Cool on a wire rack, and cut into squares. Serve with Butterscotch Sauce. Serves 15.

BUTTERSCOTCH SAUCE:
2 cups packed brown sugar
⅔ cup light corn syrup
¼ cup butter

½ cup light cream
1 teaspoon vanilla

Combine brown sugar, corn syrup, and butter in saucepan and bring to a boil. Boil 5 minutes, then stir in cream and vanilla. Cool to room temperature and store in refrigerator. Also good served over ice cream or cake.

Oh My Stars! Recipes that Shine

Crème de Menthe Brownies

1 cup sugar
1½ cups butter, softened,
   divided
1 teaspoon salt
1 teaspoon vanilla
4 eggs, beaten

1 cup all-purpose flour
2 cups chocolate syrup
2 cups powdered sugar
2 tablespoons crème de menthe
6 ounces chocolate chips
6 tablespoons butter

Cream together sugar and ½ cup butter. Mix in salt, vanilla, eggs, flour, and syrup. Pour into a 9x13-inch pan greased on the bottom only. Bake at 350° for 30–35 minutes; let cool.

Cream together powdered sugar, remaining 1 cup softened butter, and crème de menthe; spread over top of cooled brownies. Melt chocolate chips and 6 tablespoons butter over low heat and spread over crème de menthe mixture while still warm. Refrigerate 1–2 hours or until toppings are set.

First Family Favorites

Brownie Pizza

1 (21-ounce) box brownie mix
1 (8-ounce) package cream
   cheese, softened

½ cup powdered sugar
1 pint strawberries, stemmed,
   sliced

Make brownie mix according to box instructions. Spread mix onto greased pizza pan. Mix cream cheese and powdered sugar until smooth and spread on top of brownie. Bake 10 minutes at 350°. Top with strawberry slices.

The Westwood Clubhouse Cookbook

The state's capitol building in Richmond houses the only statue for which George Washington ever posed.

Black Forest Truffles

3 cups semisweet chocolate
  chips
1 (14-ounce) can sweetened
  condensed milk

½ cup chopped dried bing
  cherries
2 teaspoons almond extract
Cocoa powder

Melt chocolate chips with sweetened condensed milk in a medium saucepan over medium heat. Remove from heat and add cherries and extract. Chill in refrigerator 2 hours or until firm.

Once firm, shape into 1-inch balls and coat with cocoa. Place truffles in 50 mini-muffin tin liners, foil or holiday printed, and chill in refrigerator 1 hour. Allow truffles to sit at room temperature 30 minutes before serving. Makes approximately 50 truffles. Store tightly covered in refrigerator.

A Taste of Prince William County Cookbook

Turtles

60 Kraft caramels, unwrapped
1 stick margarine
⅓ cup evaporated milk

3 cups chopped pecans
1 pound chocolate bark

Melt caramels in margarine and milk in double boiler. Remove from heat and add pecans. Mix well. Drop by teaspoonfuls onto greased cookie sheets. Freeze.

Place chocolate bark in a deep pyrex dish and microwave for 2½ minutes; stir well. If not melted enough, heat again for 30 second at a time until melted.

When caramel mixture is frozen, dip each one in melted, but cooled, chocolate. Lay on wax paper until chocolate is set. Makes about 60 pieces.

Note: When removing these from freezer, take out a few at a time—you want the turtles to stay frozen until dipped.

Just Like Mama's

Tidewater Toffee

2 cups sugar
1 pound butter (do not substitute
  margarine)

1½ cups chopped pecans,
  toasted

Melt sugar and butter in a saucepan over medium heat. Bring to a boil, stirring often; bring temperature of mixture to hard-crack stage of 300°–310° (you must use a candy thermometer). Watch carefully and do not burn.

Stir chopped and toasted pecans into butter and sugar mixture; mix well. Pour quickly onto a lightly greased 10x15x1-inch baking pan. Cool to the touch; score top. Cool completely and crack into pieces. Serves 12.

Toast to Tidewater

English Toffee

2 cups slivered almonds,
  divided
1 cup butter
1½ cups sugar

3 tablespoons light corn syrup
3 tablespoons water
1 (12-ounce) package semisweet
  chocolate chips

Line a 12x18-inch baking pan with foil and spray with cooking spray. Sprinkle about 1 cup of the almonds over the pan and set aside. In a medium saucepan, melt butter. Remove from heat, and stir in sugar, corn syrup, and water. Cook, stirring occasionally, until mixture reaches 300° on candy thermometer. Remove from heat and pour out into prepared pan, spreading mixture with back of a spoon to fill the pan. Evenly distribute chocolate on toffee mixture and when melted, spread with off-set spatula. Sprinkle melted chocolate with remaining almonds. Refrigerate 20 minutes to set chocolate. Break candy into 2-inch pieces. Candy may be stored in an airtight container at cool room temperature for up to 1 week; use parchment paper to separate layers.

A Taste of Prince William County Cookbook

Date Loaf Candy

½ cup sweet milk
2 cups sugar
¼ cup butter

1 cup dates, chopped
1 teaspoon vanilla
1 cup broken pecans

In saucepan, boil milk, sugar, and butter to 240°, or until mixture forms soft ball in cold water. Remove from heat and add dates and vanilla. Heat until dates melt. Add pecans and beat until cool. Pour onto wet cheesecloth and form a ball or log. Let cool and unroll from cheese-cloth. Slice candy roll or log every ½ inch or so.

First Family Favorites

Peanut Butter Candy

2 cups sugar
¾ cup milk
2 teaspoons butter

3 tablespoons peanut butter
1 teaspoon vanilla
Chocolate chips (optional)

In saucepan, cook sugar and milk to soft-ball stage. Stir in butter, peanut butter, and vanilla, beating until creamy. Chocolate chips may be added if you prefer a chocolate candy. Pour into buttered dish and let set until firm, then cut into squares.

The Riggs Family Cookbook

The creator of "Mr. Peanut," invented in 1916, was a 13-year-old boy named Antonio Gentile of Suffolk, who won $5 in a design contest that was sponsored by Planters peanuts.

Microwave Pecan Brittle

1 cup granulated sugar
½ cup white corn syrup
1 cup pecan pieces

1 teaspoon butter
1 teaspoon vanilla
1 teaspoon baking soda

In a 1½-quart casserole, stir together sugar and syrup. Cook in microwave on HIGH setting 4 minutes. Stir in pecan pieces. Microwave on HIGH 3–5 minutes, until light brown. Add butter and vanilla to syrup, blending well. Microwave on HIGH 1–2 minutes more. Pecans will be lightly browned and syrup very hot. Add soda, and gently stir until light and foamy. Pour mixture onto lightly greased cookie sheet or unbuttered nonstick cookie sheet. Let cool ½–1 hour. When cool, break in small pieces, and store in airtight container.

Note: Cooking times may vary with the wattage of your microwave.

Food, Family, and Friendships

Old-Fashioned Peanut Butter Fudge

3 cups sugar
1½ cups milk
Pinch of salt

1 teaspoon vanilla
1 stick butter, softened, divided
2 cups peanut butter

In a medium saucepan, mix sugar, milk, and salt, and cook to soft-ball stage. Remove from heat and add vanilla, ¾ stick butter, and peanut butter. Beat well. Use remaining butter to grease bottom of a square baking pan. Pour candy mixture into pan. Let cool, then cut into squares.

Virginia Cook Book

Microwave Fudge

3 cups semisweet or milk chocolate chips
¼ cup margarine

1 (14-ounce) can condensed milk
½ cup chopped nuts

Place all ingredients, except nuts, in a large bowl. Best to layer with chips, margarine, sliced, then milk. Microwave on HIGH or MEDI-UM-HIGH approximately 5 minutes, or until chips are melted. Stir once or twice during cooking. Stir in nuts and pour into greased square baking dish. Refrigerate until set (3–4 hours); slice into squares.

Note: May use 2 cups milk chocolate chips and 1 cup semisweet chips.

Kids in the Kitchen

Pies and Other Desserts

PHOTO © FRANKEE LOVE, WWW.BEACHWEDDINGSVIRGINIA.COM

Virginia beaches offer the sound of the surf, warm, salty breezes, spectacular sunrises, a view that goes on forever . . . and beach weddings! A perfect example that truly "Virginia is for lovers."

Bird's Nest Apple Pie, 1890s

6 cups sliced apples	1 cup sour milk
2 cups all-purpose flour	2 egg whites
1 cup sugar	¼ cup sugar
1 teaspoon baking soda	½ teaspoon ground cinnamon
½ teaspoon cream of tartar	¼ teaspoon ground nutmeg

Divide apples between 2 greased 9-inch pie plates. Set aside. In a bowl, combine flour, sugar, soda, cream of tartar, sour milk, and egg whites. Mix well. Divide batter and pour over apples. Bake at 350° for 30 minutes or until lightly browned. Invert onto serving plate.

Combine sugar, cinnamon, and nutmeg. Sprinkle over apples. Let stand 5 minutes.

Celebrating Our Children Cookbook

Applets

1½ cups all-purpose flour	1 egg
2 teaspoons baking powder	⅓ cup milk
½ teaspoon salt	1½ cups finely chopped or
½ teaspoon nutmeg	shredded Granny Smith apples
⅓ cup Crisco	¼ cup butter, melted (more if
½ cup sugar	needed)

Sift together flour, baking powder, salt, and nutmeg. Cream Crisco and sugar; add egg. Mix in milk alternating with flour mixture. Stir in apples. Bake in greased mini-tart or muffin pan at 400° for 20–25 minutes. Let cool. Dip each tart in melted butter. Do not store in airtight container, because the applets will get "soggy" after a day or two.

Taste & See

Sweet Potato Pie

3 medium sweet potatoes
½ stick margarine
1¼ cups sugar
½ teaspoon salt
4 eggs, beaten

2 cups milk
1 teaspoon vanilla extract
1 teaspoon lemon extract
1 (9-inch) deep-dish pie crust

Boil potatoes until soft; peel and mash while warm. Add margarine to hot potatoes. Add sugar and salt. Add beaten eggs, milk, vanilla, and lemon extracts (mixture will be thin). Mix well. Pour into unbaked pie shell. Bake at 350° for 1 hour.

Garden Gate Recipes

Blueberry Cream Pie

¾ cup sugar
½ teaspoon salt
¼ cup cornstarch
2½ cups milk
3 egg yolks
1 tablespoon butter
1 teaspoon vanilla

1 envelope unflavored gelatin
2 cups fresh blueberries (do nut
   substitute canned or frozen)
1 (9-inch) pastry shell, baked
1 cup whipping cream
¼ cup sifted confectioners'
   sugar

Combine sugar, salt, and cornstarch in a heavy saucepan. Gradually add milk, stirring until blended. Cook over medium heat, stirring constantly, until mixture thickens and comes to a boil. Boil 1 minute, stirring constantly. Remove from heat. Beat egg yolks. Gradually stir about ¼ of hot mixture into yolks. Add to remaining hot mixture, stirring constantly. Cook over medium heat 2 minutes. Remove from heat. Add butter and vanilla, and sprinkle gelatin evenly over top. Stir in until evenly distributed throughout. Gently stir in blueberries. Pour into pastry shell. Cool pie. Beat whipping cream until foamy. Gradually add powdered sugar. Spread over cooled pie. Chill well before serving. Refrigerate leftovers.

My Table at Brightwood

Deep~Dish Pear Pie

FILLING:

2 pounds pears
1 tablespoon lemon juice
3 tablespoons flour
1 cup sugar
Dash of salt

½ teaspoon cinnamon
½ teaspoon nutmeg
1 tablespoon butter or
   margarine

Peel pears; cut in halves and core. Arrange in a 1½-quart baking dish. Sprinkle with lemon juice. Mix flour, sugar, salt, cinnamon, and nutmeg together; sprinkle over pears. Dot with butter.

PIE CRUST:

1 cup all-purpose flour
½ teaspoon salt
⅓ cup shortening

¼ cup grated Cheddar cheese
2–3 tablespoons water

Sift flour and salt together; cut in shortening until mixture resembles coarse cornmeal. Mix in cheese; stir in 1 tablespoon water at a time until pastry holds together. Chill. Roll pastry in a circle a little larger than top of baking dish. Slash in several places and arrange over pears, crimping pastry to edges of dish securely. Bake 30–40 minutes in a 350° oven. Serve with whipped cream, if desired. Yields 6 servings.

Taste of the Town II

Ten~Minute Chocolate Chess Pie

½ stick butter or margarine
3½ tablespoons cocoa
1½ cups sugar
Pinch of salt

1 (6-ounce) can evaporated milk
2 eggs, beaten
1 teaspoon vanilla
1 (9-inch) pie shell, unbaked

Preheat oven to 350°. Melt butter in small saucepan and cool. Combine in mixing bowl the cooled butter and remaining ingredients. Pour into unbaked pie shell. Bake 45 minutes.

The Ham Book

Mud Pie

1½ cups crumbled chocolate
   wafer cookies
3 tablespoons butter, melted
½ gallon coffee ice cream,
   softened

1 (16-ounce) can fudge topping
Cool Whip or whipped cream
Chocolate sprinkles

Make a crust of crumbs and butter in deep-dish pie pan. Freeze. Spread softened ice cream over crust. Freeze. Top with Cool Whip or whipped cream. Freeze. Sprinkle with chocolate sprinkles at time of serving.

Thought for Food

Chocolate Silk Pie

Wonderful!

1 stick butter or margarine,
   softened
¾ cup sugar
2 ounces baking chocolate,
   melted

1 tablespoon vanilla
2 eggs (Eggland's Best)
1 (9-inch) pie shell, baked
Whipped cream, Cool Whip,
   or ice cream

Cream butter, sugar, and melted chocolate. Add vanilla and 1 egg. Beat with mixer 5 minutes. Add other egg and beat 5 additional minutes. Pour into baked pie shell. Top with whipped cream, Cool Whip, or ice cream.

Our Best to You!

White Chocolate Pecan Mousse Pie

1 (15-ounce) package refrigerated
  pie crusts, divided
1 teaspoon flour
2 tablespoons butter
2 cups chopped pecans
1 cup vanilla milk chips or white
  chocolate baking bar, chopped
¼ cup milk
2 cups whipping cream
⅓ cup sugar
1 teaspoon vanilla extract
Grated chocolate or
  chocolate-flavored syrup
  (optional)

Preheat oven to 450°. Prepare 1 pie crust according to package directions for unfilled crust. Refrigerate remaining crust for later use. Place prepared crust in a 10-inch springform pan or 9-inch pie pan; press in bottom and up sides of pan. Flute top edge of crust with fork dipped in flour. Generously prick bottom and sides of crust with fork dipped in flour. Bake in preheated oven until golden brown, 9–11 minutes. Cool completely.

In a 10-inch skillet over medium heat, melt butter. Stir in pecans; cook, stirring constantly, until pecans are golden brown, about 6 minutes. Cool completely, about 1 hour. In a small saucepan over low heat, stirring with a wire whisk, melt vanilla chips and milk. Cool completely, about 1 hour.

In a large bowl, beat whipping cream until stiff peaks form. Fold in sugar, vanilla, melted vanilla chips mixture, and pecans; blend well. Spoon mixture into cooled crust. Refrigerate 4 hours before serving. Just before serving, garnish with grated chocolate or chocolate syrup, if desired.

Virginia Traditions

Explorer William Clark was born on August 1, 1770, in Caroline County. He and Meriwether Lewis led the Lewis & Clark expedition from 1804–1806.

I Would Kill for a Piece of Virginia Pie

1 (8-ounce) package cream
  cheese, softened
1 (14-ounce) can condensed
  milk
1 (16-ounce) carton frozen Cool
  Whip, thawed
1 stick margarine
½ cup flaked coconut
½ cup chopped pecans
½ cup caramel ice cream
  topping
2 pie crusts, baked

Combine cream cheese and condensed milk; fold in Cool Whip. Set aside. In frying pan, lightly brown margarine, coconut, and pecans. Let cool slightly. Divide cream cheese mixture into 4 parts. Divide caramel topping into 4 parts. Divide coconut-pecan mixture into 4 parts. Into each cooled pie crust, make a layer of cream cheese mixture, drizzle a layer of caramel topping over this layer; sprinkle a layer of coconut-pecan mixture over this. Repeat to make another layer of each in each crust. Chill until time to serve.

Pungo Strawberry Festival Cookbook

Coconut Pie

3 eggs
1 cup sugar
1 cup evaporated milk
½ stick butter
1 teaspoon vanilla
1 cup flaked coconut
1 unbaked pie shell

Mix eggs, sugar, and milk. Melt butter and pour into egg mixture with remaining ingredients. Mix and pour into unbaked pie shell. Bake at 350° for 45 minutes.

Country Cookbook

White Christmas Pie

1 tablespoon plain gelatin
¼ cup cold water
1 cup sugar, divided
4 tablespoons all-purpose flour
½ teaspoon salt
1½ cups milk
¾ teaspoon vanilla
¼ teaspoon almond flavoring

½ cup whipping cream,
   whipped
3 egg whites
¼ teaspoon cream of tartar
1 cup shredded coconut, plus extra
   for sprinkling
1 (9-inch) pie shell, baked

Soften gelatin in cold water. Mix together in a saucepan ½ cup sugar, flour, and salt. Gradually stir in milk. Cook over low heat, stirring constantly until it boils. Let boil 1 minute. Remove from heat and stir in softened gelatin. Cool. When partially set, beat with beater until smooth. Blend in vanilla and almond flavorings. Gently fold in stiffly whipped cream.

Beat egg whites and cream of tartar to make meringue. Gradually add remaining ½ cup sugar, and beat until peaks stand up. Carefully fold gelatin-cream mixture into meringue. Then fold in 1 cup shredded coconut. Pour into pie shell and sprinkle with coconut. Chill until set, at least 2 hours. Serve cold.

Gather 'Round Our Table

Butterscotch Meringue Pie

1 cup brown sugar
4 tablespoons cornstarch, or 8
   tablespoons flour
¼ teaspoon salt
2½ cups milk

3 eggs, separated
6 tablespoons butter
1 teaspoon vanilla
1 (9-inch) pie shell, baked

Combine brown sugar, cornstarch, and salt in a heavy saucepan. Stir in milk. Cook over medium heat, stirring constantly until thick. Remove from heat and stir a little hot mixture into beaten egg yolks (reserve whites for Meringue). Pour back into saucepan and boil 1 minute longer. Remove from heat; stir in butter and vanilla. Pour into baked pie shell.

MERINGUE:

3 egg whites (from above)
¼ teaspoon cream of tartar

6 tablespoons sugar

Beat egg whites with cream of tartar until soft peaks form. Gradually beat in sugar; continue to beat until stiff peaks form. Spread Meringue over filling, sealing to edge of crust. Bake at 350° until Meringue is golden brown, about 12–15 minutes. Cool away from drafts.

Granny's Kitchen

Peach Cobbler

15 medium peaches, sliced	2 cups sugar
1 tablespoon lemon juice	2 teaspoons ground ginger
⅓ cup all-purpose flour	1 teaspoon salt

Combine ingredients, mix well, and set aside.

PASTRY:

3 cups sifted all-purpose flour	½ cup water
2 teaspoons salt	3 tablespoons butter
1 cup shortening	

Combine flour and salt. Cut in shortening. Sprinkle with water. Press dough into a ball. Roll out ⅓ of the dough and cut into thin strips. Roll out remaining dough for top crust.

Pour ½ the peach filling into a buttered 9x13-inch baking dish. Cover with pastry strips. Add remaining filling. Dot with butter, and cover with top crust. Slit center of top crust several times. Bake in 350° oven 1 hour. Makes 12 servings.

Food, Family, and Friendships

Prize Peach Cobbler

¾ cup all-purpose flour	2 tablespoons margarine
⅛ teaspoon salt	2 cups fresh, sliced peaches
2 teaspoons baking powder	1 teaspoon cinnamon
¾ cup sugar	Sugar to taste
¾ cup milk	

Sift flour, salt, and baking powder; mix with ¾ cup sugar. Slowly stir in milk to make a batter. Melt margarine in 8x8x2-inch pan. Pour batter over melted margarine. Do not stir. Taste peaches and add cinnamon and sugar to your taste; mix well. Carefully spoon peaches over batter. Bake one hour at 325°. Great served warm with ice cream.

A Taste of Heaven

Old-Fashioned Apple Dumplings

PASTRY:

2 cups all-purpose flour
2½ teaspoons baking powder
½ teaspoon salt

⅔ cup shortening
½ cup milk

Sift flour, baking powder, and salt together. Cut in shortening until particles are about the size of small peas. Sprinkle milk over mixture and press together lightly, only enough to make dough stick together. Roll dough as for pastry and cut into 6 squares. Set aside.

APPLES:

6 medium apples, whole, pared, cored

4 teaspoons cinnamon
¼ cup sugar

Place an apple on each of the pastry squares. Mix cinnamon and sugar; fill each apple cavity with mixture. Pat dough around apples and pinch together at top. Place dumplings 1 inch apart in greased baking dish.

SYRUP:

2 cups brown sugar
2 cups water

¼ cup butter
¼ teaspoon cinnamon or nutmeg

Mix all ingredients together in saucepan and simmer 5 minutes. Pour over dumplings. Bake at 375° for 35–40 minutes, basting occasionally.

Vesuvius, Virginia: Then and Now

Built in 1735, Blandford Church in Petersburg has one of the world's largest collections of Tiffany windows. In 1901, fifteen windows were designed and executed by Louis Comfort Tiffany and placed in the church as a memorial to Confederate soldiers.

Sallie's Chocolate Tarts

2 eggs
1 stick margarine, melted
1 cup sugar
1 cup packed light brown sugar
3 tablespoons flour
3 tablespoons baking cocoa

⅓ cup milk
1 teaspoon vanilla extract
12–14 unbaked tart shells
Sweetened whipped cream for
   garnish

Beat eggs lightly in a large bowl. Add margarine, sugar, brown sugar, flour, and baking cocoa; mix well. Add milk and vanilla and mix until well blended.

Arrange tart shells on a baking sheet. Divide chocolate mixture evenly among tart shells. Bake at 350° for 25 minutes or until filling is set. Cool tarts on wire racks. Garnish with sweetened whipped cream. Serves 12–14.

In Good Company

Chocolate Delight

1 cup all-purpose flour
1 stick margarine, softened
½ cup chopped nuts
1 cup confectioners' sugar
1 (8-ounce) package cream
   cheese, softened

1 (16-ounce) carton Cool Whip,
   divided
3 cups cold milk
2 (3-ounce) packages chocolate
   instant pudding

Mix together flour, margarine, and nuts like pie dough. Press into 9x13-inch baking pan. Bake at 375° for 15 minutes. Mix together confectioners' sugar, cream cheese, and ½ the Cool Whip. Spread over crust layer. Mix cold milk and pudding mixes together. Spread over cream cheese layer. Top with remaining Cool Whip. Store in refrigerator for several hours or overnight.

Favorite Recipes: Bayside Baptist Church

Cherry Holiday Dessert

1½ cups boiling water
1 (6-ounce) package or 2 (3-ounce) packages sugar-free cherry Jell-O
1½ cups cold water
1 (21-ounce) can sugar-free cherry pie filling
4 cups cubed sugar-free angel food cake
3 cups cold milk
2 (3-ounce) packages sugar-free vanilla pudding
1 (8-ounce) carton whipped topping, divided

Stir boiling water into gelatin in large bowl at least 2 minutes until completely dissolved. Stir in cold water and sugar-free cherry pie filling. Refrigerate 1 hour or until slightly thickened and consistency of unbeaten egg whites.

Place cake cubes in 3-quart serving bowl. Spoon gelatin mixture over cake. Refrigerate about 45 minutes or until set but not firm (gelatin should stick to finger when touched and should mound). Pour milk into large bowl. Add pudding mixes. Beat with wire whisk 1 minute. Gently stir in 2 cups whipped topping. Spoon over gelatin mixture in bowl. Refrigerate 2 hours or until set. Top with remaining whipped topping and garnish as desired.

Editor's Extra: Can also be layered in a glass trifle dish for a beautiful presentation.

Favorite Recipes: Bayside Baptist Church

Not Your Ordinary Banana Pudding

2 (7¼-ounce) bags Pepperidge
  Farm Chessmen cookies,
  divided
6–8 bananas, sliced
2 cups milk
1 (5-ounce) box French vanilla
  instant pudding

1 (8-ounce) package cream cheese,
  softened
1 (14-ounce) can sweetened
  condensed milk
1 (12-ounce) container frozen
  whipped topping, thawed

Line bottom of a 9x13-inch dish with 1 bag of cookies and layer bananas on top. In a bowl, combine milk and pudding mix and blend well using a mixer. In another bowl, combine cream cheese and condensed milk and mix until smooth. Fold whipped topping into cream cheese mixture. Add cream cheese mixture to pudding mixture and stir until well blended. Pour mixture over cookies and bananas. Top pudding mixture with remaining bag of cookies. Refrigerate at least 2 hours before serving.

G.W. Carver Family Recipes

Surprise Dump Pudding

1 (29-ounce) can sliced peaches
1 (20-ounce) can crushed
  pineapple
1 (18¼-ounce) package Duncan
  Hines Deluxe Yellow Cake Mix

2 cups flaked coconut
1 cup chopped pecans
1 stick margarine, melted

Dump undrained peaches in 9x13-inch pan and chop. Dump in undrained crushed pineapple. Dump in cake mix and stir up. Sprinkle top with coconut and pecans. Drizzle melted margarine over top of all. Bake at 350° for 45 minutes to 1 hour. Yummy!

Not By Bread Alone Cookbook

Old-Fashioned Cold Bread Pudding

4 eggs
4 cups milk, divided
1½ cups sugar
2 teaspoons vanilla

6–8 cold biscuits
½ stick butter or margarine
½ teaspoon nutmeg

Preheat oven to 350°. Beat eggs with 1 cup milk. Add sugar, and beat to dissolve. Then add remaining milk and vanilla. Beat well. Pour in greased 9x13-inch dish. Crumble biscuits into it; lightly press into milk. Dot with butter or margarine and sprinkle nutmeg over all. Bake at 350° for 50–60 minutes until as brown as you like it.

Note: Can be baked in 2 medium-size baking pans, or halved for 1 medium-size pan.

Grandma's Cookbook

 Robert E. Lee, commander of the Army of Northern Virginia during the Civil War, was born January 19, 1807, at Stratford Hall in Westmoreland County.

Pistachio Delight

CRUST:

1 stick butter, melted   **½ cup chopped nuts**
1 cup plain flour

Mix and press into a 6x9-inch pan. Bake 25 minutes at 350°. Cool.
(May use graham cracker crust—then it doesn't have to be baked.)

FIRST LAYER:

1 (8-ounce) package cream cheese,   **1 cup confectioners' sugar**
   softened   **1 cup Cool Whip**

Mix together cream cheese and confectioners' sugar; mix in Cool Whip
and spread over Crust.

SECOND LAYER:

2 (3-ounce) packages pistachio   **1 cup Cool Whip**
   instant pudding   **Chopped nuts for garnish**
3 cups milk

Mix well and spread over cream cheese mixture. Spread additional
Cool Whip and chopped nuts over top. Chill well.

Church Family Favorites

Sleeping Meringue

1 angel food cake, sliced
   horizontally into halves
6 egg whites
¼ teaspoon salt
½ teaspoon cream of tartar
1½ cups sugar

1 teaspoon vanilla
1 cup whipping cream
2 cups sliced fruit, such as
   strawberries, peaches,
   blueberries, or a combination

Preheat oven to 450°. Place half the angel food cake in a buttered deep-dish springform pan with a hole. Beat egg whites in a large bowl until stiff peaks form; add salt and cream of tartar while beating. Add sugar and vanilla gradually, and beat 15 minutes. Pour meringue over cake half in pan. Place in oven. Turn off the heat, and go to bed (8–10 hours). Remove dessert from pan to a serving plate just before serving time. Whip whipping cream in a bowl, and spread over top of dessert. Garnish with fruit. Makes 8–10 servings.

Note: There is half a cake left over, so you can double the recipe and make two desserts, or just nibble on that extra half of the cake. I consider that a cook's benefit.

Celebrate Virginia!

 No one knew more about the geography of North America in his own day than Thomas Jefferson. A skilled surveyor and cartographer, he was engaged in a lifelong search for geographic knowledge. Jefferson studied the history of geography and amassed a remarkable collection of explorers' accounts, geographic works, and maps for his personal library. Although Jefferson himself never traveled any further west than Warm Springs, Virginia, he was promoter of four attempts to reach the Pacific, and he personally planned the successful expedition led by Meriwether Lewis and William Clark from 1804–1806.

Ice Cream Flower Pot

2 tablespoons chocolate cookie
   crumbs, divided
1 scoop chocolate ice cream
Green sprinkles

Gumdrops
Cookies or peanut butter cups
Candy spearmint leaf

To make the"dirt,"place 1 tablespoon chocolate crumbs into bottom of a small clear plastic cup. Add a scoop of softened chocolate ice cream, followed by a second layer of cookie crumbs. For grass, put green sprinkles on top. Place a cut straw into center of flowerpot and freeze.

Meanwhile make a "flower" by sticking gumdrops into sides of a cookie or peanut butter cup with toothpicks. To serve, press the flower into the straw. Add a candy spearmint leaf. Makes 1 pot.

All American Recipes

Mama Lois' Homemade Ice Cream

2 packages unflavored gelatin
1 pint milk
2 cups sugar
1 teaspoon vanilla extract
1 quart half-and-half cream

2 cups fruit (peaches, strawberries,
   blueberries, etc.)
Enough whole milk to fill a
   1-gallon container

Mix gelatin and milk together in a saucepan. Heat over low heat until gelatin melts. Stir constantly and be careful not to get the mixture too hot. Pour into a large bowl and add sugar, vanilla, half-and-half, and fruit. Add enough whole milk to make the total volume 1 gallon. Pour into freezer container (no more than ¾ full) and crank until frozen. Remove from freezer and pack into gallon container (or several quart containers) for refrigerator freezer.

Variation: For chocolate ice cream, leave out the fruit. Add 2½ tablespoons cocoa powder into the sugar before adding sugar to milk/gelatin mixture. You can also use 1 small can chocolate syrup instead of cocoa.

Kitty Caters

Lemon Lush Dessert

STEP ONE:

1 stick margarine, melted	**½ cup chopped nuts**
1 tablespoon sugar	**1 cup self-rising flour**

Combine all ingredients and press into ungreased 9x13-inch baking dish. Bake at 350° for 15 minutes.

STEP TWO:

1 cup powdered sugar	**1 (12-ounce) carton frozen Cool**
1 (8-ounce) package cream cheese,	**Whip (unthawed), divided**
softened	

Mix powdered sugar and cream cheese with 1 cup Cool Whip. Reserve remaining Cool Whip for topping:

STEP THREE:

1 (5-ounce) package lemon	**3 cups cold milk**
instant pudding mix	

Prepare pudding as directed on package, and pour over cream cheese mixture. Top with remaining Cool Whip and chill well. Cut into squares. Serves 12.

Note: Chocolate pudding may be used in place of lemon.

Tangier Island Girl

 Born into a prominent political family on February 9, 1773, Virginia native William Henry Harrison gave the longest ever presidential inaugural speech, and served the shortest term. His nearly two-hour address was delivered in a snowstorm in March 1881, and consequently he caught pneumonia and died thirty days later.

Éclair Cake

1 (5-ounce) package vanilla
  (or French vanilla) instant
  pudding
3 cups milk
1 (8-ounce) container frozen
  Cool Whip, thawed

1 box graham crackers
1 (15-ounce) can chocolate fudge
  frosting

Mix pudding and milk; fold in Cool Whip. In a 9x13-inch dish, place a layer of whole graham crackers, then a layer of pudding. Alternate layers, ending with graham crackers. Heat frosting in microwave just enough to spread over top layer of graham crackers. Keep refrigerated. Serves 8–10.

Taste & See

Wilda's Baked Apples

May be used as accompaniment or dessert.

3 pounds apples (Winesap or
  Stayman)
1 (3-ounce) package raspberry or
  strawberry gelatin

½ cup margarine
1 scant cup flour
1 cup sugar

Peel and slice apples. Generously fill an 8-inch-square baking dish. Apples will shrink in baking. Sprinkle on dry gelatin. Combine margarine, flour, and sugar. Sprinkle crumb topping over apples. Bake in 350° oven 45 minutes.

Recipe submitted by Mary Frances Houff, Augusta
Country Treasures

Bristol is legally two cities—one is in Virginia and one is in Tennessee. Although they share the same main street, they each have their own government and city services.

Empanaditas
(Pastry Tarts)

½ cup milk
1½ teaspoons lemon juice
½ cup butter or margarine,
  softened

1 egg yolk (save egg white)
2 cups all-purpose flour, sifted

Combine milk and lemon juice until milk curdles. Cream butter and yolk until light and fluffy. Sift flour onto creamed butter mixture, alternating with sour milk, while mixing. Gather into a ball, wrap with wax paper, and chill about 1½ hours.

On a lightly floured surface, roll out chilled dough ⅛ inch thick, and cut into 3-inch rounds using cookie cutter or jar rim. Put a teaspoonful of Filling on center, and fold dough to half-moon shape. Seal edges with egg white and press down with fork tines. Bake on greased sheet in preheated 350° oven 15–20 minutes, or until light brown.

FILLING:
1 cup chopped almonds or
  cashews
½ cup honey

¼ cup sugar
2 tablespoons butter

Combine all ingredients in saucepan and cook slowly until sugar is dissolved.

Note: Dough may be shaped into little boats and filled. Or spread Filling on rolled uncut dough, roll like a jellyroll to 1½-inch diameter, and cut into ½-inch pieces or coins.

Philippine Cooking in America

Fruit Pizza

1 (20-ounce) package refrigerated
  sugar cookie dough
1 (8-ounce) package cream
  cheese, softened
1 (12-ounce) container frozen
  whipped topping, thawed

½ cup sugar
Fresh strawberries
Fresh peach chunks
Banana slices
Canned pineapple chunks,
  drained

Cut cookie dough roll in ½-inch slices. Arrange on 12-inch pizza pan and press edges to form solid crust. Bake at 350° for 15–20 minutes, or until light golden brown. Combine cream cheese, whipped topping, and sugar, mixing until smooth. Spread filling on cooled crust. Arrange fruit in circles on filling. Serves 8–12.

Children's Party Book

Catalog of
Contributing Cookbooks

In Yorktown, visitors can experience 18th century homes and revolutionary battlefields while strolling along picturesque streets that are the backdrop for art galleries, specialty shops, and antiques.

Catalog of Contributing Cookbooks

All recipes in this book have been selected from the cookbooks shown on the following pages. Individuals who wish to obtain a copy of any particular book may do so by sending a check or money order to the address listed by each cookbook. Please note the postage and handling charges that are required. State residents add tax only when requested. Prices and addresses are subject to change, and the books may sell out and become unavailable. Retailers are invited to call or write to same address for discount information.

ALL AMERICAN RECIPES
from Virginia Beach 911 Dispatchers

C. Gough, Chairperson
Virginia Beach 911 Scholarship Fund
2509 Princess Anne Road
Virginia Beach, VA 23456

Recipes collected from Virginia Beach 911 dispatchers and their families as a fundraiser for the 911 scholarship fund. Eight categories within 121 pages.

$15.00   Retail price

Make check payable to VB 911 Scholarship Fund

BEREA'S HOME COOKING FAVORITES

Attn: Betty Spraker   Phone 276-686-5792
Ladies of Berea Christian Church
265 Spaker Road
Crockett, VA 24323

A compilation of over 630 favorite recipes from two publications by Ladies of Berea, which have sold more than 2,600 copies. The book of southwestern Virginia home-cooking includes a section of old-timey recipes that embrace the regional heritage.

$10.00   Retail price
 $5.00   Postage and handling

Make check payable to Ladies of Berea Christian Church

THE BEST OF VIRGINIA FARMS COOKBOOK

by Cici Williamson
Menasha Ridge Press   www.menasharidge.com

Combining useful information, agricultural history, and over 260 recipes, *The Best of Virginia Farms Cookbook* will entertain and educate you about Virginia's land, people, and food. This book is currently out of print.

CELEBRATE VIRGINIA! COOKBOOK

by Rowena J. Fullinwider, James A. Crutchfield, and Winette Sparkman Jeffery

Rowena's, Inc.   Phone 800-627-8699 • Fax 757-627-1505
758 W 22nd Street   www.rowenas.com
Norfolk, VA 23517   rowena@rowenas.com

Celebrate Virginia! is a fabulous book full of outstanding favorite family recipes. Includes 400 years of Virginia history, humor, interesting tidbits, and facts on every page. This includes not only Virginia's great food but its well-known great tradition of hospitality. 320 pages. Hardcover.

    $19.99   Retail price   Visa/MC/Disc/Amex accepted
    $4.50   Postage and handling   ISBN 1-93060-496-3

Make check payable to Rowena's, Inc.

CELEBRATING OUR CHILDREN COOKBOOK

Gretna Elementary PTO   Phone 434-656-6412
Compiled by Katherine T. Giles
3989 Rockford School Road
Gretna, VA 24557

Our 166-page cookbook was designed to be a family heirloom for each student who contributed and a celebration of our children and our community. From Nana's Pasta and Shrimp to Pookies' Bread and Butter Pickles, to Yorkshire Beef.

    $12.00   Retail price
    $3.00   Postage and handling

Make check payable to Katherine T. Giles

CHILDREN'S PARTY BOOK

Junior League of Hampton Roads   Phone 757-873-0281
729 Thimble Shoals Boulevard, Suite 4-D   Fax 757-873-8747
Newport News, VA 23606   www.jlhr.org • volunteer@jlhr.org

Children's Party Book contains over 25 preplanned children's parties, complete with invitations, menus, activities, decorations, and games. A unique gift for teachers, caregivers, and new or expecting parents. First published in 1984, it was updated in 1996 to include multi-cultural holidays such as Hanukkah and Kwanzaa.

    $13.95   Retail price   Visa/MC accepted
    $.70   Tax for Virginia residents   ISBN 0-9613600-3-8
    $3.50   Postage and handling for each additional book

Make check payable to Junior League of Hampton Roads

CHURCH FAMILY FAVORITES

Kenbridge United Methodist Church   Phone 434-676-8134
3339 Pleasant Hill Lane   Fax 434-676-3211
Kenbridge, VA 23944   joverman@mailstation.com

Five hundred recipes collected over the years by our members and former members and friends. These recipes are favorites and some are exclusive to "southside" Virginia.

    $8.00   Retail price
    $4.00   Postage and handling

Make check payable to Kenbridge United Methodist Church

THE COLONIAL WILLIAMSBURG TAVERN COOKBOOK

The Colonial Williamsburg Foundation
P. O. Box 1776
Williamsburg, VA 23187-1776

Phone 1-800-446-9240
www.williamsburgmarketplace.com

It's six o'clock, stomachs are rumbling, and suddenly you have a yearning for the Crab and Shrimp Stuffed Flounder you enjoyed at Christiana Campbell's Tavern. No problem. Pull out this cookbook, roll up your sleeves, and in an hour, you'll enjoy the tastes and aromas of Williamsburg.

$21.00   Retail price
Plus postage and handling

Visa/MC accepted
ISBN 0-609-60286-1

COME COOK WITH US

Hellenic Woman's Club
Attn: Cookbook Chairman
7220 Granby Street
Norfolk, VA 23505

Phone 757-587-8470 (Pat Garrett)

A thesaurus of Greek cooking dedicated to the preservation of the culinary traditions of ancient and modern Greece for the benefit of our children . . . for future generations of Greek-Americans . . . and for our friends.

$18.00   Retail price
$5.00   Postage and handling

Make check payable to Hellenic Woman's Club

COOKIN' FOR THE CURE

Relay for Life Team "Shining Stars for a Cure"
110 E. Main Street
Salem, VA 24153

Phone 540-389-3564
Fax 540-378-1532
mstaples@fnbonline.com

Cookin' for the Cure is a collection of over 400 favorite recipes contributed by co-workers and supporters of the American Cancer Society's Relay for Life. All profits benefit this great cause. Hardcover book with 192 pages, dividers, index, and more.

$12.00   Retail price
$2.00   Postage and handling

Make check payable Shining Stars for a Cure

COOKING WITH ARK ANGELS

Area Rehabbers Klub
1811 Capeway Road
Powhatan, VA 23139

Phone 804-598-7615
Fax 804-598-6308
www.welcome.to/arkva • arkva@prodigy.net

A unique assortment of 300 recipes from dedicated volunteers that care for Virginia wildlife. There are recipes for our wildlife friends, as well as vegetarians in our midst. You'll also be informed of ways to help wildlife around you.

$10.00   Retail price

Make check payable to Area Rehabbers Klub

COOKING WITH GRACE

Grace and Holy Trinity Church   Phone 804-359-5628
8 N. Laurel Street   Fax 804-353-2348
Richmond, VA 23220   www.ghtc.org • barbara@ghtc.org

Cooking with Grace is a compilation of traditional southern recipes and current regional fare. You will find helpful hints from Grace church's "The Kitchen Queen," as well as savory dishes for a weeknight supper or an elegant dinner party.

   $24.95   Retail price
    $7.00   Postage and handling   ISBN 0-9762159-0-X

Make check payable to *Cooking with Grace*

COUNTRY COOKBOOK

Oak Grove Baptist Church
Virginia Beach, VA

Favorite family recipes with simple, easy-to-follow directions. This book is currently out of print.

COUNTRY HOME FAVORITES

Peggy Gebauer/Vida Parker
1404 Niagara Road   Phone 540-344-0787
Vinton, VA 24179   gebauerchef@worldnet.att.net

Country Home Favorites includes 300 recipes, all quick and easy. This is a great cookbook to bring the family back to the table. Also makes a great gift.

   $15.00   Retail price
    $.75   Tax for VA residents
    $4.05   Postage and handling

Make check payable to Peggy Gebauer

COUNTRY TREASURES
from Virginia Farm Bureau Kitchens

Virginia Farm Bureau   Phone 804-290-1000
W & YF Department
P. O. Box 27552
Richmond, VA 23261

Country Treasures from Virginia Farm Bureau Kitchens is a collection of favorite farm family-tested, treasured recipes from all over the Commonwealth. Spiral-bound with coated cardstock cover and more than 700 pages. Nearly 1,300 recipes from farm families throughout Virginia.

   $20.00   Retail price

Make check payable to Virginia Farm Bureau

CULINARY SECRETS OF GREAT VIRGINIA CHEFS

by Martha Hollis
Thomas Nelson Publishers
P. O. Box 141000
Nashville, TN 37214

Phone 800-251-1000
www.thomasnelson.com

Culinary Secrets reflects the heritage of Virginia cuisine, which is steeped in historic tradition and grounded in impeccable taste. This is both a cookbook of more than 200 of the best recipes from the finest chefs, and their "trade secrets."

ISBN 1-5585333-5-4

DELIGHTFULLY SEASONED RECIPES
from Your 911 Family and Friends

2508 Princess Anne Road
Municipal Center Building 30
Virginia Beach, VA 23456

This book was developed as a fundraiser for our 911 scholarship. Family and friends of Virginia Beach 911 dispatchers contributed recipes in eight categories. 244 pages.

$15.00   Retail price

Make check payable to VB 911 Scholarship

DISCOVERY TOUR 2006 COOKBOOK

Breaks District Boy Scouts
P. O. Box 1016
Gundy, VA 24614

Phone 276-935-8878
gfhmullins@yahoo.com

This padded hardcover, three-ring-binder cookbook was created by the Boy Scouts of the Appalachian region of southwest Virginia with many authentic mountain recipes. This collection is 254 pages with 499 recipes, including many wild game and traditional Boy Scout, Dutch oven recipes.

$15.00   Retail price
$5.00   Postage and handling

Make check payable to BSA Troop 740

FAVORITE RECIPES
Barbara's Best Volume II

by Barbara D. Boothe
2886 Lake Road
Lottsburg, VA 22511

Phone 804-529-7049
Fax 804-529-5030

This hardcover cookbook is packed with over 350 tried-and-tried, downright delicious, country cooking recipes. Enjoy dishes such as Banana Split Salad, Crockpot Macaroni and Cheese, Taco Pizza, Working Woman's Favorite Fast Dinner, Microwave Peanut Brittle, and many more.

$15.00   Retail price
$2.00   Postage and handling

Make check payable to Barbara Boothe

FAVORITE RECIPES

Bayside Baptist Church Women's Ministry   Phone 757-460-2481
1920 Pleasure House Road   Fax 757-460-4452
Virginia Beach, VA 23455   www.baysidebc.org • kent@baysidebc.org

This cookbook contains 335 pages and over 985 recipes from the cooks of Bayside Baptist Church, including over 90 slow cooker and casserole recipes, and over 122 diabetic and sugar-free recipes. Fabulous but simple recipes for everyday family meals.

  $18.00   Retail price
   $3.00   Postage and handling

Make check payable to Bayside Baptist Church

THE FINE ART OF DINING

Muscarelle Museum of Art   Phone 757-221-2709
P. O. Box 8795   Fax 757-221-2711
Williamsburg, VA 23187   www.wm.edu/muscarelle • caluca@wm.edu

The Fine Art of Dining from the Muscarelle Museum of Art is a collection of 300 tried-and-true recipes. The cookbook includes updated versions of old favorites plus new recipes perfect for our busy lives. Because Williamsburg is near the Chesapeake Bay, seafood recipes abound.

  $15.00   Retail price   Visa/MC accepted
    $.75   Tax for VA residents
   $4.00   Postage and handling

Make check payable to Muscarelle Museum of Art

FIRST FAMILY FAVORITES

First Baptist Church of Woodbridge Women's Ministry
13600 Minnieville Road
Woodbridge, VA 22193   jblue@fbcwoodbridge.org

The Women by Design ministry team learned that missionaries had a difficult time getting pure drinking water while serving in remote locations. Jane Blue and Sherry Howard decided to create a fundraiser cookbook; proceeds were enough to not only pay cookbook expenses but to purchase several water filters.

  $15.00   Retail price (Includes S&H)

Make check payable to FBCW

FOOD, FAMILY, AND FRIENDSHIPS

by Mary M. Darden and Margaret T. Proffitt
2617 Majesty Lane   Phone 757-496-9680
Virginia Beach, VA 23456   HooklUp@verizon.net or maryjim@infionline.net

This collection of favorite recipes and memories from the authors' families and friends reflects regional cooking in the southern tradition. Old and new recipes make the book easy to use and fun to read. Now in 12th printing.

  $19.95   Retail price   ISBN 0-9654643-0-8
   $4.00   Postage and handling

Make check payable to Mary M. Darden or Margaret T. Proffitt

FOOD TO DIE FOR:
A Book of Funeral Food, Tips, and Tales
Jessica Bemis Ward
Southern Memorial Association   Phone 434-847-1465
Old City Cemetery, 401 Taylor Street   Fax 434-856-2004
Lynchburg, VA 24501   www.gravegarden.org • occ@gravegarden.org

A lighthearted cookbook about funerals and the customs surrounding them. The cookbook contains 180 pages of funeral etiquette, anecdotes, and over 100 delicious recipes. Illustrated with black-and-white photographs of the Old City Cemetery in Lynchburg. National Winner of the 2005 Tabasco Community Cookbook Award.

  $25.00   Retail price   Visa/MC/Disc accepted
    $1.25   Tax for VA residents   ISBN 0-9759822-0-6
    $5.00   Postage and handling

Make check payable to Old City Cemetery

FOR MEN WHO LIKE TO COOK, WANT TO COOK (OR HAVE TO!)
by John M. Shenk   Phone 540-434-8220
1560 College Avenue   Cell 540-476-3658
Harrisonburg, VA 22802   je4c@comcast.net

These recipes will inspire men to explore the world of cooking, beginning with quick and easy recipes. Men can cook at home, not just in famous restaurants. (Women and children will enjoy this book, too.) Included are 292 recipes, cooking tips, famous quotes.

   $ 9.50   Retail price
   $1.50   Postage and handling

Make check payable to John M. Shenk

FROM CHANEY CREEK TO THE CHESAPEAKE
Family and Friends of Giles Dickenson Wise and Lenora Amburgey Wise
4827 Lee Avenue
Virginia Beach, VA 23455

This cookbook is 115 pages of recipes that originated in the southwestern region of Virginia. Tried-and-true recipes such as Butterscotch Pie and Pulled Chicken Barbeque are balanced with innovative entries such as Stuffed Pears and Zucchini and Feta Gratin.

  $10.00   Retail price
   $4.00   Postage and handling

Make check payable to Patti Holt

G.W. CARVER FAMILY RECIPES
G.W. Carver Elementary School   Phone 540-387-2492
6 East Fourth Street   Fax 540-375-4105
Salem, VA 24153   gwcarver@salem.k12.va.us • tbyington@salem.k12.va.us

G.W. Carver Family Recipes is a collection of favorites from our teachers, aids, custodians, and clerical staff. We put together some special foods and ideas in memory of a special son of one of our teachers. You'll love it!

  $10.00   Retail price
   $1.00   Postage and handling

Make check payable to G.W. Carver Elementary School

GARDEN GATE RECIPES

United Methodist Women for Belle Haven Methodist Church
Attn: Jessie Gladstone
P. O. Box 96   Phone 757-442-7383
Belle Haven, VA 23306

Heartwarming book full of recipes from every mother's heart for her family. These recipes have been enjoyed from great grandmothers to the great grandchildren with love. There are 267 pages and 902 recipes.

$10.00   Retail price
$2.50   Postage and handling

Make check payable to United Methodist Women

GATHER 'ROUND OUR TABLE

by Edith Vick Farris
168 Kaylor Circle   Phone 540-289-7311
Massanutten, VA 22840-2132   farris46@aol.com

More than 250 pages of 400+ recipes, pictures, and stories from the Doughtie family of Virginia and North Carolina. Laminated, custom-designed cover; plastic comb, imprinted binding; 7x8½ inches.

$15.95   Retail price
$3.00   Postage and handling

Make check payable to Edith Vick Farris

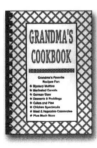

GRANDMA'S COOKBOOK

Don Hopkins/Hopkins Enterprises
P. O. Box 224   Phone 276-957-4873
Spencer, VA 24165   stonecrossmountain@comcast.net

Grandma's Cookbook contains the private collection of recipes of Grandma Hallie Hopkins, including secret family recipes and her own secret cake recipes. These family secret recipes are not found in other cookbooks. In one year, Grandma baked and sold over 1,000 cakes.

$14.95   Retail price
$.75   Tax for VA residents
$2.00   Postage and handling

Make check payable to Hopkins Enterprises

GRANNY'S KITCHEN

by Theone L. Neel   Phone 276-988-6472
6983 Clearfork Road
Bastian, VA 24314-4532

Granny's Kitchen was written as a labor of love, which was a gift to the author's grandchildren. The simple kitchen-tested recipes call for ingredients that most cooks have on hand. Over 800 recipes, plus menu ideas and cooking tips sprinkled throughout. Index. 409 pages.

$12.00   Retail price
$3.00   Postage and handling

Make check payable to Theone L. Neel

THE HALL FAMILY COOKBOOK

by Gene R. Hall and Pamela D. Hall
Virginia Yankee Press
P. O. Box 21306   Phone 540-989-1650
Roanoke, VA 24018   virginiayankeepress@att.net

Over seventy treasured family recipes presented in an easy-to-follow format. Recipe preparation difficulty levels range from very easy to somewhat challenging. A variety of appetizers, entrées, and desserts will spice up everyday dining and delight the guests you entertain.

  $19.95   Retail price   ISBN 0-9779118-0-2
   $1.00   Tax for VA residents
   $4.00   Postage and handling
Make check payable to Pamela Hall

THE HAM BOOK

by Robert W. Harrell, Jr. and Monette R. Harrell
Harrell Hams
407 W. Riverview Drive   Phone 757-539-2447
Suffolk, VA 23434   ham5ham5@yahoo.com

This historical cookbook about ham has over 350 of the most delicious recipes using ham of all types, and includes accompanying delights from appetizers to desserts. Was selected as one of the Top Fifteen Virginia Cookbooks by *Virginia Living Magazine*.

  $14.95   Retail price
   $.67   Tax for VA residents   ISBN 0-915442-14-0
   $2.00   Postage and handling
Make check payable to Harrell Hams

HOLIDAY FARE: Favorite American Recipes

by John R. Gonzales
The Colonial Williamsburg Foundation   Phone 1-800-446-9240
P. O. Box 1776   www.williamsburgmarketplace.com
Williamsburg, VA 23187-1776

Chef John Gonzales serves up fun fare for the holidays. Featuring more than sixty genuinely American recipes, *Holiday Fare* combines the history and local flavors of Colonial Williamsburg's famed Christmastide festivities.

  $16.95   Retail price   Visa/MC accepted
Plus postage and handling   ISBN-10: 0-87935-196-9
                             ISBN-13: 978-0-87935-196-0

IN GOOD COMPANY

Junior League of Lynchburg   Phone 434-846-6641
2101 Rivermont Avenue   Fax 434-845-5569
Lynchburg, VA 24503   www.jrleaguelynchburg.org • jlloffice@verizon.net

In Good Company is a superb collection of recipes, menus, and restaurant favorites compiled by the Junior League of Lynchburg. Features menus for entertaining, entertainment tips, favorites from nineteen area restaurants, and historical tidbits about Lynchburg and the surrounding area.

  $14.95   Retail price   Visa/MC accepted
   $.75   Tax for VA residents   ISBN 0-9614766-1-3
   $3.00   Postage and handling
Make check payable to Junior League of Lynchburg

IT'S DELICIOUS!

Hospital Hospitality House
The Dietz Press
612 E. Marshall Street
Richmond, VA 23219

Phone 804-828-6901
Fax 804-828-6913
www.hhhrichmond.org
bjacksonhhh@yahoo.com

A 219-page collection of over 300 recipes contributed by staff, volunteers, donors, and former guests of Hospital Hospitality House, a 112-room nonprofit facility that provides lodging for patients/family members who come to Richmond for specialized medical care.

$28.95   Retail price
$1.45   Tax for VA residents
$2.95   Postage and handling

Visa/MC/Amex accepted
ISBN 0-87517-119-2

Make check payable to Hospital Hospitality House of Richmond

JOY IN SERVING

by Ladies of Berea Christian Church
Attn: Betty Spraker
265 Spaker Road
Crockett, VA 24323

Phone 276-686-5792

Over 350 southwestern Virginia recipes compiled by ladies who are known for their great home cooking. Preserving their local heritage, the book has a special section for home canning and a more modern section of slow cooking.

$10.00   Retail price
$5.00   Postage and handling

Make check payable to Ladies of Berea Christian Church

JUST LIKE MAMA'S

by Judy Hensley
204 Parker Estate
Gate City, VA 24251

Phone 276-386-9861
dellh@mounet.com

Continuing the torch of hospitality and cooking that she learned from her mother, Judy Hensley's cookbook preserves the "old-timey" traits and traditions learned from Edna Mae Vanzant, who gave birth to five daughters that still today cook and bake *Just Like Mama.*

$18.00   Retail price (includes shipping)
Make check payable to Judy Hensley

KIDS IN THE KITCHEN

O. T. Bonner Middle School
300 Apollo Avenue
Danville, VA 34540

Phone 434-799-6446

In homes today, as always, life is centered around the kitchen. It is with this thought in mind that we have compiled these recipes. Some recipes are treasured family keepsakes and some are new; however, they all reflect the love of good cooking.

$10.00   Retail price
$2.00   Postage and handling

Make check payable to O. T. Bonner Middle School

KITTY CATERS

by Catherine Kellam
P. O. Box 386   Phone 757-331-3820
Cheriton, VA 23316-0386   bkkellam@aol.com

Kitty Caters contains 219 pages of 319 original recipes. I've worked hard and had lots
of fun compiling this cookbook. I hope that my family and friends will treasure this
book of old favorites, and that those who find a copy passed along to them will treasure it, too.

$16.00   Retail price
$.80   Tax for VA residents
$1.50   Postage and handling

Make check payable to Catherine Kellam

A LAUGH & A GLASS OF WINE

by Bonnie L. DeLelys   Phone 540-899-7606
711 Caroline Street   Fax 540-899-6837
Fredericksburg, VA 22401   bbinnsittr@aol.com or rjohnstoninn@staffnet.com

This book was written as a joke with great recipes gathered over the years. Includes
a few jokes and an interesting photo dedicated to my son, and acknowledges my true
girlfriends who never judged but always listened.

$18.00   Retail price
$3.00   Postage and handling

Make check payable to Bonnie L. DeLelys

LONG HILL BED & BREAKFAST

Rhoda W. Kriz   Phone 866-450-0341
547 Apple Pie Ridge Road   www.longhillbb.com
Winchester, VA 22603   rkriz@visuallink.com

When you are wishing for the luxuriousness and comfort of a bed and breakfast experience, satisfy your desires with dishes from this collection of *Long Hill Bed &
Breakfast's* Award Winning Breakfasts. You will find 27 recipes and interesting facts in
this easy to use 24-page, spiral-bound booklet.

$5.00   Retail price
$1.75   Postage and handling

Make check payable to Rhoda W. Kriz

LOVING, CARING AND SHARING

by Cordelia Higgins   Phone 434-645-2299
620 East Tennessee Avenue
Crewe, VA 23930

Third-time cookbook author, Cordelia Higgins shares her talent, time, and treasure of
a life-long collection of outstanding recipes in this fantastic, 166-page book that is
sure to become a kitchen favorite! The common ingredient in each of these recipes
. . . love.

$12.00   Retail price

Make check payable to Cordelia Higgins

MRS. ROWE'S FAVORITE RECIPES

Mike DiGrassi
Mrs. Rowe's Restaurant and Bakery
74 Rowe Road   Phone 540-886-1833
Staunton, VA 24401   mrsrowes@intelos.net

Opened in 1947 by Mildred Rowe and still run by her family, Mrs. Rowe's is one of the best home-style restaurants in Virginia. This cookbook includes dishes served at the restaurant, plus southern favorites contributed by Mrs. Rowe's family and friends.

$12.95   Retail price   Visa/MC accepted
$.60   Tax for VA residents   ISBN 0-9708304-0-8
$3.00   Postage and handling

Make check payable to Rowe's Family Restaurant

MY TABLE AT BRIGHTWOOD
Southern Cooking on a Country Road

by April Miller   Phone 434-432-4223
Brightwood- 501 Marilla Lane
Chatham, VA 24531

With today's emphasis on "lite" foods, we shouldn't forget the recipes of our grandmothers that called for butter, lard, and heavy cream. The wonderful taste of these "heritage" foods can sometimes be incorporated into any diet. Go for it!

$10.00   Retail price
$.50   Tax for VA residents
$2.50   Postage and handling

Make check payable to April Miller

NOT BY BREAD ALONE COOKBOOK

Mt. Olivet United Methodist Church
c/o Theone Neel   Phone 276-988-6472
6983 Clearfork Road
Bastian, VA 24314-4532

Church members and friends submitted 554 taste-tested family and potluck recipes in this cookbook. It is made up with ten sections, including one on healthy recipes. Household hints are included and spirit-lifting quotations are sprinkled throughout. Index. 260 pages.

$10.00   Retail price
$2.00   Postage and handling

Make check payable to Mt. Olivet U.M. Church

OH MY STARS! RECIPES THAT SHINE

Junior League of Roanoke Valley   Phone 540-343-5512
541 Luck Avenue, Suite 317   Fax 540-343-5512
Roanoke, VA 24016

Oh My Stars! is a collection of recipes that will appeal to the everyday cook, the gourmet, or the entertainer. More than 200 pages of delicious savory and sweet choices—from Spicy Shrimp Salsa to Fresh Apple Brownies—make this book a must-have!

$24.95   Retail price   Visa/MC accepted
$1.25   Tax for VA residents   ISBN 0-9679497-0-X
$3.50   Postage and handling

Make check payable to JLRV

OUR BEST TO YOU!

The Edwards Family of Franklin, Virginia
3716 Bellevue Road   Phone 919-571-9131
Raleigh, NC 27609   lucillecarter@earthlink.net

A conglomerate of recipes (200) from a very large, very close, fun-loving and well-fed family. Having been so well-fed, we wanted to pass along our favorites. The book has 223 pages.

  $14.95   Retail price   Cash or Checks accepted
    $1.05   Tax for VA residents
    $4.00   Postage and handling

Make check payable to Lucille Edwards Carter

PHILIPPINE COOKING IN AMERICA

by Marilyn R. Donato, RD   Phone 540-345-2033
3707 Alton Road, SW   Fax 540-345-2033
Roanoke, VA 24014-3003   www.philamcookbook.com • tomardonat@yahoo.com

This 200-plus-page cookbook includes a great selection of easy-to-follow Philippine recipes adjusted to common American ingredients. First published in 1972, *Philippine Cooking* (because of its high demand) is now on its seventh revised edition. Also includes a helpful hints section.

  $19.95   Retail price

Make check payable to M. Donato

PUNGO STRAWBERRY FESTIVAL COOKBOOK

Pungo Strawberry Festival   Phone 757-426-7832
643 Princess Anne Road   Fax 757-721-9335
Virginia Beach, VA 23457-1313   www.pungostrawberryfestival.com
                                   pungofestival@aol.com

Pungo Strawberry Festival Cookbook presents over 400 recipes spiral-bound in a hard-cover, 164-page book. Contains simple, tasty recipes from many "country" cooks in Virginia Beach, featuring, but not limited to, recipes of the strawberry crops being honored.

  $15.00   Retail price

Make check payable to Pungo Strawberry Festival

RECIPES FROM HOME

by Fontaine Ruritan Club
Attn: Ann Huffman   Phone 276-632-6298
16 Lawless Drive   Fax 276-632-2341
Fieldale, VA 24089   anng7@comcast.net

This delightful cookbook has 300 tried-and-true favorite recipes submitted by the Fontaine Ruritan Club members. Also includes history of Fontaine club and a helpful hints section in the back. From appetizers to desserts, *Recipes from Home* has it all!

  $10.00   Retail price
    $5.00   Postage and handling

Make check payable to Fontaine Ruritan Club

THE RIGGS FAMILY COOKBOOK

Patricia Isbell
Route 1, Box 7
Braggs, OK 74423

Phone 918-487-5692

The Riggs Family Cookbook contains a brief family history, two generations of birth dates, two photos from the early 1900s, and approximately 250 recipes on 85 pages. One special section consists of recipes from one sister's early 1900 cookbook. These recipes are priceless!

$8.00 Retail price
$1.25 Postage and handling
Make check payable to Patricia Isbell

SHARING OUR BEST

Antioch United Methodist Women
4392 Planters Road
Dolphin, VA 23843

Phone 434-848-0902
chjon53@aol.com

Sharing Our Best is a 202-page cookbook with recipes submitted by local people with their best "down home" cooking. Includes a shopping list in the margin. Also includes a base for easy viewing.

$10.00 Retail price
Make check payable to Antioch United Methodist Women

THE SMITHFIELD COOKBOOK

The Woman's Club of Smithfield
P. O. Box 754
Smithfield, VA 23431

Phone 757-357-3063
sgewell@charter.net

This collection of traditional local recipes and stories of historical significance define the town of Smithfield and Isle of Wight County. The customs and traditions of the area are reflected in the food and dining practices of past generations, and the cookbook is a record of such to be handed down and preserved.

$15.00 Retail price
$.75 Tax for VA residents
$2.00 Postage and handling
Make check payable to The Woman's Club of Smithfield

TANGIER ISLAND GIRL

by Patsy Parks Young and Shirley Parks Taylor
Attn: Shirley P. Taylor
26329 Parks Road
Parksley, VA 23421

Phone 757-787-2169
st67@verizon.net

Tangier Island Girl is a unique collection of stories, sayings, and facts about this tiny island in the Chesapeake Bay discovered by Captain John Smith. Patsy Young, an island native, has compiled 150 simple, yet delicious recipes, such as coconut pound cake, lemon lush dessert, and a wonderful entrée or dip: oven-baked crabmeat.

$10.00 Retail price
$3.50 Postage and handling
Make check payable to Shirley P. Taylor

TASTE & SEE

Philadelphia United Methodist Church   Phone 434-577-2104
14179 Dry Bread Road
Emporia, VA 23847

This attractive 240-page, three-ring binder cookbook contains nearly 500 recipes of friends and family members of Philadelphia United Methodist Church, located in Brunswick County, Virginia, the original home of "Brunswick Stew." The recipe is included here. Taste a bit of Brunswick County history—you'll like it!

  $15.00   Retail price
   $6.00   Postage and handling

Make check payable to Philadelphia UMW

A TASTE OF HEAVEN

Attn: Janice Rhodes
Rockingham Group   Phone 540-564-8807
633 East Market Street   Fax 540-434-0390
Harrisburg, VA 22801   jrhodes@rockinghamgroup.com

While the book is full of delicious recipes, it also celebrates the little-considered role of food in human relationships, and the people who prepare it. This cookbook was compiled by the Rockingham Group to raise money for the United Way.

  $11.00   Retail price

Make check payable to Rockingham Group

A TASTE OF PRINCE WILLIAM COUNTY COOKBOOK

Prince William SPCA   Phone 571-222-0033
P. O. Box 6631   www.pwspca.org
Woodbridge, VA 22195   pwspca@pwspca.org

Regional cookbook with 350 recipes and 173 pages. Hardback and spiral-bound, featuring 15 recipes for your pets; 9 categories of recipes ranging from very easy to gourmet.

  $12.00   Retail price
    $.60   Tax for VA residents
   $3.00   Postage and handling

Make check payable to Prince William SPCA

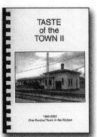

TASTE OF THE TOWN II

Woman's Club of Windsor
Attn: Dorothy G. Gwaltney   Phone 757-242-6607
1418 Five Forks Road   Fax 757-242-9212
Windsor, VA 23487   nfmema@aol.com

Published in celebration of the Windor's centennial year—2002, this cookbook contains a synopsis of the town history with photos of Windsor through the years. The recipes were contributed by our civic leaders, elected officials, and residents of the community. 196 pages. 585 recipes.

  $10.00   Retail price
   $5.00   Postage and handling

Make check payable to The Woman's Club of Windsor

A TASTE OF TRADITION

Temple Family
3333-24 Virginia Beach Boulevard
Virginia Beach, VA 23452

Phone 757-340-8001
Fax 757-340-0998
akilmer@esgco.com

Country cooking at its best. Recipes have been passed down through the generations of the Temple family. Profits fund the annual family reunions. 177 pages of outstanding recipes.

$20.00   Retail price (includes shipping)

Make check payable to Andrea M. Kilmer

A TASTE OF VIRGINIA HISTORY

by Debbie Nunley and Karen Jane Elliott
John F. Blair Publishers
1406 Plaza Drive
Winston-Salem, NC 27103

Phone 800-222-0706
Fax 336-768-9194
www.blairpub.com

Virginia is the perfect subject for a book offering a variety of dining experiences in historic restaurants. *A Taste of Virginia History* features 120-plus restaurants and 300-plus recipes that will satisfy your appetite for the best the state has to offer.

$18.95   Retail price
$5.00   Postage and handling

Visa/MC accepted
ISBN 0-89587-293-5

Make check payable to John F. Blair, Publisher

TASTE TREK!

Heimdal Science Fiction Club
63 Knollwood Drive
Rustburg, VA 24588

Phone 434-845-7517 or 434-426-1646

Taste Trek! contains 186 "out of this world" recipes. We are a science-fiction group, so some of our recipes have a science-fiction flavor. Diabetic recipes are included in each section.

$10.00   Retail price
$4.00   Postage and handling

Make check payable to Heimdal Science Fiction

TASTY TREASURES FROM JOHNSON'S CHURCH

United Methodist Women of Johnson's United Methodist Church
Machipongo, VA

This cookbook is a treasure chest of homemade delights from members and friends of Johnson's Church. It contains over 400 recipes (144 pages) separated into seven sections and thirteen pages of helpful information. Johnson's is known for its good cooks. This book is currently out of print.

THOUGHT FOR FOOD

Goodwin House
Alexandria, VA

Someone once said, "Anything worth doing is worth doing well." This cookbook has been the combined effort of many people, including staff and residents of Goodwin House, who submitted recipes, art, and poetry. This book is currently out of print.

TIDEWATER ON THE HALF SHELL

The Junior League of Norfolk-Virginia Beach, Inc. Phone 757-623-7270
P. O. Box 956 Fax 757-623-3932
Norfolk, VA 23501 www.jlnvb.org • info@jlnvb.org

Since its first printing in 1985, *Tidewater on the Half Shell* has sold over 150,000 copies. This cookbook of casual elegance captures the classic yet contemporary flavor of Hampton Roads' distinctive cuisine with 566 fine Virginia recipes.

$18.95 Retail price Visa/MC accepted
$.95 Tax for VA residents ISBN 0-9614767-0-2
$5.00 Postage and handling
Make check payable to JLNVB

TOAST TO TIDEWATER

The Junior League of Norfolk-Virginia Beach, Inc. Phone 757-623-7270
P. O. Box 956 Fax 757-623-3932
Norfolk, VA 23501 www.jlnvb.org • info@jlnvb.org

Toast to Tidewater features 167 triple-tested recipes that share the ingredients and culinary delights of the Tidewater region. Over half of the recipes are paired with Virginia wines, ciders, and beers. *Toast to Tidewater* received the National First Place 2004 Tabasco Community Cookbook Award.

$27.95 Retail price Visa/MC accepted
$1.40 Tax for VA residents ISBN 0-9614767-1-0
$5.00 Postage and handling
Make check payable to JLNVB

TRIED AND TRUE RECIPES

by Joan Dimengo
13536 Heathrow Lane Phone 703-815-1586
Centreville, VA 20120 jdimengo@hotmail.com

As a retired Army wife, I've had the opportunity to enjoy food and collect recipes and cookbooks from the USA and Europe. Now that we have settled in Virginia, I've taken the time to gather my 400 favorite recipes.

$12.50 Retail price
$3.50 Postage and handling
Make check payable to Joan M. Dimengo

VERY VIRGINIA

Junior League of Hampton Roads
729 Thimble Shoals Boulevard, Suite 4-D
Newport News, VA 23606

Phone 757-873-0281
Fax 757-873-8747
www.jlhr.org • volunteer@jlhr.org

Over 400 triple-tested recipes emphasizing fresh ingredients and foods indigenous to Virginia. It was first published in 1995. Adding to the uniqueness of the book, it includes wine suggestions from Williamsburg Winery as well as a "Kids in the Kitchen" section.

$17.95 Retail price	Visa/MC accepted
$.90 Tax for VA residents	ISBN 0-9613600-2-X
$3.50 postage and handling	

Make check payable to Junior League of Hampton Roads

VESUVIUS, VIRGINIA: THEN AND NOW

The Vesuvius Community Association, Inc.
P. O. Box 304
Vesuvius, VA 24483

Phone 540-377-5756
Fax 540-377-5756
vesuviusva@earthlink.net

Over 180 recipes are a taste of Vesuvius and its history—from its beginning as an iron furnace to its heyday as a station on the N&W Railway. There are vintage photographs and even a diagram of the Vesuvius mine.

$10.00 Retail price	Check or PayPal only accepted
$4.05 Postage and handling	

Make check payable to VCA

VINTAGE VIRGINIA: A History of Good Taste

Virginia Dietetic Association
P. O. Box 439
Centreville, VA 20120

Phone 703-815-8293
Fax 703-815-8293
www.eatright-va.org • vdahdqtrs@aol.com

A unique collage of timeless recipes, historical facts, and cooking and nutrition tips that reflect Virginia's rich culinary traditions and heritage. Artist P. Buckley Moss created the cover for this hardback limited edition cookbook from the Old Dominion. 192 pages. 190 delicious recipes.

$10.00 Retail price	ISBN 0-9673874-0-X
$5.00 Postage and handling	

Make check payable to Virginia Dietetic Association

VIRGINIA COOK BOOK

Compiled by Janice Therese Mancuso
Golden West Publishers
4113 North Longview Avenue
Phoenix, AZ 84014

Phone 1-800-658-5830
Fax 602-279-6901
www.goldenwestpublishers.com
order@goldenwestpublishers.com

Virginia is home to rich history and great food. These recipes reflect the many flavors of Virginia and highlight its celebrated heritage.

$6.95 Retail price	Visa/MC/Disc accepted
$.56 Tax for VA residents	ISBN 1-885590-45-8
$5.00 Postage and handling	

Make check payable to Golden West Publishers

VIRGINIA FARE

Junior League of Richmond
205 West Franklin Street
Richmond, VA 23220

Phone 804-643-4886, ext. 11
Fax 804-643-4887
www.jlrichmond.org • mwbryan@jlrichmond.org

Join the Junior League of Richmond for a culinary view of our Commonwealth. *Virginia Fare* includes a photographic tour of the Old Dominion, menus for entertaining, grilling, and marinade recipes, and a journey through the state by syndicated columnist Guy Fridell.

$15.00 Retail price
$.75 Tax for VA residents
$4.00 Postage and handling

MC/Visa accepted
ISBN 09614056-1-9

Make check payable to Junior League of Richmond

VIRGINIA HOSPITALITY

Junior League of Hampton Roads
729 Thimble Shoals Boulevard, Suite 4-D
Newport News, VA 23606

Phone 757-873-0281
Fax 757-873-8747
www.jlhr.org • volunteer@jlhr.org

Virginia Hospitality is a 300-page community cookbook first published in 1975. It features 600 triple-tested recipes, sketches, and histories of famous Virginia houses and discussions of cooking and entertaining. This cookbook is in its 19th printing. Inducted into the McIlhenney Tabasco Community Cookbook Hall of Fame in 1991.

$17.95 Retail price
$.90 Tax for VA residents
$3.50 Postage and handling

Visa/MC accepted
ISBN 0-9613600-1-1

Make check payable to Junior League of Hampton Roads

VIRGINIA SEASONS

Junior League of Richmond
Richmond, VA

In Virginia, food is part of every season, and Virginians have made food part of every celebration, from the first Thanksgiving, held at Berkeley Plantation on the James River in 1619, to a tailgate picnic at the Strawberry Hill Races. If you can't join us at our festivals, join us at our table. Currently out of print.

VIRGINIA TRADITIONS

GFWC Junior Woman's Club of Hopewell, Inc.
P. O. Box 932
Hopewell, VA 23860

jwchopewell@msn.com

A local favorite since 1994 and sure to become one of yours! Easy-to-follow recipes from appetizers and beverages to desserts and for every part of the meal in between. (Over 675 recipes, 521 pages.) Includes themed menus. Proceeds benefit charity.

$15.00 Retail price
$5.00 Postage and handling

Make check payable to GFWC Junior Woman's Club of Hopewell, Inc.

THE WESTWOOD CLUBHOUSE COOKBOOK

Attn: Jerry Craft   Phone 540-372-7700
The Westwood Clubhouse of Brain Injury Services, Inc.   Fax 540-372-3438
507 Westwood Office Park   www.braininjurysvcs.org
Fredericksburg, VA 22401   jcraft@braininjurysvcs.org

This nonprofit agency improves the lives of individual's affected with brain injuries by
community-based services, education, and advocacy in the Fredericksburg and surrounding area. Profits from the sales of this cookbook will be used for direct services
to survivors of brain injuries.

$15.00   Retail price
$4.00   Postage and handling

Make check payable to Brain Injury Services, Inc.

WHAT CAN I BRING?

Junior League of Northern Virginia   Phone 703-442-4163
P. O. Box 9980   Fax 703-761-413
McLean, VA 22102   www.jlnv.org • cookbook@jlnv.org

If you want delicious meals that will leave your guests begging for "your" recipe—this
is the cookbook for you. The Junior League of Northern Virginia compiled a unique-
ly diverse selection of double-tested recipes and added ideas for presentation, cooking hints, and entertaining tips.

$19.95   Retail price   Visa/MC accepted
$1.00   Tax for VA residents   ISBN 0-9667722-0-2
$5.00   Postage and handling plus $2.00 each additional book

Make check payable to Junior League of Northern Virginia

Virginia Timeline

Presented below is a brief chronology of historical Virginia events.

1584: The name "Virginia" is suggested for America's East Coast—named for Queen Elizabeth I of England (known as the Virgin Queen).

1607: Jamestown is the first permanent English settlement in the Americas.

1613: John Rolfe makes first shipment of tobacco from Virginia to England.

1619: First legislative meeting held at Jamestown.

1621: The first Thanksgiving is shared between the Indians and the pilgrims.

1640: The first elected separate legislative body is formed—Virginia House of Burgesses.

1644: A peace treaty is signed with the Powhatan Indians.

1661: Slavery is legalized in Virginia.

1699: Jamestown is burned in an Indian uprising, and the capital of Virginia is moved to Williamsburg.

1693: The College of William and Mary is founded.

1732: George Washington is born in Westmoreland County on February 22nd.

1753: Patrick Henry delivers the famous "give me liberty" speech at the House of Burgesses.

1776: Virginia adopts its first constitution and declares independence.

1780: The capital of Virginia moves to Richmond.

1788: Virginia becomes the tenth state.

1789: George Washington becomes the first president of the United States.

1831: Nat Turner leads a slave revolt against white slave owners, killing 57.

1861: Virginia's state flag is adopted; Virginia secedes and joins the Confederacy; the Civil War begins; first battle of Manassas begins.

1865: Civil War ends; President Lincoln is assassinated.

1870: Virginia reenters the Union.

1875: Civil Rights Act adopted, barring racial discrimination in public facilities.

1943: Pentagon opens in Arlington. The construction of the Pentagon costs $83 million dollars.

1964: The Chesapeake Bay Bridge-Tunnel is completed.

1989: L. Douglas Wilder of Virginia becomes first African-American governor.

2005: Federal Census: state population = 7,332,608; white = 5,259,281; African-American = 1,397,192; Hispanic = 438,789; all others 237,346.

2007: The 400th anniversary of the founding of the nation is held at Jamestown.

Index

PHOTO ©DOUG WILSON / VIRGINIA TOURISM CORPORATION

The Tomb of the Unknowns in Arlington National Cemetery (a.k.a. Tomb of the Unknown Soldier) is dedicated to American soldiers from World Wars I and II, the Korean Conflict, and the Vietnam War who died without their remains being identified. The Tomb is guarded 24 hours a day by specially trained members of the 3rd United States Infantry.

INDEX

INDEX

INDEX

INDEX

INDEX

INDEX

INDEX

INDEX

INDEX

BEST OF THE BEST STATE COOKBOOK SERIES

Best of the Best from
ALABAMA
(all-new edition)
(original edition)*

Best of the Best from
ALASKA

Best of the Best from
ARIZONA

Best of the Best from
ARKANSAS

Best of the Best from
BIG SKY
Montana and Wyoming

Best of the Best from
CALIFORNIA

Best of the Best from
COLORADO

Best of the Best from
FLORIDA
(all-new edition)
(original edition)*

Best of the Best from
GEORGIA
(all-new edition)
(original edition)*

Best of the Best from the
GREAT PLAINS
North and South Dakota,
Nebraska, and Kansas

Best of the Best from
HAWAI'I

Best of the Best from
IDAHO

Best of the Best from
ILLINOIS

Best of the Best from
INDIANA

Best of the Best from
IOWA

Best of the Best from
KENTUCKY
(all-new edition)
(original edition)*

Best of the Best from
LOUISIANA

Best of the Best from
LOUISIANA II

Best of the Best from
MICHIGAN

Best of the Best from the
MID-ATLANTIC
Maryland, Delaware, New
Jersey, and Washington, D.C.

Best of the Best from
MINNESOTA

Best of the Best from
MISSISSIPPI
(all-new edition)
(original edition)*

Best of the Best from
MISSOURI

Best of the Best from
NEVADA

Best of the Best from
NEW ENGLAND
Rhode Island, Connecticut,
Massachusetts, Vermont,
New Hampshire, and Maine

Best of the Best from
NEW MEXICO

Best of the Best from
NEW YORK

Best of the Best from
NO. CAROLINA
(all-new edition)
(original edition)*

Best of the Best from
OHIO

Best of the Best from
OKLAHOMA

Best of the Best from
OREGON

Best of the Best from
PENNSYLVANIA

Best of the Best from
SO. CAROLINA
(all-new edition)
(original edition)*

Best of the Best from
TENNESSEE
(all-new edition)
(original edition)*

Best of the Best from
TEXAS

Best of the Best from
TEXAS II

Best of the Best from
UTAH

Best of the Best from
VIRGINIA

Best of the Best from
VIRGINIA II

Best of the Best from
WASHINGTON

Best of the Best from
WEST VIRGINIA

Best of the Best from
WISCONSIN

*Original editions available while supplies last.

All BEST OF THE BEST STATE COOKBOOKS are 6x9 inches
and comb-bound with illustrations, photographs,
and an index. They range in size from 288 to 352
pages and each contains over 300 recipes.
Retail price per copy $16.95.

To order by credit card, call toll-free **1-800-343-1583** or visit **www.quailridge.com.**

- -

Ⓠ Order form
Use this form for sending check or money order to:
QUAIL RIDGE PRESS • P. O. Box 123 • Brandon, MS 39043

❑ Check enclosed

Charge to: ❑ Visa ❑ MC ❑ AmEx ❑ Disc

Card # _____

Expiration Date_____

Signature _____

Name _____

Address _____

City/State/Zip _____

Phone #_____

Email Address _____

Qty.	Title of Book (State) or Set	Total

Subtotal _____

7% Tax for MS residents _____

Postage ($4.00 any number of books) **+ 4.00**

Total _____